Battered Cherub

Battered Cherub

THE AUTOBIOGRAPHY OF

JOE GORMLEY

To BERT

Best Wishes

Joe Gormley

HAMISH HAMILTON

LONDON

First published in Great Britain 1982
by Hamish Hamilton Ltd
Garden House 57–59 Long Acre London WC2E 9JZ

Copyright © 1982 by Joe Gormley

British Library Cataloguing in Publication Data

Gormley, Joe
   Battered cherub.
   1. Gormley, Joe 2. National Union of Mineworkers—Biography
   I. Title
   331.88'12'2330941   HD6668.C/G/
   ISBN 0-241-10754-7

Typeset by Topset Typographics Ltd
Printed and bound in Great Britain by
Richard Clay (The Chaucer Press) Ltd, Bungay, Suffolk

Contents

1   Clogs and Ferrets   1
2   Up Bonk and Down Bonk   11
3   Sylvesters and Gablocks   26
4   All Directions at Once   40
5   In Place of Strife   60
6   222 Euston Road   78
7   Strike   95
8   Heath and Wilson   119
9   The Wreckers   146
10 Miners v Tories   173
11 The Philosophy of a Democratic Socialist   183
12 The Future of Energy   199
    Postscript   207
    Index   212

To Jeremy Hornsby, without whose tolerance and endeavour this book could never have been written. His hours of research along with people such as Paul Noble, David Branton and Steve Bundred made my task far easier. This warrants my deepest gratitude.

To Nellie my wife, whose guidance kept me on the straight and narrow.

And to all others who in any way contributed.

Chapter One

Clogs and Ferrets

I suppose, looking back at it all, that my first experience of mining came when I was about ten. A gang of us were digging in one of the sandhills on the common near my home. We were digging into the side of it, when suddenly the whole thing collapsed on top of me. My feet were sticking out from that sand, but the rest of me was underneath, and to this day I can remember the thoughts racing through my mind for the few seconds that I was trapped. Ten years old certainly wasn't too young to conjure up the terror of being buried alive.

Luckily, some adults were nearby, and they rushed over and got me clear, and I've no doubt we all got a regular ticking off. It would have been no more than we deserved. We were all the sons of miners, and I suppose we should all have known better—but there we were, burrowing tunnels in the sandhills, and without a thought of the dangers we were running.

It was to be only six more years before I knew those dangers for real, when I brought my first dead colleague out of a mine. He was a collier, and a huge stone had fallen on him and killed him outright. Then I understood. The understanding was helped when my father died down the mine, and then later when my son was badly injured down the mine, and then his understanding was helped when there was a disaster at his mine, and he in turn had to bring out dead colleagues.

I write this with no bitterness. They are facts of life—and death. And, although we have fought over the years to make them less likely to happen, they remain the hard facts of mining life. And a hard life it is.

*

I was born on July 5, 1917, in the village of Ashton-in-Makerfield, midway between Wigan and St Helens in Lancashire. I've always thought of it as a village, though it had about 19,000 people in it even then. It was all coal and cotton. Today, they've both gone.

For people like us, there was no going to hospital to have a kid in those days, so my first view of the world was our little cottage, one of fourteen in Duke Street, very much the rough and tough end of Ashton. There were already a brother and two sisters in the family when I arrived, and there were another brother and two more sisters to come, so I suppose you could say that I was born into a negotiating position—not that I could do much about it then. My elder brother John would get the new clothes, and they'd be passed to me as hand-me-downs, and by the time I'd worn them out there would have to be a new set for younger brother Bob.

It wasn't too good a deal, really, but then we were very poor. My father was a miner. His father had brought him over from Ireland to work on the farms around Ormskirk, but after a while he went down the pits in St Helens. My mother, Lizzie, was a Williams, half-Welsh and half-Irish. She only stood five foot and a bit, but she ruled that house with the proverbial rod of iron, which in her case was the boiler stick she used primarily for poking the clothes around in the big old copper, but also for lambasting us when we were disobedient.

Mind you, she had to take a bit of stick, too. On Saturday nights. Maybe it was the strain of working in the mine conditions of that time, I don't know, but like a lot of miners my father, Johnny, would go out on a Saturday night, get drunk, and come home and lay into my mother. Because of what you could call our bleak economic situation, my elder brother had gone to live with our grandmother at Newton-le-Willows as soon as he got old enough, so I was the oldest lad in the house. And I remember lying in bed on Saturday nights, frightened to death of my father coming home drunk again and starting on mother, leaving it to me to go downstairs and remonstrate with him, something I had to do from a pretty early age.

I'm no saint, but that experience made me vow that when I got married my wife wouldn't have to put up with all that.

On the other hand, it was only because of occasionally having too much to drink. All the rest of the time, I thought of my father as a great character. He was a pretty good catch-as-catch-can wrestler in his spare time. During Haydock Park races they had wrestling competitions on Ashton Heath, near the racecourse, and many's the time I've seen him win three or four quid there, which was the equivalent of a week's wages. He used to teach us a bit, as well, wrestling on the mattress at home, how to defend yourself, a bit of boxing and so on, and there were a couple of occasions when that was to come in handy. In fact, I believe it was he who instilled in me what I most believe in today—the ability to show people you can do a job, and do it without fear of criticism.

And he did work hard, with such a large family to keep, and what little relaxation he had came with his pigeons and his ferrets. Pigeons were always a big thing with a lot of miners. Every Sunday, in the pub, they'd have the 'sweeps', which was when they drew out the discs which told the owners the different points from which they had to release their pigeons. It was very much the luck of the draw, and if you drew a position which gave your bird a tail wind, you'd have a good chance of winning—and woe betide anyone who moved while the pigeon was circling to come in, with my father standing there shouting it home. His were short distance pigeons, and I used to help with the training. This involved putting the bird in a basket, taking it about two miles away, and then releasing it. The only trouble was, the pigeon would be home in about two minutes, and I'd have to walk all the way back again. Pigeon-training didn't really appeal to me.

As for the ferrets—my father used to go out in the fields hunting rabbits and rats with them. The ferrets lived at the bottom of the backyard, next to the toilet,and the midden, where you threw the ashes from the fire, which were emptied once a month by the council men, who took them away in horse-carts. Well, those ferrets lived in a cage on the wall, and one day-nobody ever knew how it happened-one of them escaped. It was a Sunday, and you'd have thought there was a near national disaster, because every one of our neighbours, as well as us, was out looking for that ferret.

The reason was that most people had an allotment nearby, where they grew vegetables to supplement their wages. And most people kept a few hens. It didn't take much to know that with a ferret loose you could end up with a few dead hens knocking around. So there was a great hue and cry-but we never did find that ferret.

For us lads, the game was football. At the bottom of Duke Street was Princes Road, the main road leading out of the centre of town. Opposite that road was a little railed-off piece of green, with a brook running through it, which was the only piece of ground where we could play cricket or football. The trouble was, there were only two mining families living in Princes Road—all the rest were other trades, and they thought they were a cut above the mining families from the streets where we lived.

So there were regular running battles between us and those families. They used to come after us with brooms, shouting, 'Go and play somewhere else. Go and play outside your own house.' But of course we couldn't, because there were the allotments in front of our houses. There was a policeman, too, who came down there every day on his regular beat, which threaded round to Ashton Heath, next to Haydock Park racecourse. If he saw us, he'd chase us too. He was a tall, thin fellow, about six foot three, with a bit of a tache, and I remember him shouting at us one day, 'You're all stacked up and fed off shovels, you lot.' Even in those days I didn't care much for authority, except for my mother and father.

We played our football in clogs, with irons on them. In fact, if you'd worn a pair of football boots, you'd have been regarded as Lord Muck. A lot of the old miners never had any shoes at all. They'd have a pair of clogs for best, with leather uppers, wooden soles, and irons on the soles. And I really preferred clogs to shoes. They were healthier, because they were shaped to your foot and kept your foot firm. And there'd be hell to pay if your irons wore down and you didn't tell so that they could be replaced, because that would mean you wouldn't get so much wear out of the clog. The women who worked in the mills wore clogs with irons on, too, and one of my deepest memories is that sound of everybody clip-clopping down the street.

Being a pretty poor family, we sometimes got help from the Church, and on two or three occasions I had to go down there to get a voucher for a new pair of clogs, because our mum couldn't afford to buy us a new pair. The Church played a large part in our life. Mother was a strong Catholic, and every Sunday we had to go to Mass at nine in the morning. We weren't allowed to eat or drink anything from Saturday supper until after we came back from Mass on Sunday. That was when my father used to get the breakfast ready. We had half an egg each, and bread and butter.It was the luck of the draw whether you got the bigger or smaller bit of the egg. A piece of bacon was a rare and special event.

For church on Sunday we'd wear our best suits, which were actually our only suits, and we had to make them last a hell of a long time. For us, getting dressed normally was pulling on a sweater, a pair of trousers held up by belt or braces, then stockings and clogs. Underwear was unheard of, and would have been regarded as the height of luxury. We did have shoes to go to church in, but we had to take them off the moment we got home to Dad's breakfast.

And, if that breakfast sounds a bit thin, I should say that we were never what we call in Lancashire 'clemmed', which is to say 'starved'. Mother always said that whatever else was available or not, we must make sure the food was right. Not that it was ever fancy.There was pea soup, and lentil soup. Potato pie, with the potatoes and beef cooked in an earthenware dish with a crust on top. And Lob Scouse, the traditional Lancashire dish, made of meat and vegetables all boiled in a pan—and for a family our size it needed a pretty big pan.

The kitchen was also the living room, and the dining room, and the place where we washed, so it was really the bathroom as well. Dad being a miner got cheap coal, which was packed under the stairs, so there was always a roaring fire. There was a table in the middle, and a hand-pegged rug in front of the fire, and one easy chair, which of course was father's. When mother was doing the washing, there'd be a coal fire under the copper, and then the actual washing was done in a wooden dolly tub. We had two of those tubs, and that was where we had our baths on Saturday nights, two of the lads in one, and two of the wenches in the other, and Auntie Maggie, one of mother's sisters, coming to help give us a scrub.

When we all got older, of course, the lads weren't allowed in while the girls were bathing, or vice versa, and by then we'd gravitated to a tin bath. When Dad had his, there'd be just him and mother—not that miners liked bathing too much. There was a belief that having too many baths weakened your back, and on weekdays they mostly just made sure their head and shoulders were washed. There were no pithead baths then, but even when they came in, that distrust of baths persisted.

Next to the living room—which really *was* a living room, because most of life took place in there—was the parlour. That was hardly ever used, only for Christmas, births, deaths and marriages. It had a three piece suite, and a carpet, and a stand for ornaments, and the things in it never wore out because it was used so rarely. Like the rest of the house, it was lit by gas.

Upstairs there were just the three bedrooms. My parents' had two double beds in, one for them, the other for my younger sisters Kathleen and Margaret. I remember Margaret being born, and us being locked out of the house while it was going on, and me and Kathleen sitting on the step and saying, 'Wonder why they won't let us in?' There was a double bed in each of the other rooms, too, one for Bob and me, the other for my elder sisters Molly and Winnie.

And that was home for the eight of us—nine when John came to see us at holidays—except that, when I was about ten, Dad decided to build an extension at the back. That taught me something too, because, as always happened on such occasions, everyone from our little area came round to chip in with a bit of work to help build it.

At the time I was born, my father was away fighting in the First World War. He was a private in the Lancashire Fusiliers, and he was on the Somme, and then later at Gallipoli; when I became old enough to understand, I remember sitting enthralled as he told us about his exploits in the war.

When he returned, he went back down the mine, and became a chargeman. This was the old system; to understand it, it might be simpler if you thought of him as a contractor, although he always had to be elected by the team he worked with, which might be about forty men.

That team would be paid as a team, and it was up to the chargeman to negotiate a price with the managers for the work they were going to do, and then sign the contract. You might have a coal face, say a hundred and fifty yards long, and each man would have a section to work. But there had to be someone in charge—the chargeman—who would allot them all their patches. You couldn't just divide the length of the face by the number of men in the team, and say 'Each man take five yards' or whatever it was, because that might mean one man working in a part of the face where conditions were bad all the time, making it harder to clear off the coal. So it was the chargeman's job to make sure, as far as possible, that everyone in the team had the same amount of physical effort to put in during the day.

Mind you, the chargeman had to do his own stint at the face, as well as liaising with the deputy and the manager for whatever supplies his team needed—roof supports, powder for shot-firing, and things like that. Then at the end of the week, on the Friday afternoon, he would get paid all the money, which he then shared out among the lads. And everyone got exactly the same, the chargeman included.

The strange thing was that he was never very politically-minded, nor did he get much involved with the union—perhaps he was too keen on his pigeons, and his ferrets. And when the General Strike came, in 1926, when I was nine, I never heard him talk about it. But I assume he must have been for it, because he was in it, and I never heard any regrets expressed in our house.

Still, you can't forget a time like that. We used to be given meals at school, usually pea soup with lumps of fat in it. I loved anything like that, though there was another lad who hated it. I always made sure I sat next to him in the playground while we were eating this stuff, and that way I'd usually end up with two bowls instead of one. On Saturdays we went to the school for a meat and potato pie, and then a meat pie on Sundays. You were expected to take it home, but by the time you did get home there wasn't much left of the pie in your hand.

The miners themselves were digging coal in the dirt rooks—the piles of waste material from the mines—and selling it to people for a few pence to help tide things over. A few mates and I thought we'd have a go, too, so we went to the rook and dug ourselves a bag of coal. Then the man with the cart came along and picked it up with all the rest, and delivered it to our house. My mother played all hell with us, because most of it was dirt, and she'd had to pay the man twopence for transporting it. That was twopence when literally every penny counted.

Being especially poor, our family qualified for 'relief', which was a few shillings a week. But of course it all had to be paid for when the strike was over. For years afterwards, every week without fail, the relief man came to collect threepence a week. He was a gaunt old scarecrow of a fellow, and he also went to a lot of others who'd been in our position. Threepence a week for years and years.

The Church had helped too, of course, but then they never asked for any return, except once in a roundabout sort of way. My father had been brought up a Catholic, but he'd stopped going. Like myself, he didn't reckon that running to church all the time was the salvation of life. Then one day the priest came to our house, and said to him: 'Come on, Johnny, why don't you come to church? Why don't you come to confession?'

After a bit my father was persuaded, and off he went. When he came back, I asked him: 'How did you go on, Dad?'

'Well,' he said, 'I went in the box and the father asked me what sins I had to confess. I told him, 'It's been so long since I confessed, it must be everything only murder, Father'!'

I have the same attitude. I believe in the Catholic religion simply because I was brought up in it, but I don't believe you have to go to church every Sunday to be a good, or even a religious, person. I think that if it's in you to do good for people, the best you can do is help them in their physical life, and leave the spiritual life to the priest.

A lot of people think that running to church all the time makes them good. It doesn't. I remember one Sunday, when I was about seventeen, coming home from church at about half past ten. My aunt Maggie, who only lived back to back with us in Peter Street, was in there talking to my mother and pulling one of our neighbours to pieces.

'Maggie,' I said, 'don't you think you're a hypocrite? You've just come away from church, and you go there to pray for people's souls and the well-being of men, and you go to Mass nearly every day, and yet here you are pulling people to bits and castigating them. Don't you think it's a lot of hypocrisy?' She slammed out of the house and didn't speak to me for six months.

There were a lot of Catholics in Ashton at that time, perhaps fifty percent of the people, and no doubt it had to do with all the Irish who came over to do the heavy grafting work in the pits. But, as in a lot of mining areas, Methodism was pretty strong too. A lot of the original union leaders were Methodist lay preachers. There were Baptist churches, too, and Protestant churches, but I never once had any sense that your religion made you different from anyone else. Politics, yes. How rich or poor you were, yes. Religion, never.

The rich and poor part of it I did my best to equalise by doing a paper round with my brother Bob. But I got the worst half of it, because every morning I had to rush up to the station with a trolley to collect the papers, while Bob, who was younger, stayed in bed till I'd brought them back. I've never let him forget it. Then on race days at Haydock we'd queue up to get the job of selling the *Sporting Chronicle* at the start of the meeting, and the *Evening Chronicle* at the end of it. When that was done, we'd wait for the bookies coming out on their way to the station, and say, 'Carry your bags, sir?' If they'd had a bad day, the replies tended not to be very polite.

The lads from our area were split into two groups, based roughly on age. Bob was the leader of the younger group, and he was a bugger for fighting. He'd fight at the drop of a hat. He'd challenge anyone. But I was the youngest, and smallest, of the older group, and it took a lot to hold my own. I didn't have Bob's fiery temper, and I've always taken a lot of rousing, but when the chips were down I had to stand my corner and make sure I didn't get whacked too often. Nor did I, thanks perhaps to my father's coaching.

It may also be from my father that I got the love of a gamble that's stayed with me all my life. He often took us on a Sunday afternoon up to the moor where they played pitch and toss, and we'd help to keep an eye open for the police. They played it with two coins. One man held the bank, and another threw the coins up. The betting was whether they'd both land heads, or both tails. A head and a tail was no bet.

Someone might say, 'I'll have a fiver on heads, if someone wants to cover it.' That's the sort of money they played for, and it was a lot in those days, considering my father was only earning about £3 a week. I had an uncle, Frank, who once headed them about ten times in a row. He kept doubling up till there was about fifty or sixty quid lying there—and then they came down tails, and the lot went.

People made their own entertainment, and Ashton certainly helped them do it. It had thirty-nine pubs—as I was to discover one by one as I got older—and about twenty clubs, Miners' clubs, Labour clubs, Tory clubs, Working Men's clubs, and so on. My mother was a prominent member of the women's section of the Labour Party, which was a bonus for us, because on Friday or Saturday night she'd come back with the big enamel dishes that they'd made potato pie in. Scraping out what was left in those damn dishes was one of the highlights of our life.

Clubs could be a hazard, too. On our way to school we had to pass the Conservative Club, and every day of the week, going to and from school, we had running battles with the lads from that area, who reckoned they were a cut above us. Fighting was very much a part of daily life—in fact, I had a pet dog, an Airedale, and on St Paddy's Day we used to tie a green ribbon round its neck. Inevitably, when it came home, that ribbon would be torn off, because *he'd* been in a fight.

Years later, when I was married, I got in a bit of a scrap, and came home with the collar ripped off my sweater. Nellie, my wife, said: 'What on earth have you been doing?'

The first thing I could think of to say was: 'I've slipped on a bit of orange peel.'

'What, and ripped your collar off?'

'Aye,' I said, a bit lamely.

'Well,' she said, 'if you expect me to believe that, you'll expect me to believe the moon is made of green cheese. I think you take after that dog of yours.'

School, which was a mile and a half or so from home, was run by St Oswald's, the main Catholic church in Ashton. There was a boys' school, and a girls' school, which were a little way apart, and I started in the juniors when I was four. I remember crying my eyes out that first day, because my mother had left me there. Not surprisingly, it was pretty church-orientated, and the first hour every day was religious education. I sang in the choir for quite a few years, too, and played for the cricket team.

I used to enjoy cricket, except for one game during the holidays, when we were playing up against a telegraph pole. I was the stumper, and when I turned suddenly to stop a ball I hit that pole and broke one of my front teeth clean in two. It was with me for ages, because there wasn't any question of going to the dentist. You had to pay for the dentist, and we didn't have any money. The bit of tooth that was left got blacker and blacker, and used to hurt like hell, but I had to suffer it for years until it was finally pulled out. Then I had a gap there for years, but in the end vanity won out and I got it filled. There was nothing fancy about my childhood.

Holidays were spent at home. In fact, although he'd have Bank holidays off, I can't remember my father ever having a week's holiday, let alone go away for it. Holiday agreements were non-existent, and you certainly couldn't afford a week off work. You worked six days a week, and if you had a day off sick you didn't get paid for that, either. So we stayed at home—so much so that the only time I went out of that village, until I was about seventeen, was when one of the Labour clubs took us on a day trip to Southport. I hadn't even been to Wigan, which was only four and a half miles away.

You'd think the colliery owners might have done something for the kids, but the only ones who did were the Smethurst Colliery group. Every year they had what they called the Smethurst outing, when they took the kids of the people who worked at their pits to Blackpool. It was looked on as one of the perks of working at those pits, and sometimes the men would sell their tickets so that some of the other kids could go.

When I was eight, I went up from the junior school to the seniors. I was quite bright, and got on so well that I was one of the few lads they picked out every year to study at night, and in their spare time, with a view to taking a scholarship to go to grammar school, which would have been either the big Catholic grammar school in Wigan, or the non-denominational grammar school in Ashton. So I worked hard, and by the time we got near to taking the exam things were looking quite good.

Then one night I was on the stairs at home, when my father had come back from work and was talking to my mother in the living room. Then I heard her say: 'I don't know what we'll do if our Joe passes that exam,

Johnny. We can't afford a school uniform, and the books he'll need, so I don't know what we're going to do.'

Well, as chance happened, there was trouble at school the following morning. There were about ten of us working for that exam, and every morning they looked at our homework. This particular day, most of the others had got their homework wrong, and I don't know what got into Mr O'Brien, the headmaster, that day, but he caned the lot of us, even though mine was right. It was a big cane, that, over a foot long and about half an inch in diameter. You got it on your hands, and he really used to make it rattle.

That, combined with what I'd heard the night before, made up my mind for me. I thought, 'There's no future in this.' So on my way home that night, I walked down to the bottom of the market place, where there was a stream called Market Brook. It ran under a bridge, and then through to the centre of the village, and I stood on the bank and took all my books—all those books I'd been working so hard with—and I threw them into that brook and watched them sail merrily down under the bridge. Where they ever finished up I'll never know.

The following day I told the headmaster what I'd done, and he looked at me and said: 'Well, that's it, you'll always be a navvy.' Then he caned me again. I was eleven, and nobody passed the exam that year. But, when it was over, the headmaster said to me: 'Gormley, you'd have walked it.'

'That's okay,' I said, 'it's done with, any road.'

Regrets? I don't know. In some ways yes, and in some ways no. But I do know that if you look back and start regretting what you've done in life, you never make any progress. All my life I've found myself in a position of leadership, but perhaps if I'd gone to grammar school I'd have ended up in commerce. Who knows? That's why it's pointless to regret things, because you can never know how they would have turned out. As for university—that thought would have been a million miles from the minds of a mining family in those days.

So at fourteen I left school. Now, it was the ambition of most of the mining families to try to keep their sons out of the pits, because it used to be said that once you got in the pits you could never get out. My parents were no exception, and they started me off working in a greengrocer's shop. I stuck it for a few months. But most of my mates from the group I was in, all of them older than I, had already gone into the pits. That made me feel out on a limb.

So I left the apples and oranges to themselves, and went down the mine.

Chapter Two

Up Bonk and Down Bonk

My mother was against it, of course. But, with all my mates down the pits, I said: 'Ah, come on, mother, it's no good for me, that shop job.'

So she relented, and one Saturday morning, in January 1932, she took me down to Wood Pit, near St Helens, which was where my father worked. We went into the pit yard and met Jim Turtington, who was the manager, and my mother said I wanted a job.

He looked me up and down and then said to her: 'By God, he's only a littl'un, isn't he?'

'Aye,' she said, 'but littl'uns have to eat as well as big 'uns, you know.'

'All right, then,' he said, and took me on there and then, and I started on the Monday.

The pit was one of many owned by the Richard Evans company, which had most of the pits in the Haydock area, but it was in some trouble, and had gone into the hands of the bank the year before, so that the bank was laying down the conditions of employment for everyone at the pit. In fact, many of them had to take a drop in pay just to keep the pit open. But this was 1931, the year of the Depression, and any job was better than none.

I started, like all the lads, as a haulage hand on the day shift. My job was what they call 'riving' the tubs, which is hooking the empty ones on to the haulage system as they came out of the cage at the pit bottom. The haulage hands were paid as the lowest of the low, underground, and at the end of the week I went to collect my pay. It was ten shillings and threepence.

But I saw very little of it. The first thing was that, as soon as I got paid, my father said: 'You see that window over there? Go and get joined in the union.' He wouldn't take no for an answer, even though he didn't have much to do with the union himself. The window he was talking about was on the trade union cabin, which was just outside the pit gates, because the owners wouldn't allow the trade union branch secretary to have an office on the premises.

Joining the union was voluntary, then, and it cost threepence a week. It seemed a hell of a lot to me at the time, and it still does, when you compare the percentage we ask our members to pay today for far better services.

Then when I got home, as was expected, I 'tipped' my wages to my mother. We were paid our money, not in packets, but little round tins, just about big enough for a half-crown to fit into, and when you were a youngster, living at home, it was regarded as right and proper that you should tip out that tin to your mother. Out of what was left, after the union money, she gave me a shilling for pocket money. It wasn't really as bad as it seems; for a penny you could go to the pictures.

But the job at Wood Pit didn't last long. A few weeks before the end of the year, the bank put it into liquidation—not that there was any connection with my presence, I should add! We finished on the Saturday, and on the Monday we all went looking for work.

My choice was to try my luck at Stones Pit, as Garswood, which was an area of Ashton which also contained Smethurst Pits, the ones which gave the children the annual outing. There was a large house there called Garswood Hall, owned by Lord Gerard, who was a big land-owner in the area, and who I think must have had some connection with the Colliery company, since he would have owned most of the local mineral rights—and indeed 'Smethursts' was the local name for the Garswood Hall Colliery Company. There were accidents in a lot of the company's pits, and while I was still fourteen there was a very bad explosion at their Number Nine Pit, in which many lads were killed.

Well, that was the way of things, and I needed the work, so on that Monday morning I queued up with a lot of others at Stones Garswood. By then, with those few months' experience behind me, I was already a bit wise to the ways of the pits, and I knew that the standard question asked of any lad who wanted a job on the haulage was, 'Can you lash on?'

Lashing on meant taking a ten-foot chain with a hook at one end and a link at the other. One end had to be coupled on to the tubs, which could be either full or empty, and twisting the other end round the haulage rope and attaching it so that it pulled the tub with it. You had to be pretty fast to do this job, because the haulage was moving all the time—there was no stopping to give you a chance to attach the tub before it set off down the incline.

Now, of course, I'd never lashed on in my life, but in the first place I knew that only about one haulage hand in eight actually got given the job of lashing on, and in the second place I was in desperate need of a job. So when it came to my turn in the line, and the under-manager asked the inevitable question, I said cheerfully: 'Oh aye, of course I can lash on.' To myself I thought, 'The law of averages says I won't have to do this job.'

Unfortunately, the law of averages didn't work out too well, because that very first day there I was given the job. I thought, 'That's it. I'm going to be straight out on my ear.' But luck was with me, in the shape of Seth Merry, a young fellow, a few years older than myself. They put me to work with him, and as soon as we were alone I said: 'Well, mate, I'll never do this job. I haven't a clue.'

'Don't worry,' he said, 'I'll show you how to do it.'

You worked in pairs, because one would attach a chain at the front of the tub, and the other at the back, so that it was firmly secured to the haulage rope both on its way down, and later on its way back up—'Up brew and down brew,' we used to call it. In the Midlands they say 'Up bonk and down bonk,' and in some places simply up hill and down hill. But that hill, or brew, or bonk, was a one-in-four incline, so you had to make sure those tubs were secure, or there could be a bad accident.

Well, that morning I was sweating away, doing my best to put the chains on the front while Seth put them on the back, when I was suddenly aware that the under-manager was looking at me. And then, to my horror, he came over to us.

'I thought you said you could lash on,' he said.

Racking my brains, I came up with the only answer I could think of. 'I can,' I said, 'but I've always been used to back-lashing, and I've not done front-lashing before.'

Looking back, it was the daftest thing to say, and he knew perfectly well I was lying, but he must have had a heart in him, because he just laughed and walked away.

After a while, I moved from lashing on to 'thrutching'. And that *was* a job. It was still classified as being on the haulage, but it was a bit more important, because it was that much closer to the men at the coal face, and they were the kings.

It worked like this—they had two-man teams, a collier and a drawer. The collier was the man who filled the tubs with the cut coal, and the drawer pulled the tub out from the seam to join it on to the haulage. Now, there were certain stretches where the drawer could manage on his own. But there were other places where you'd have an incline, maybe as much as a hundred yards long, which could be as steep as one in five or one in six.

That's where the thrutcher came in, because thrutching means pushing, or perhaps a little more than pushing. It really means pushing your bloody brains out. You'd wait at the bottom of the incline until the drawer came out from the seam, and then nip behind the tub and push, often with your head. There were some drawers who gloried in their own strength, but a lot of others, in their forties or fifties, who were a bit past it, and then you'd have to push your guts out.

What's more, one thrutcher would be looking after perhaps six drawers, so that, for every journey up the brew a drawer made, the thrutcher would do six, and since those drawers were all on piece work they'd be in and out like fiddlers' elbows. I spent a few years thrutching, and I don't suppose many jobs come much harder. The roofs of the tunnels could be less than four feet high, and there'd be splinters in them where the supports had split a bit. I used to come home with my back covered in cuts and sores, from my shoulder-blades to my backside.

In those days, all the props were made of wood. Later, when steel props were introduced, many of the miners argued that the wooden props were better, because they creaked and gave a bit more of a warning if they were going to give. But that was really a fallacy. The fact is that steel props will support about five times the weight of the wooden ones, but of course they're much heavier. And when you've spent all day underground working with a heavy pick, or shovel, or hammer, you don't want to be shifting heavy props around. So, when the steel ones were introduced, the colliers would make it their business to get to the prop store early, to ensure they got as many wooden ones as possible.

It was the same as the argument about not wanting too many baths because they would weaken your back. For many miners, the truth was that they just didn't like having baths. And even when compulsory safety helmets were introduced there were those who said, 'Oh, I can't wear a helmet, it makes my head ache,' or similar nonsense. When I started, they certainly weren't compulsory, and I never saw my father in anything but a flat cloth cap when he went down the mine.

We didn't have electric lamps then, either, only oil lamps which you hung from your belt. But they could detect gas—ventilation wasn't so good then, and you always had to be on the look-out for pockets of methane.Today, there's a methanometer to do that job, though the deputies still carry the safety lamps down with them to make sure there's enough oxygen in the air. When I started, they were still taking canaries down to help with that job—if the canary keeled over, you knew there wasn't much left worth breathing.

When I started, it was on day shifts only. We got a twenty-minute break for eating—down the mine, of course—and it was called 'snap time' because you'd take your food in what were known as snap tins, or bait tins. I usually took two or three sandwiches, which my mother made up for me, and a bottle of cold water or cold tea to drink—a thermos flask would have been an expensive luxury.

Sometimes I used to concoct my own mixtures for the sandwiches, like cheese and jam together, or anything to make it a bit moist. That's what you need when you've been working in the dust. Bob, my younger brother, used to love raw onions, and when he joined me down the pit at Stones Garswood he used to go deliberately to the windward side of where everybody else was eating, so that whatever they had in their snap tins, they ended up eating raw onion as well.

There was a lot of tobacco-chewing down the pit, too. About a year after I started I tried it, just the once. All the lads used to try it, but I'm afraid that like a lot of the others I ended up swallowing it, and for about two hours I wasn't much use to anyone—I was in the return airway being sick as a dog. I thought, 'To hell with that game', and never tried it again from that day.

The point of it was to keep moisture in your mouth, so that you could spit out the coal dust. A sweet wouldn't last very long, and you'd get sick of chewing the same piece of chewing gum. So, as I got to working nearer the coal face, I took to sucking a piece of coal. I'd find a hard bit of coal, clean it off, and suck that same piece all day. You'd be surprised how well that managed to keep the mouth moist. Later, when snuff became the habit, as it still is for a lot of miners, I tried that, too, but I found it would set me sneezing for the rest of the day, so I dropped that as an idea and went back to my lump of coal.

The average height of the coal seams in Lancashire was about four feet, though I've worked in some as low as eighteen inches, and anyone suffering from claustrophobia had a problem. It was bloody hard work, and because of the low roofs most men preferred to work kneeling, with knee-pads on to protect them. Later on, when I was filling coal with a spade, I could fill twenty tons and more working on my knees, though when you stood up afterwards you used to get what we called 'Nan in the back', and I don't suppose I need explain what *that* means.

But you would get used to working in that position, and in that environment, and if they then sent you to work in a six- or eight-foot seam you'd be frightened to death. Everything seemed so strange. So the men preferred to stay in the lower seams they knew, even though the work was half-killing them.

And dangerous it was. The way they worked it then was that the cutter would cut along the bottom of the seam, and as he did so the gap would have to be 'spragged'—held up with temporary props. Then, when the whole length of the face had been cut, a borer would go along, followed by the shotfirer, who fired the boreholes, causing the main bulk of the coal in the seam to be broken up. That was all right as long as it fell and broke into small pieces, but sometimes it would come down in one big lump, which could knock out one of the permanent supports from the day before. And it doesn't take much imagination to see what could happen then.

Once the coal had fallen, it would be loaded on to the tubs or conveyors, and permanent supports would be put in place, and the whole operation would start again the next day.

Another system was the pillar-and-stall method. Instead of cutting along the seam, they would cut straight into it, forming small roadways, or stalls, separated by, and supported by, walls or pillars of stone and coal which they left standing. That was how I came to see my first fatality.

I was sixteen, and by then was working on the three-shift system. One week would be on the day shift, from six in the morning till about two in the afternoon. The next week would be the afternoon shift, from two till about ten at night. And the third week on night shift, from ten till six in the morning. It was night shift we were on that week, two of us operating the haulage system. The particular seam we were working on was a tall one, about seven or eight feet high. The drawer had just gone back to the face, to fetch out another tub from his collier, when suddenly he came running out again shouting for help. It seems that it was too late anyhow because, when he'd got to where the collier was working, he found this huge stone had fallen off the top of one of the pillars and killed him just like that.

So we went back with him and helped carry the poor fellow out, and if I'd ever needed waking up to the hard realities of life, I didn't after that.

As the tradition was then, all the men on that shift walked out of the pit. It doesn't take long for news like that to spread through all the workings. It wasn't in any sense a strike, or a protest, but simply a mark of respect for the dead. That tradition carried on for many years, and in most cases they'd have a collection for the widow, though the amount of it would always depend on how well a man was known and liked.

The Fatalities Scheme, introduced many years later, was designed to give dependants a more reliable, and of course an equal, benefit, and one of its conditions was that after a fatality the men should remain at work. But it took a long time to break that tradition down, and even today, in some parts of the country, there's a feeling that it's not right, and that a dead man's colleagues *should* leave the pit out of respect.

Exactly twenty years later, in 1953, my father was to die down the pit. He'd done every job down there, and done it when it was hardest, chipping coal with the picks, and filling it by hand into the tubs, before the first coal-cutting machines were installed. He actually worked at the pit face until he was over sixty.

It was just before Christmas, and he'd had a heavy cold, and we were talking in the Labour Club. I asked him: 'Why the hell don't you retire, Dad?'

'I've no money to retire, Joe,' he said, 'the job I'm on it's only just a question of going.'

'If you can't retire at sixty-five,' I said, 'you'll not be able to at seventy-five.'

He was on the night shift at the time, in charge of a haulage engine for bringing men and materials up the inclines. No one ever knew exactly what happened. Perhaps he jumped up to answer the phone in a hurry, or something like that, but anyway he just collapsed and fell down dead.

By that time I was getting to be a bit known in the union, and I had the job of telling mother that in effect he did her a good turn, because we'd had a doctor's report that with the condition of his heart he could have dropped dead running for a bus—and as it happened, being a very active man, he often did run from the pit head to catch the bus home.

But, since he had died down the pit, she got a lump sum of two or three hundred pounds from the Fatalities Scheme, which was by then in force. It didn't really help. She died only a few years later, and I'm certain it was of a broken heart. I don't think she ever forgot.

And I know I'll never forget what it was like down the mines, even in the Thirties, when I started. What made it extra hard was that it was all contract work, piece work, so that people worked themselves half to death just to get a barely living wage. I'm all for agreements and incentives to keep productivity up, but the way it worked in those days was half-way towards slave labour.

As I said earlier, the colliers were the kings. Even though we all paid our own contributions, the union was very much regarded as being a colliers' union, and the majority of union work was done on their behalf.

Each collier would have a set of tallies—metal strips with a number punched on them, and a bit of string attached that would be threaded through a hole in each of the tubs the collier filled, to show that they were his—and done in such a way as to make it hard for someone else to take it off and cheat by putting his own on. That was the drawer's job. Then, when the tub had been checked at the top, the tallies were taken off and collected, and the collier, or his drawer, would take them down again the next day.

The checking system itself was a vital part of the whole operation, and often caused a lot of bitterness. When the tubs reached the top, they went over a weighing machine, next to what was called the checkweighman's office. In there, you had one man representing the employers, and one representing the union. That checkweighman was elected by the colliers, and they paid his wages, and he was a very important part of the union structure.

The checkweighmen were brought in to counteract a whole range of malpractices by the management. For example, if they found three hundredweight of dirt in a one-ton tub of coal, the manager had the discretion to disallow all the coal as well, so that the collier and the drawer between them had shifted seventeen hundredweight of coal for nothing. There were many abuses like that, until the checkweigh societies came to be formed. In my opinion, they were the forerunners of the strong trade union movement we have in the mining industry today.

In those days, the checkweigh societies ran parallel with the union, and the colliers contributed to both. But in many places they became totally entwined, since the checkweighman was inevitably one of the branch officials, needing the strength of the union behind him to get his point of view across. In fact, at Stones Garswood, the checkweighman was the union branch secretary.

And he needed to be tough, because the management would play hell if they didn't think the tubs had the right weight in them. Mind you, it was generally accepted that there had to be some dirt with the coal, and they used to reckon a tub weighing a ton as representing nineteen hundredweight of coal. But every so often they'd take one of the tubs out of the haulage stream and tip it over for checking.

'They' were the 'pit brew girls', big, bonny, strapping wenches, who could whip those wagons over as fast as you could see, strong as any fellow. They could wield a shovel as well as any man, too, separating the dirt from the coal in the tub they'd tipped over, then filling the coal back in again and making a note of the amount of stone and debris that had been mixed in with it.

But, if the colliers had their battles with the management, we had our grouses with the colliers, too, because while we on the haulage were working like slaves, it was the colliers who were taking all the money home. A lot of the lads were pretty disgruntled about this, and we had a bit of a meeting about it. For some reason they looked on me as their leader, so I went down on their behalf and told the colliers that, if they weren't prepared to fork out on a Friday, they weren't going to fill much coal the following week—because of course the number of tubs they filled depended on our speed in getting them in and out.

All we were asking for was a bit of a tip, which we could share out between us, and which would mean us each getting about a dollar each, which doesn't sound much, but in those days represented a nice bit of pocket money. It obviously sounded reasonable to them, because they all agreed except for this one collier. I remember him to this day, a big, bombastic bloke, and he started shouting the odds and saying 'I'll get you stopped' and all that sort of thing. Some of the colliers were the pets of the bosses, what we called 'soft-coal' colliers, meaning that they liked the easy life. And he was one of them.

So I just said: 'All right, don't worry.' And he didn't fill much coal the following week. Then he threatened to get me sacked, but he couldn't, because I was always pretty good at my job. And after a week or two he capitulated, and said he'd fall in line with the rest of them.

He had no choice. As long as the total contracted amount of coal was coming out of the pit, the management didn't care which of the teams was getting it. And, although they wondered why this fellow suddenly wasn't getting so much coal, it wasn't their concern. But he knew. And, even in those days, there were lots of little ways you could use to put your point of view over. In his case, for instance, you could arrange that his drawer would 'get off the road' in a very difficult position, making it hard for him to get on again. And, while he was trying to get back on, all the other drawers would be running in and out with their tubs.

But life wasn't *all* work. And like my father I used to follow working hard with playing hard, mostly gambling and girls—and naturally the occasional drink as well!

The gambling came in the person of one Jack Clark. He was the bookies' runner, and when I was on afternoon shift he'd call round in the morning and I'd have three threepenny doubles and one threepenny treble 'on the strap', which means to say on credit. If any of those horses I backed ever won it was a miracle, and by the end of the week I'd usually owe Jack Clark three or four shillings. Now, even by the time I was sixteen, I was only getting about four bob a week pocket money, so I'd have to pay Jack the strap, and then borrow it back again to go out with at the weekend.

I was continually in debt, and that wasn't helped by Jack Clark's other activity, which was running a card school in a little shed at the end of his backyard. There would be ten or twelve of us at this little table, and the game was always three-card brag. It was a halfpenny in the kitty, and then so much for the candle—it was dark in there, and we needed a candle to see by. The only trouble was, Jack Clark paid for the candle by taking a halfpenny out of every kitty.

Now, we'd often play for eight hours on a Saturday, and then again on a Sunday, so it isn't hard to work out what happened. By the time the game was over, Jack Clark had got most of the money, and the players would have precious little left between them. But we were young and daft, and it was some years before I realised what was happening. Jack Clark never worked in his life. He brought up a whole family on the dole and his outside activities, and yet he was the only one who could afford to go into the pub and order halves of bitter all round.

Saturday was our night for a drink—if Jack hadn't got the lot—and often as not a few pints would leave us broke till next pay day. But I enjoyed the pub, as I still do, and I enjoyed giving them a song. In fact, there was a friend of mine called Blackwell who had a band in Wigan, and I sometimes used to go over and sing with them. Eventually they asked me to go singing full-time. I turned it down, but who knows, I might have ended up a pop-star! After all, at the Cross Keys, one of the pubs I used in Ashton, they used to have talent contests on a Friday night, and I won it once—singing 'Russian Rose'! I still love singing, and many years later, at one or other of the parties during the NUM annual conferences, I'd end up giving them a ditty.

When we did go for a drink, of course, it was only with our own kind. There was no social mixing. For a start, you never even *saw* the pit owners, even though in the case of Stones Garswood they were a local family. The colliery managers would live in Ashton, and perhaps near the pit, but in those days they were regarded as very important men in the community, and it would have been unheard of to meet them in the pub for a drink, as would happen today. We didn't even mix with the middle managers, or the deputies.

But there were a few exceptions, and one of them was a Major Hart, who was manager of a colliery in the Leigh area. He ran the Bickershaw Brass Band, which was a big one, and they always said that if you were a good band player you could always get a job in that colliery. He used to buy their instruments for them, and if they were good players they got a good job at the pit, too. That sort of paternalism was common. Very occasionally you might see a favourite collier having a drink with the manager, but never the run of the lads like ourselves.

Once I had gone down the pit I stopped playing sport, because we had little enough free time, though I did often go to watch Wigan, whom I supported, play rugby league, especially after I got married. A lot of miners in that area of Lancashire played rugby league, and there used to be a saying at Wigan that if you wanted a good prop forward you only had to shout as much down the nearest pit-shaft and there'd be a good one come up in the next cage.

In those days, they'd get gates of about twenty thousand, where now it's down to two or three, and they played thirteen a side, because there had been the split between League and Union. It was very much not done to talk League and Union in the same pub. In the pubs and clubs in the centre of Wigan it was League, and on the outskirts it was Union.

And then there were the girls. Peter Street, which was back to back with Duke Street, where I lived, faced on to open fields, and four miles across those fields was the village of Golborne. That was a happy hunting ground, because there were a lot of mills there, and of course a lot of mills meant a lot of mill girls. I used to go and meet them in those fields for a bit of what we called 'sparking'. I don't suppose that needs explaining, but we certainly weren't playing hoop-la. I've always been one to enjoy the ladies.

Another favourite spot was a place called Skitters Woods, which was the only patch of trees in the area open to the public. I used to be full of bluebells, and a fair covering of courting couples as well, but now, like the fields, it's all been smothered over with houses. And there was Lord Gerard's estate, a vast place surrounded by a wall, with big trouble if you got caught on the wrong side of it. But of course we did hop over when we could, because there were hundreds of rabbits to be poached in there. Now, that park's been cut clean in two by the M6 motorway, and Ashton, shorn of its pits and its mills, has become a dormitory suburb for Liverpool.

I was nineteen when I met Nellie. Her real name was Ellen Mather, and she came from Ashton, the eldest daughter of Levi Mather, who was the youngest of five brothers. They all worked in the pits, and her father was one of the finest machinists I've ever seen in a coal mine. he was a part-time farmer as well, which is something that still happens—lads with smallholdings or farms who work down the pits.

Levi was a hell of a fellow, good at football and cricket and darts, and billiards and snooker, too. On top of all that he won a medal for bravery down the mine. I think his family were either Methodist or Church of England, but his wife was a Catholic, and that's how Nellie was brought up. Like my mother, Nellie's was one of the founder members of the women's section of the Labour party in the district. And another was a certain Mrs Blackwell, who was my mother's aunt.

Well, Mrs Blackwell had a son called Tommy, who I suppose was a sort of cousin of mine, and Tommy was having a party for his twenty-first birthday, to which I was invited. Nellie was not. But she and a friend of hers called Esther decided to gatecrash it. There were mostly lads there, but a few girls, one of whom was with me. The moment I saw Nellie, though, I decided I rather fancied her—well, to be honest, I'd already fancied her from afar, because I had seen her a few times waling in the street. She was slim, and very good-looking, and in the context of a mining village I always thought she looked rather regal.

Someone was playing the piano, and I did some sort of party trick— Nellie says that I was just standing there and twiddling a coat-hanger round and round, which doesn't sound much of a trick, I must say—and then I went over to her and said: 'Well, now I've done that, you'll have to give us a song.' She wasn't too keen. As she puts it, she sings like two cats under a door. But her friend Esther told her they had to do it, and up they got together and sang, of all things, 'The Old Rugged Cross'. She's never known why that particular song, but I know it sounded so terrible it brought the house down.

That's when I decided to go over and ask if I could take her home. 'Not likely,' she said, 'you're with that other girl.'

It was on a Saturday night, that party, and the following day, after church, Tommy and I and another friend called Billy Cunningham went on what was called 'the parade'. Gerrard Street was the main street in Ashton, and on Sunday evenings everyone would walk up and down it, with the lads whistling at the girls, and the girls pretending not to notice. But luckily for me, when we saw Nellie and Esther parading, and gave them the customary whistle, they stopped to talk, and Billy Cunningham and I made a date to take them to the pictures the following Saturday, me with Nellie and Billy with Esther.

That was fine, and we made another date for the following week. But unknown to me at the time, Esther didn't fancy Billy one little bit, and she asked Nellie if she minded changing partners. Nellie went along with the idea, but then it turned out she didn't fancy the poor fellow either, and she never turned up. For some reason or other I didn't turn up either, so the unfortunate Esther was left with Billy and nothing she could do about it. But the following day I met Nellie again at the parade, and from that moment we started going out together regularly.

It wasn't exactly a jet-set romance. I was on shift work, so I'd say to Nellie, 'Can we go to the pictures next Saturday?', and when she agreed I'd say 'Well, book the tickets, will you, and I'll give you the money later.' To this day she reminds me that I never paid her back for all those tickets she bought.

She would never go in the bottom doors, where all we rough buggers went, and where it was only a penny. She insisted on the top doors, which were twopence, to sit in the balcony. And to book seats cost threepence, so I reckon she did lay out quite bit.

Nellie worked as a silk warper in one of the mills in Golborne, that same Golborne where our son Frank now works in the pit, and where there was a very bad explosion a couple of years ago. When she was on afternoon shift, I'd walk across to meet her at the mill, and then we'd walk back through the fields. She lived with her parents, which was a bit farther than our house, and she'd usually have her bike, but we'd walk together and let one of the tyres down and pretend she'd had a puncture. Or sometimes I'd borrow my brother Bob's bike, and we'd go for rides together. Pubs never. For a start I couldn't afford it, and then again, the pub was really a place where you drank with the lads. You'd very seldom see single girls in there.

So it was mostly the fields—many's the time I was so late with her that I had to run like hell to get back in time for the night shift—and, like a lot of other young couples who fell in love and courted in those fields, we reached the position where it was necessary to go to the church. It was never considered any disgrace. If fact, from the time we started going out together I think it was assumed we'd get married. I don't think her mother was overjoyed, but her father and I got on like a house on fire, so there were no threats of a thumping, or anything like that.

Nellie was nineteen, and we got married on October 2, 1937. It was a Saturday, and as usual I'd tipped my wages to my mother the night before, and she'd given me seventeen shillings and sixpence for pocket money. That was what we had to get married on. And it didn't last long. When we went into the vestry to sign the book, the priest, Father Lancaster, said: 'Well, Mr Gormley, it's usual to make a small donation to the church.' I thought, 'I'll give him a dollar,' but before I could get the money out he quickly added: 'It's usually ten shillings.' I gave it to him with what I confess was a great deal of reluctance.

That left seven and sixpence. But luckily we had a very generous helper in Nellie's mother, who paid for the taxi to the church, which was ten shillings, and for the first week's food bill. We had a good party at the Caledonian Hotel on the Town Green in Ashton, and then went back to their house, which was where we began our married life. It was so much like going back home, in a way, that I'd forgotten to bring any clothes with me, and all I had to wear for the wedding night was the frilly shirt I'd worn at the church—not that it really mattered.

On the Monday morning I went back to work at Stones Garswood, and Nellie went back to work at the mill, which was just as well, because if I was bringing two pounds a week home, that would have been a good week, so it helped that Nellie was getting a fair wage. She never showed her pregnancy much, and on February 11 I went off to do night shift quite unaware that anything was in the offing. I came home the next morning to find myself the father of a bouncing boy, delivered at home by Nurse Davey, the midwife.

It seems it took Nellie by surprise, too, because she'd been getting a bit fed up sitting around, and suggested to her mother that they go to the pictures. 'You can't go to the pictures like that,' her mother had said, but Nellie had insisted, and as soon as they got there she started to go into labour. There wasn't much to spare by the time they'd managed to get her back home again.

In the late summer of that year, 1938, we had another piece of good luck. Nellie's mother had always had her eye on a certain double-fronted house in the same road in Ashton, and sure enough it became vacant and she was able to get hold of it. So I went to see Mr Sunderland, who owned the houses, and asked if we could stay on in their house, where we'd been living with them for six months by then. I was pleased as Punch when he said 'Yes', and not quite so pleased when he added: 'But we'll have to put your rent up. It'll be ten shillings a week.' Many weeks, that would be nearly half my wages, but we still jumped at the chance of having a home of our own.

But, as chance would have it, something else happened at that time. The daughter of the colliery owner was getting married, and they came round asking everyone for a contribution for a wedding present.

I'd never even seen the girl, so when they came to me I said: 'No. I'm not contributing to any present. When I got married not so many months ago, nobody contributed for a present for us. So why the hell should I contribute to a present for someone who's got a lot more money than me anyway?'

Nothing was said, but the following Friday they came round at paytime with little boxes of wedding cake for everyone but me. I wasn't bothered. After all, that was the day we were going to have our own home for the very first time, and I was just looking forward to being together with Nellie and our new baby, whom we'd called Frank.

Now, of course, we couldn't afford for me to take a day off work to help Nellie's parents move, so she borrowed a handcart to carry all their heavy stuff up to their new house, and then set to scrubbing and cleaning to make everything nice for when I came home, and arranging what little bits of furniture we had—a couple of armchairs, a sideboard, and an old table of her mother's, which she scrubbed and scrubbed to get all the paint off. Then, after doing all that, she cooked the meal ready for me, because she knew how excited I'd be, and wanted everything to be as right as she could make it.

Well, at ten that night I got home from the shift, and sat down, and she brought the food for me, and I just looked at it and said: 'I just can't eat it.'

'What on earth's the matter with it?' she asked, obviously very upset after all her hard work.

'I'm sorry, love,' I said, 'but I've got some bad news for you. I've got the sack.'

I might not have got the wedding cake, but when I'd opened my pay packet I found a note to tell me I was fired. Naturally I'd gone straight in to ask them what it was all about, but they just said: 'Ah well, Joe, you know why.' And, in those days, there was nothing to be done about it. The immediate cause was obviously the business about the wedding present, but I also think they hadn't forgotten the episode with the collier a couple of years before.

In any case, they didn't need valid reasons for doing anything in those days, and the funny thing is that I never even bothered going to the branch secretary of the union. The branch officials were a bit complacent and inactive anyway, and I think I was something of an embarrassment to them. They preferred a placid life to one of continual arguments with the colliery managers.

Nellie, not surprisingly, burst into tears when I told her the news, and I wasn't exactly dry-eyed myself. One moment on top of the world, with our first evening in our own home—then disaster. In the end, none of the meal got eaten.

'Never mind, love,' I said finally, 'something will come of it.' And so it did. The following morning I went to see my father at Boston Colliery, where he and my elder brother Johnny were working. He had a word with the manager there, and straight away I signed on and started work at Boston on the Monday, a fine September morning of 1938.

It was to be one of the many coincidental turning points which have marked every stage of my life.

Chapter Three

Sylvesters and Gablocks

I started at Boston as a general dogsbody. By then I was pretty expert in most of the things that went on down at the pit, so I could do any general repair work, or most other things that needed doing.

But, after I'd been there a few weeks, the deputy came up and asked me if I wanted to earn more money.

'Of course I do,' I said, 'I always want more money.'

'Well,' he said, 'I've got a job going as second man on a coal cutter, if you want it.'

Want it? I jumped at the chance. It meant doing a regular afternoon shift, instead of changing shifts every week, and it meant an extra sixpence a shift. That was important, when I was trying to keep a good level of housekeeping money to give Nellie every week, especially now that we had a child.

The coal cutter was the skilled man. He'd be one of the older miners, normally in his fifties. And the second man acted as his general runabout. The machine was an undercutting machine, which took a six- to eight-inch slice out of the bottom of the seam. As the cutter took it along, one of my jobs was to put the 'sprags', or wedges, under the rest of the coal in the seam, to keep it from breaking up.

Another of the jobs was taking care of the picks. The machine had a jib, with an endless chain, like a bandsaw, driven by compressed air, and the picks were slipped into the chain. It was my responsibility to make sure those picks were always clean and sharp, and the amount of work involved depended on the state of the seam. On some, you could do perhaps a two-hundred-yard run and never need to change the picks, while on others you'd be renewing the picks all the time.

At the end of the day it was my job to carry out all the dulled picks for resharpening at the colliery surface, and many's the time I've carried seventy or eighty of those things on my shoulders. Seventy of them would weigh about thirty pounds, which might not seem much, except that it was about three miles, and you had to walk all the way—there were no manriders in those days.

What's more, whereas most roadways today are horizontal, we used to follow the seams down their inclinations, and believe me, the seams in Lancashire were always pretty well inclined – always sloping south, towards the river Mersey. So it wasn't so bad carrying the picks in at the start of the shift. It was carrying them out at the end I didn't care for so much. But I was young and fit, and used to take a pride in showing it wasn't any problem for me.

The seams varied in height—I've actually worked in some as low as sixteen inches—but the ones I preferred were between four feet and four feet six inches high, allowing you enough space to put pads on and work on your knees. As we worked our way along the seam, the cutter would take that slice out to a depth of about five feet. Following behind us was a man with a machine for boring holes of that same depth in the coal above where we'd cut.

After him came the shot-firer. He would 'stem', or fill, all those holes with explosive, and then fire them, blowing down all the coal above the cut. It was his responsibility to check the area round every shot-hole for any gas present. Above the coal seam there is a 'parting', where the strata separate once the coal has been dropped by the shot-firing. That's where gas accumulates—in what we called the 'wastes', an area behind you as you worked at the face, and which had been fired and excavated a few days previously. Normally, the current of air at the coal face is strong enough to carry away any gas, but it was still a risky business, and if there was any hint of gas at all, the shot-firer wouldn't fire till it had cleared.

Happily, modern mining methods have removed a lot of that risk, and few shots are fired, except occasionally at the 'headings', that is, at each end of the seam being cut. But even that's being eliminated by machines which cut out the holes you need.

The shot-firing took place on the night shift. Then, on the morning shift, the colliers would come in and load the coal on to the conveyor belts, each man shifting up to twenty tons or more a day. And following them, in the afternoon, we would come back with the cutters and the whole process would start again. With us came the conveyor men, whose job it was to move the conveyor system forward to the next piece of the seam to be cut. It was a permanently rotating system.

Above us, as we worked, the earth, for perhaps a mile up to the surface, was supported by the props. Behind them were the 'packs', about six yards wide, made of stone from the waste material, and packed tight up to the roof. Then behind that the area called the waste, and behind that another pack. The theory was that this system would prevent subsidence, but today it has been discarded.

As the seam advanced, of course, the props had to be removed, to be replaced by a new line of packs, and the removal was also the packers' job, which they did using winches called 'sylvesters' or 'gablocks' to drag out the props. The whole idea was to tip the weight of the earth away from the face itself—and, I might add, the men working at it.

So the whole system was totally inter-related. If one group of workers had a dispute, it immediately affected all the others, because it only needed one link to be missing from the chain and the rest was useless. It wouldn't operate. Most important of all, everyone down the mine had to rely on everyone else to do his job properly in order to minimise the risks. I think that's the basic reason why miners have traditionally been such a close-knit group of workers.

But, even though we were all so interdependent, each operation was still separate, and paid for on a separate contract—the colliers for so much coal filled, the cutters for so much coal cut, the borers for so many holes bored, and the packers for so many yards packed and waste removed.

Each mine was divided into 'districts', each of which might have a couple of coal faces in production. There might be five or six districts to each mine, and each district would have a deputy to oversee it and to be reponsible for the safety in that district. The deputies came from among the miners, and to get the job they had to pass some pretty stiff exams, to make sure they knew every detail of what went on, and what should go on, down the mine. Today, the managements try to get the necessary production from a colliery using far fewer coal faces, which reduces the problems of transport and materials. But, in those pre-nationalisation days, all the company was interested in was getting as much coal from the pit as possible, and that meant working as many faces as possible. Why should they worry? They thought nothing of it if times got bad and they had to close the pit, because they had so many other irons in the fire. But at least by the time I started the battle against women working underground had been won, even though, as I mentioned earlier, they were still doing very dirty work in the screening plants. It wasn't until a few years after the Second World War that we finally got them out of that, too. Then, many of them went to work in the canteens, which is why today we have women canteen workers in the NUM.

In later years, I was frequently asked what the Union's attitude would be if a woman asked to work down a mine. My reply was always that we'd considered it, and made a decision on it. That decision is hidden from nobody. We said quite openly that we would not allow women to work underground in British coalmining. We had a long battle to get them out of the pits, and the Union is not prepared to undo that achievement.

The law was framed in such a way as to suggest that women would only be allowed to go underground if the main content of the job didn't entail staying underground regularly. We objected even to that. We said, 'Not on your life!'

This puts the Coal Board in a bit of a cleft stick. We've told them that the first time they employ a woman underground, we would say, 'That's it. She's not to be employed, or there'll be trouble.' So they know our feelings on the matter. Successive governments have known our feelings on the matter. We just hope that none of these modern young ladies tries to create a situation, by deliberately applying for a job on the coalface, because the Coal Board would have to say 'No' to her.

We don't mind women doing jobs on the surface, as they are doing, but we believe that working underground in a mine is no fit place for a woman. We're quite specific about this, and strong enough to insist on it, so nobody need have any other thoughts on the matter.

But, in those pre-War days, the strength of the union was far less. Any general negotiations in the area would go on between the miners' agent and the owners' agent. We had a famous one, who was always known as 'Mr No'. He'd sit there behind his desk and, no matter what claims were put to him, he'd only have the one stock reply—'No'. I don't think he knew the meaning of the word 'Yes', because he certainly never used it, and it's surprising we didn't give him more trouble than he got.

If you *really* wanted to improve your conditions, there was no alternative to fighting your own battle with the colliery managers. That's where I won my first small victory. In those days, the colliers, who were regarded as the élite, and the leading cutters, were given concessionary coal as a perk of the job. No one else got it, and I didn't think that was right—not right for me, anyway.

So I went to see the management about it. They wouldn't have it. So I wrote out my notice. Well, they talked me out of it, but when I asked a second time for concessionary coal, they again refused, and again I wrote out my notice. This went on for about six weeks. Nellie used to bring Frank in his pram down to the pit to see me, and she'd say: 'Oh no, Joe, you're not putting in your notice *again,* are you?'

I'd say: 'I bloody well am. If I don't get what I want, I'll keep these notices going in.' And in the end I did get what I wanted, in the form of twenty-four hundredweight of coal for ten shillings, delivered to my door every six weeks. A lot of the other lads came up afterwards to ask me about it, of course, and I just told them: 'It's up to you. Get in there and claim it.' But I was the only one who succeeded.

We needed every bit of extra help we could get, because, working on piece work, there were good weeks and bad weeks. I got a broken finger once, and had to miss a few days, so that at the end of the week I only had two days pay to draw. So on that occasion I gave it all to Nellie. She gave it straight back and said: 'You can keep the bloody thing. If you can't give it me when it's a full week, you can keep the two days.'

I knew what she meant. We just couldn't afford to be off work. I got a bad elbow once, when a big lump of coal came off the face and knocked me spinning. My elbow and shoulder were badly bruised, but I was back at work the following day. If you got a cut on your face, or something like that, you'd just rub a bit of coal dust on it and carry on. Many times I've had fingernails ripped off, or had black nails through hitting them with a hammer. If that happened, I'd relieve the pressure by getting a piece of wire from one of the detonators and sticking it down the back of the nail to let the blood spurt out.

There were no doctors at the pits, and if you got something like a broken finger, the first aid man would treat you. Then it would be up to you whether you went to hospital or to your own doctor. But unless it was really serious you wouldn't bother, because you couldn't afford to. If you were off work sick for a week, you only got about fifteen shillings, and our rent was ten shillings to start with.

So you had to be pretty hard, to work in the mines, and whether it was a good thing or a bad thing I'm not sure, because it was only as a result of economic reasons forcing us to work when we weren't fit. Proper sickness benefit was a dream, but a dream which, as socialists, we fought for, always with the memory of what it used to be like. Those benefits are what a lot of people complain about nowadays, but then they didn't have to suffer under the old system. As far as I'm concerned, if a person is genuinely sick, or genuinely injured, or genuinely unemployed, he shouldn't have to go shopping at a different shop.

Working on the coal-cutter led to another instance when I had to decide what I really thought about life. Down the mine, although we were a mixture of all religions, it was never a topic of conversation. Come to think of it, we never discussed politics either—it was always assumed that all miners were supporters of the Labour Party anyway. And religion was simply a man's own business.

But then a young Irish priest came to Ashton. Now, one of the main shifts for coal-cutters was on the Sunday morning, to get the coal ready for the colliers on the Monday morning. If we didn't cut on Sunday, they didn't work on Monday.

One day this young priest came to our house and asked to speak to me. Then he asked me why I worked on Sundays. I said: 'Well, I don't think I'm any less religious by doing what I'm doing than by coming to church. Because, if I don't work on a Sunday, a lot of other people are going to be out of work on a Monday.'

'That's no argument,' he said. 'Have you forgotten what's laid down for the Lord's Day?'

That got me mad. 'Surely,' I said, 'the Lord laid down rules that have to be looked at with a bit more elasticity than you're showing. You can be just as religious without having to run to church. And I intend to make sure that my colleagues aren't put out of work on Mondays just because of some religious rules. If I want to do that, I could get sacked, and if I get sacked, who's going to look after my family?'

He didn't have an answer, and he left.

When war came, in 1939, I was twenty-two and very frustrated. Most of my mates were able to go into the Army—though many of them, like that same Billy Cunningham who'd been on my first date with Nellie, were sadly to get killed—and I wanted to join them, but being by then a specialist miner I wasn't allowed to join up. In the early years they called up some miners, but later on they got so short of coal that they wouldn't allow any miners to go into the forces. Those who were left were supplemented by the so-called 'Bevin boys', brought into the pits under the scheme devised by Ernest Bevin to give people an alternative to going into the Army.

I've often, in the years since, reminded people that at that time it was a straight choice between war and the pits.

They were a mixed bunch. One young fellow, who was sent to work with me, came from Warrington, which wasn't a traditional mining area. But he didn't take long to learn. I was then a leading man on a coal cutter, and he became my second man, and very efficient too. It got to the point where, if for some reason I wasn't there, he could take over the cutter himself. He became really skilled, and I thought he would have stayed on after the War. But like most of them, once he was told he could go, he went, even though he'd made such a wonderful job of it.

But there were others who wouldn't do a thing. There was one, the son of a doctor, who never had any intention of doing any work, and all they could get him to do was sit in one of the refuge holes in the workings, with a book in which he ticked off the number of loads that came past him. They couldn't get him to do a damn thing else, so he just sat the War out that way.

We knew all about the War, of course, with all the planes coming over to bomb Manchester and Liverpool, and dropping quite a few on Ashton on the way. After I'd finished my shift, at two in the morning, I'd often walk back to an empty house, with the door wide open, and wonder where everyone was, until I realised that they'd either be at Nellie's mother's house, which was only sixty or seventy yards away, or in the air-raid shelters. But that wasn't for me.

I always used to say: 'To hell with it. If a bomb hits me, it'll hit me in bed, and the best of luck to it.' I never once went into those shelters. I've always had this feeling that if you're going to be a true man, you have to be a little bit of a fatalist. If it's going to happen, it'll happen. If you're going to get killed, you'll get killed. If you weren't a little bit of a fatalist you wouldn't do some of the jobs we had to do in the mines – like seeing a roof starting to deteriorate and then getting under it to put supports up.

It was in 1940, on October 9, that our second child, Winnie, was born. We'd been to the pictures the night before, but although Nellie had said she felt a bit rough, she didn't say it was that. I remember that day. It was pouring with rain, and I was on afternoon shift. We'd taken the bed downstairs to the parlour, and it turned out that just as Nellie was giving birth the damn curtains fell down.

The black-out was strictly in force, and within a few seconds there was an air-raid warden shouting, 'Will you put those lights out.' Nurse Davey, the midwife, shouted back that there was a woman inside giving birth, and all he could shout back was, 'I can't help that.' Nor he could. By the time I got home I had a daughter, so I missed both my children's births through being down the mine.

The other impact the War had on us was through all the troops billeted nearby. They used Haydock racecourse as a camp, as well as Lord Gerard's estate, so Ashton became a real centre for troops, and the girls had a wonderful time. When I was on night shift, and there were no more buses, I'd have to walk home past the racecourse during the black-out, and there'd always be a sentry shouting, 'Stand and deliver,' or whatever it was. I'd just shout back, 'Get the hell out of it,' and in the end they got to know us. But we still got those challenges every morning.

There were all sorts of nationalities stationed at Haydock—Free Poles, Free French, Yugoslavs, Italians, Czechs. We got to know a lot of them. There was never any sneering at young men, like myself, who were not in uniform, because everyone understood that it was a mining area, and that that was the reason. But I still felt my resentment at not being allowed to join up, and my reaction, whenever I saw a soldier in uniform, was to take him home for tea and then go out and get him drunk, especially on Friday nights, the lads' night out, which were known as 'Amami' nights, so-called because that was the name of the shampoo with which the lasses titivated their hair.

Then, shortly before D-Day, we got this vast invasion of thousands and thousands of Americans, the Yankees. We had a lot of friends among them—Lou Gordioso, Gene Lamagna from the Bronx, Tall Thomas from Mexico. Nellie used to have them lined up for her to press their pants for them, and they'd bring her tins of fruit and cream, from which she made cakes for them.

They were all young lads, and didn't have a clue about anything. They came to Ashton, flashed their money about because they didn't know what to do with it, got a bit of training, and then a load of them were sent off to some abortive landing where thousands of them got slaughtered. Cannon fodder. A lot who were our friends never came back. But I think it was that first exposure to so many different nationalities that gave me the feeling for internationalism which has stayed ever since.

On Saturday afternoons, though, it was Wigan, always Wigan. If they were playing in a cup-tie away from home, Nellie would make a flask of tea and go down to the rugby league ground to queue for the tickets. We followed that team all over the country, and one of the proudest moments of my life was in 1981 when my grandson, Frank's boy, got picked to play for Lancashire. Mind you, a couple of years earlier he cost me the most expensive tie in the country. He was playing for a youth team, and I said I'd sponsor them so much for every point they got. The trouble was, they were the runaway winners of their league, and it cost me about £150. All I got for it was a present of one of their club ties, and a lot of pleasure.

In the early years of the War, when I was a coal cutter, I would negotiate with the manager on behalf of my cutting team. There were area agreements, made between the agents, but there was still room for the individual to manoeuvre, and it could mean that I'd have a different agreement to what they'd managed to achieve at the next door pit. It just depended on how good a negotiator you were. Then, in 1942, I had a disagreement with the management, and I moved to pan-shifting – moving the shaker-pans of the conveyor system forward to the coal face.

Like my father before me, I became the chargeman, and it was my job to get all the wages and split the money up among the men according to how many shifts they had worked. It was a hell of a system, a pernicious system. You could have a chargeman, acting like a contractor, who would arrange the contract for the job and then never even go to work at the pit. He'd just turn up on a Friday, collect the money, and pay the men off. He'd end up with more than they did, even though they'd been working all week and he'd done nothing. So I determined to break this so-called 'butty' system.

I went to the management and told them: 'If there's four men in a team, they'll get four equal wages out of the money we earn on the contract. But don't give it to me. You divide it up. You give four men four wage packets.'

In the end they agreed. Later, others followed. But it was I who effectively broke that system.

In 1943 we had our first-ever holiday. We went to a pub in North Wales, on the banks of the Conway at Llanwryst. There was nothing much to do but walk around in the fields, and nothing much in the fields but sheep and sheep muck and bluebottles as big as horses. I had more hair in those days, and as was the fashion I used to smooth it down with vaseline. Those flies loved that. They kept landing on it, and I remember my lad pulling up a big fern to waft them away with.

The kids loved it all, of course, and the first time we went down to the river, on a lovely hot day, they couldn't wait to get in. So we stripped them off, put on their costumes, and in they went. I'll never forget the roar of fury from farther down the bank. It turned out that it was a special fishing section of the river, and all the fishermen there reckoned the kids were ruining their sport.

Our second holiday was a week in Blackpool, right at the end of the War. We stayed in a boarding house in Dickenson Road, and for most of the week none of the other people there talked to one another at all. But then Germany surrendered, and it was VE night, and suddenly we all got together and decided to go out to celebrate. Unfortunately, there was a shortage of beer, so there wasn't much to celebrate *with*, but then someone said that at Knott End, across the river from Fleetwood, there was a pub which somehow always managed to have something to drink. So we all got on a tram to Fleetwood, and took the ferry across to Knott End.

Nellie's parents were there, together with Nellie and me and the kids, and we all got blotto. It's always the way – when you haven't been able to get something for a while, and then you can, you tend to hog yourself. And we did. I remember as closing time came, and we started to leave, I saw this little round table full of half-drunk glasses of rum. 'I'm not leaving these,' I thought, and drank the lot. I walked, or staggered, back to the ferry, and it was only through someone restraining me that I didn't walk straight off the jetty into the river. And I know we were singing in that tram all the way back to Blackpool.

Perhaps, who knows, we were all dreaming of a brave new world, which would, naturally, be a socialist world. I had joined the Labour Party at about the time I got married, and it was politics which originally interested me most, rather than the union. I would occasionally meet the union branch secretary and have a chat with him, but I never bothered to attend branch meetings, simply because I always did my own negotiating. Right from the start I'd fought for better conditions, but as an individual.

In those days, the Party's main means of expressing itself to the grass-roots members was through the Labour Clubs, many of which had been founded by the miners themselves as places for meeting and talking politics, since there was an increasing awareness that workers should become politically involved. They were social clubs as well, of course— shades of those potato pie scrapings on a Friday night!—and over the years the social side has taken over more and more, though they still contribute to local party funds.

There would be annual meetings to elect the club officials, like the president, or chairman, and the secretary, and at the time I joined there had recently evolved another post for election, that of delegate to the monthly meetings of the National Union of Labour Clubs. It hadn't been going long, and there were still only about sixty clubs affiliated, whereas today there are about two hundred. The preponderance of the clubs was around our area of Lancashire, with a few in Yorkshire as well. Ashton alone had six Labour Clubs, and it was from the Ashton Central club that I was elected as delegate to the monthly meetings.

That was around the time war broke out, and I was to stay as the delegate for most of the war years. It gave me my first taste for politics. I got on to my first platform and made my first speech. I was young, and politically ambitious, and it was there, in those monthly delegate meetings, that I received my first, practical, basic training for all that was to follow.

They listened to me, too, because I was speaking on behalf of one of the bigger clubs in the association, and meeting by meeting, year by year, I gradually made a lot of friends in the area through the medium of the Labour Club movement. Those friendships were to stand me in good stead, and many years later I was able to repay those friendships—for years and years that Association had been trying to get affiliated to the Labour Party nationally, and when I became Chairman of the Party's Organisation Committee, I was able to ensure that they finally achieved it. They even made me an honorary vice-president of the National Association of Labour and Socialist Clubs, and in spite of the fact that I haven't been able to attend many of their meetings, they haven't sacked me yet!

So now the Association sends a delegate to the Labour Party conference, and they've even had a member on the National Executive Committee in recent years, though the paradox is that nowadays, with all the concerts and bingo and so on that they get involved with, they're far less political than they used to be. But in those days it was mostly politics, real hard politics, and through being a prominent member of the Labour Club movement I also became known in the local Labour Party.

It seemed certain to me then that, apart from working down the pit, my route in life would be a political one. That was before I led my first strike.

In 1946, there had been a fire at Boston. A spark from a cutter had ignited the coal face. Luckily there weren't any fatalities, but it was serious enough to close the pit. So I moved to another pit in the area, to a mine called Lyme Pit.

Two years later, in 1948, I was a chargeman pan-shifter, or conveyor-mover, at Lyme Pit, the same job I'd had before the fire at Boston, except that now there were forty-odd men in the preparatory teams.

Now, as I described earlier, the rota system by which the mines then worked meant that we were always on afternoon shift, or sometimes nights, but never on the day shift. That was reserved for the colliers. And we were getting a bit browned off.

I remember it was snowing heavily outside, as we all sat in the canteen, talking about our grouses, but without any clear idea what to do about it. So finally I stood up.

'I think we're out of our minds,' I said. 'Here we are, we can't bring our kids up, and come to think of it we never even see our kids, because we come to work while they're at school, and when we get home they're in bed, and when we get up in the morning they've gone off to school again. It's bloody daft. I think it's time we put a stop to this regular afternoon shift. What I suggest is that we just bugger off, go and have a drink in the pub, and leave them to it. Let's see what they think.' That may not be word for word, but it expresses exactly what I said to them.

Without a murmur, all those forty-odd men who were on the preparatory work—the conveyor men, the cutters, and the borers – just stood up and walked out. It was an almost uncanny feeling to realise that my words could have that effect. At any rate, we all went to the pub, as suggested, had a few drinks, and went home.

When we arrived for work the following day, of course, the pit had come to a standstill. We went to sit in the canteen, and suddenly everyone was there, the president of the branch, and the secretary of the branch, and one of the agents, and God knows who else. They were all expressing sympathy like mad, but at the same time they were all prevailing upon us to go back to work.

We listened to them for a while, and then I said: 'Ah yes, you can give us all the sympathy in the world, but it won't change the system, you know.' So they talked a bit more, and we listened a bit more, and then I turned to the lads, who were sitting all around me, and I said: 'Well, there's plenty of sympathy here, my mates, but there's not much else, is there?'

Now, the previous day we hadn't told anyone why we were walking out, though from our grumbles over the months they knew the reason perfectly well. But this time, although we'd spelt it out, they still hadn't come up with anything constructive, so I said to the lads: 'I suggest we just sit tight and let 'em have another do.' And up we all got and walked out the second time, safe in the knowledge that, although our action was completely unofficial, no one else was going to go and do the jobs we'd been doing.

The following day I said to myself, 'We've shown them that we've as much ability to stop the pit as anyone else, and it's time to go back and see if they can work anything out.' So back we all went that afternoon, and again they came to see and talk to us.

Well, we knew perfectly well they couldn't change the system overnight. But we'd shown by our protest that it wasn't just a colliers' organisation. Before that, the colliers could have a walk-out, or a dispute, or an argument, and everyone thought it was all right, just because they were the colliers, the élite. No one ever dreamed that the preparatory shift men would be prepared, or able, to stop the pit without the colliers being involved, and what hurt them was the fact that, if we didn't work, the colliers couldn't work, and they didn't get a penny for non-working days, even if they turned up for their shifts.

So I told them: 'We want an assurance from you lot that you're going to consider the matter seriously. You have to face the fact that while some people do a regular morning shift, and are able to bring their kids up normally, others, who do a regular afternoon shift under the present system, never see their kids at all.'

Straight away they promised to look at the situation, which was really all they could do. So I turned to the men with me and said: 'Okay, lads, we've had our protest, and we've shown 'em what we can do. So come on, let's get back to work.' To a man they all stood up, and without any further protest we all went back down the pit.

It taught me a great lesson—that it's easy enough to start a strike, but you must have the guts to finish it. As I was to say on two occasions, as President of the NUM years later, 'There has to come a time when enough is enough . . . when you say that now is the time to get things started again.'

But, short as the strike had been, it soon proved to be another of those chance turning points in my life. It led directly to the start of my career in the union.

Two other quite separate factors also took a hand. The first was that, being on afternoon shifts, I'd always either been too tired, or else physically couldn't get to the branch meetings of the union, which were held on a Friday night. But they'd just started a system by which we could go home, once the work assigned to us for the day was completed.

The second factor was that, nationally, we'd just won the five-day working week, under which agreement we got the same pay that we'd previously earned by six days' work. But the Government were desperate for fuel, so they came back to us and asked us to keep the pits open on Saturdays. Many people argued that this would be a big step backwards, but in fact it was the reverse, because a lot of the lads were very happy to get the overtime for working on Saturdays.

This all took place in 1948, two years after the Attlee Government had nationalised the coal industry, their second piece of nationalisation, following their take-over of the Bank of England. No one had argued too strongly about the Bank, nor was there much dispute about the mines.

Everyone knew that the industry was extremely inefficient, and riddled with the sorts of abuses I've already outlined. And, whereas some might imagine that nationalisation would play a major part in a story like this, the fact was that it made precious little difference to us at the time. They simply came along with a lot of notice-boards which they stuck at the various pit gates, saying, 'This pit is now the property of the National Coal Board.' The deputies stayed the same. The managers stayed the same. And we never saw the owners anyway, so a change of ownership couldn't have much effect on our daily lives.

But it did mean that, as a union, we could now negotiate with one set of people rather than a host of different owners with different attitudes, and they decided to call a national conference to discuss this Extended Hours Agreement. And it happened to be our branch's turn to send a delegate, who was to be chosen at the branch meeting following our little fracas.

Because of our new working arrangements, I was able to go to that meeting, which was the first I had ever attended. The secretary, a little chap called Wilf Foster, who was also a Haydock councillor, was nominated. But a lot of the lads who had been with me in the dispute had also turned up, and they nominated me.

The President of the branch, Tommy Wilcock, was a member of the Communist Party, but he was a pretty fair chairman at meetings, and when he was asked for his opinion, he said he thought that a rank-and-filer should go. And I was duly elected.

It was the first national conference I'd ever attended, of course, and it was the first time I'd ever been to London. It was all pretty strange. We stayed at the Bonington Hotel, which was then a temperance place, which didn't exactly suit us! And I remember walking down towards Trafalgar Square to get a meal. It was just about the first restaurant I'd ever been in, and I didn't have much of a clue what to do—which is funny, thinking of latter years, when the Press seem to make a story out of it every time I go and have a meal. Rationing was still on, but we managed to get a damn good bite, with all kinds of food you just couldn't get up in the mining areas.

Following the conference, I started attending branch meetings regularly, and three or four months later we had the Annual General Meeting of the branch at the colliery, and I was nominated to stand against Tommy Wilcock, who had been President of the branch for many years. When the vote came, I defeated him quite easily. Willy-nilly, my career in the union seemed to be finding its own course.

But I still wasn't convinced that my path didn't lie in politics. I became Chairman of the local Labour Party, and I also became Secretary of the Ashton Central Labour Club, though that was to have its drawbacks.

There was one occasion when we needed someone to take over from the steward, who was going on holiday. As it happened, Nellie's father, Levi, wasn't working, because he'd had a bad attack of silicosis, so I asked him to take it over, and told him we'd give all the help we could. So he and her mother went behind the bar, and Nellie did the cleaning.

Well, Levi was in his element. Whenever anyone came in, he'd draw them a pint and give it to them to try and say, 'Isn't that smashing?' 'Aye, it's smashing, thanks very much,' they'd say, and by the end of the fortnight, instead of making money, we *owed* money. It cost me a week's wages to pay back what Levi had given away with everyone trying his bitter. I said: 'That's the last time I ever take over a pub or a club.'

In 1951, I was elected a member for the East Ward of Ashton Urban District Council, but I also decided that if I was to make anything of being a leader among the mineworkers, then I ought to have some sort of qualifications. So I went to day release classes to sit for my deputy certificate. It was pretty complicated, and you had to be an experienced miner before you could even consider taking the exams. You had, as you still do today, to know all the safety laws, detailed techniques for testing for gas, how to test the roof, and even how to stem a shot, which involved something like firing an old-fashioned cannon—you primed the explosive powder with a detonator, rammed that into the bore-hole, and followed that with the 'stemming', which was clay which had to be rammed in until it reached about four inches from the end of the hole.

They were tough exams, but I passed quite easily, and was then going on to study for my under-manager's and manager's certificates.But with all my union and Labour Party activities I found it increasingly difficult to spare the time. What's more, I was seeing less and less of Nellie and the kids. On top of everything else, there'd been a bit of niggling with relatives, and it all got a bit too much.

So at the beginning of 1952 Nellie and I decided to chuck the whole thing up and emigrate to Australia. We put in our application, and on the form it asked what our hobbies were. I put 'Trade Unionism and Politics', and we were turned down. The reason we were given was that we had no sponsor in Australia, but I was convinced it was because of my 'hobbies'. The strange thing was that ten years later, out of the blue, we got a letter asking if we were still interested in going. But by then my life had taken a very distinct direction, and we turned *them* down.

We were still determined to leave, though, and in 1953, since we couldn't go to Australia, we went to Staffordshire instead.

Chapter Four

All Directions at Once

Staffordshire was to be a clean break—or that was the idea. Nellie went to work in the potteries as a dipper, with the job of putting the liquid glaze on the pots before they were fired. And I went to the Glebe Colliery at Fenton, which now, like all the pits I worked at, with the exception of Bold, is closed.

But somehow the union wouldn't let me escape. After I had been at the Glebe about three weeks, I went to a branch meeting and was promptly elected to the committee. And it wasn't long before I was in a fight.

I was working as a collier, filling coal by spade, and it very quickly became obvious to me that I was having to fill a hell of a lot of coal to get anything near the wages that I'd left behind in Lancashire. They were still operating on piece work at the Glebe, but the price-lists that they'd negotiated for doing the various jobs were far too low. So I started raising hell, and pointing out to my colleagues that we were working for peanuts.

As a result, the miners' agent for the area, Harold Lockett, called a meeting at which there were representatives of three or four different collieries. Harold had had some of the price-list agreements sent to him from Lancashire, and he kept trying to read them out at the meeting to prove that the Staffordshire agreements were just as good. But he couldn't prove it, because they *weren't,* and besides, having been President of my branch at Lyme Pit, I had all the relevant price-lists with me.

'I don't know what you're trying to do, Harold,' I said. 'Are you trying to indicate to these men that they're being paid the same wages for the same output per man shift as they are in Lancashire?'

'No,' he said, 'I'm not saying that.'

'Well, what the hell *are* you saying?' I demanded. 'Because that's the reason we're here. I'm telling you that in North Staffordshire we're working for pounds a week less, for the same output, than in Lancashire. And I want to know what you're going to do about it.'

At least it did get them moving, and they put in for an increase in the price-list, after I'd told them that, in order to get equalisation, they should get at least a shilling a ton extra. So what happened? They came back happily bragging that they'd got the increase. But, when I asked them what they'd actually achieved, it turned out to be only eightpence or ninepence a ton.

'You must be out of your minds. It's negotiations gone mad,' I told them. 'And what's more, what are you going to do about the powder?' That threw them into another tizzy, because whereas in Lancashire the powder for blowing the coal out was always provided free, in Staffordshire they had so much a week stopped out of their wages to pay for it. 'This is bloody daft,' I said, 'the whole system down here stinks of paternalism.'

So they went away again and had themselves another meeting, and then came back to report. 'Did you get it?' I asked. 'Oh yes,' they said, 'we've got the free powder now, but we've had to agree to a penny a ton being subtracted from the price-lists.'

'You *what?*' I said. 'What sort of a gain is *that?* You've all gone bloody mad.'

One way and another I didn't reckon I was going to get rich filling coal in Staffordshire, but luckily I'd taken my deputy's exams two years before, so I applied for the job of deputy and got it straight away, at the same pit. Maybe they thought they'd have less trouble from me that way. It was certainly a full-time job, because, knowing all the jobs down the mine as I did, I would also fill in on anything that needed doing.

One of my jobs was shot-firing—the regular man who did it was off sick, or something like that, so I took over. Now the practice was that, after examining for any traces of gas, you would stem your shots, as I described earlier, and then make sure that all the approaches to the area had sentries posted, to prevent anyone wandering into the area where the firing was to take place.

Well, this particular team was driving a roadway through a fault in the seam. They were a lot of Polish lads—like the Yugoslavs, many Poles married English girls during the War, stayed behind after it was over, and went down the mines. But for many of them, of course, it was years before they could speak anything like decent English.

At any rate, I gave this Polish lad a disc, to show that he was the sentry, and sent him to a spot up the roadway where he would be out of harm's way. Then I took the others to a safe distance down the face and fired the shot. That done, I went back to stem the next hole. Suddenly I heard a voice shouting, and a light flashing, from a gap about ten yards from where the shot had been fired.

'What the hell are you doing down there?' I shouted, not knowing who it was. 'It' turned out to be the pit safety officer.

'What's up? You've no sentries up there,' he said.

'Yes I have, I've got a fellow up there,' I said, and told him his name. But, sure enough, he wasn't there, and when we went back to the face we found out what had happened—this Pole hadn't understood me properly, and instead of going where I'd sent him, he'd stayed with the rest of the crowd. Needless to say, the safety officer wasn't too pleased. 'Well okay, it's my fault,' I told him, 'there's no responsibility attached to anyone else.'

The next day, there was a bit of an inquest with the manager, but there wasn't really too much I could say about it, because it had been my responsibility. But, as it happened, I was getting a bit fed up with Staffordshire anyway. I was missing my own people, and my own traditions, and the previous weekend, when I'd been back to see some friends in Ashton, I'd met some of my old colleagues, who had asked me to go back.

So when it became obvious that the manager was going to have to do something about it, I just said: 'Nay, don't worry about me. Give me my cards, and I'll get back to Lancashire.' They settled for that, and so back to Ashton I went.

Of course, it needn't have been as easy as that. I could even have been taken to court and summonsed, because by law I was responsible for making sure there was a sentry to stop anyone approaching the shot from that side, and if that safety officer had been actually climbing through the hole when the shot was fired, he could have been badly hurt. So I was guilty. It's true that it was the normal practice just to send a man up to act as sentry, and tell him where you wanted him to be, and you'd have expected a pitman to know the rigmarole of the job. Well, maybe it was the language barrier, but he certainly didn't understand. Perhaps I should have gone there with him, posted him at the spot, and told him, 'Don't you move from there till I get back.'

But I didn't, and there it was, and not wanting to get him into trouble I just said, 'It's nowt to do with him,' and they accepted it, and back to Lancashire I went, happy that at least they hadn't sacked me, which they would have been quite entitled to do.

It was to be eight or nine months before Nellie and the kids joined me again, because of course we'd let our house go when we left for Staffordshire, and we had nowhere to come back to. But at least, as I'd been told I would, I had a job, at Bold Colliery in St Helens, and I started there the week I returned.

Nor did it take me long to get back into the full swing of the Union and politics. In 1954, I was again elected on to the council in Ashton, and a right pickle it was in, too. It was solid Labour, of course, with fifteen councillors out of fifteen. The leader was also the agent for the constituency, and on top of that the county councillor for our area. It was real Tammany Hall stuff, and he was notorious in the district. If anybody wanted a council house, all he had to do was send his wife down to see this man . . . and lo and behold they got a council house.

Being young, and fresh on the council, I said that we couldn't allow *this* sort of thing to carry on. Along with some people who thought the same way, I worked and worked until finally we got him shifted, first from the county council, then from Ashton council itself. After that he decided to retire, and then we were able to appoint a new agent for the constituency, and the whole mess was finally cleared up—as it badly needed to be, because all that had been going on was such public knowledge that the other parts of the constituency were beginning to look askance at Ashton Labour Party.

Soon after that, I was elected leader of the Labour group, with a chemist named Johnny Morris as the secretary, but the damage had been done, and we soon lost two or three seats to the Ratepayers. The curious result of that was that the council actually became far less democratic than it had been when it was a hundred percent Labour. Because then we had fifteen different sets of opinions, and no one could claim they were arguing a certain way because it was local Labour Party policy. We all fought among ourselves to get our point of view across.

But as soon as the Ratepayers arrived—they ended up having six seats in the end—we started having to hold caucus meetings, and voted together according to what was decided at those private meetings. I know people call it democracy, but its practical effect was to force the Labour group into having to be seen publicly as completely united. In *practice,* the whole thing became far *less* open-minded. I'm perfectly well aware of the dangers in that argument. I'm simply reporting what happened. It's just a fact that when we had all the seats on the council, arguments and all, we made far more progress.

While all this was going on, I was elected, in 1956, to one of the most important jobs in the union branch at Bold Colliery—as the standing delegate to the monthly meeting held in Bolton, which was the headquarters of the Lancashire miners at that time. The meetings dealt with matters on an area basis. We got reports from the agents on what was happening in their particular group of pits; reports from the Lancashire Miners' Executive Committee, which met twice a month; reports from national level.

Anyone who was a standing delegate—being the spokesman for his colliery—soon made his name, though in fact I was already pretty well-known from the time I was employed at Lyme Pits. There had been a dispute, when the Area Conference claimed concessionary coal for everybody, and this time I was on the wrong side of the fence. The plan entailed those of us who already enjoyed the concession giving up part of our take.

Lyme Pits was one of the Richard Evans group and enjoyed a concessionary coal agreement—the one I'd fought to get as second man on the coal-cutter. But, as part of the hang-over from pre-Nationalisation days, the agreement didn't extend to the rest of Lancashire. They, of course, wanted it too. Our argument went as follows: 'That's okay. We believe you're right. But you shouldn't have to reduce our concessionary coal in order to make sure everybody else gets theirs.'

Well, I was one of the leaders in that fight, but it was one I lost, even though we had legal opinion to back us. In the end I had to say: 'Okay, we're outnumbered. We've done what we can. We now have to accept Union policy that there'll be concessionary coal for everybody, as against just for a limited few.' It was only fair, of course, but it did mean that in place of those twenty-four hundredweight of coal at ten shillings, delivered every six weeks, we got just six tons a year at £2 a ton.

All those wonderful socialist ideals become a bit harder to accept when you're on the losing side of the deal!

Many of these anomalies went on for years. In fact, more than twenty years later, the Yorkshire and Nottingham areas were still battling against a national concessionary coal agreement which would mean a reduction in their area agreements. But the National Union had accepted the need for it, and the conference had accepted it, and in the end it will be inevitable, just as we'd had to give way in the Fifties.

But it was through that battle that I became really well-known in the Haydock area, especially since, at the monthly conference in Bolton, all the delegates from the St Helens pits would meet privately to discuss tactics and so on. When it came to the main meeting, we'd support each other, as much as anything else to stir things up for the area officials. It was a game, then, and today it's still being played.

If that was a game, then the next big turning point in my career, the one which was to push me heavily in the direction of the union rather than politics, was decided on an even more frivolous level—by the toss of a coin.

At that time, the Lancashire miners had two representatives on the National Executive Committee of the NUM. One was always an area official, and the other a rank-and-filer. As still happens, they were nominated and elected every two years, and each area in the county would put forward its candidates. The St Helens group of collieries got together and nominated two of us for the rank-and-file seat. But the pits were divided exactly evenly on which of us they wanted, and we had to make a decision. So I said: 'Oh hell, flip a coin to decide which of us goes.' I've never been able to remember whether it came down heads or tails, but whichever it was, I won.

So when it came to the ballot, I had the full support of the St Helens collieries, which were a pretty powerful group. I came second in the voting, and the post was won by someone from one of the pits over in the West of Lancashire, who was the man in possession, the sitting member of the NEC.

Then Chance took another hand in my life. Within about six months, quite unexpectedly and prematurely, he died. And since I had come second in the ballot, I was called on to fulfil his term of office. At the age of forty I found myself, unbelievably to me, a member of the national executive committee of my union. What's more, Lancashire was the only area which always had a rank-and-filer as one of its representatives, and for three years I was the only one on the NEC. I was still working down the mine, of course, and I used to say that I was the only cloth-cap miner on that national committee. But on it I was, and I was to stay on it, without a break, until my retirement.

I think it was salutary to have at least one man on the executive who was still actually doing the job. It was a way of keeping the other members on their toes—after all, it's easy enough for the top officials in any union to lose touch with the fact that they're representing real people doing real jobs.

My job was certainly real enough—it was while I was at Bold that we had a terrible accident involving a St Helens lad. I was one of the first to get to him. He was caught up in the drum shearer, and he had literally been scalped. There wasn't any ordinary first-aid which would help, so I did the only thing possible and simply stuck the top of his head back on again. Then we took him out on a stretcher, not that I held out much hope for him.

But it seemed they'd managed to patch him up, because within nine months he started back to work, and I remember exclaiming, 'That's a bloody marvel,' when I saw him. I put him back on his old job, to get him back his confidence, and although he was never quite the same again, they'd done a miraculous job in sewing him together and making him able to lead a normal life.

That was how Nellie found out what had happened. All I had said at the time was that there had been a bad accident. That's fairly standard among miners. They'll talk among themselves about something that occurs, but there's a sort of unwritten rule that the womenfolk don't get told the details. I suppose it's something like the deep-sea fishermen—their wives have enough to worry about simply knowing that the men are out there, or in our case down there, without giving them extra gory details to fret over.

On other occasions, it could be a bit of a farce, too. There was one lad there who was shouting about how something bad had happened to his leg. So we put him on a stretcher, and carried him out. It was up a long, long incline, and by the time we got to the top we were sweating cobs.

The moment we got there, hey presto, he got off that stretcher and just walked away. I said: 'If I get hold of him, he'll have two broken legs next time!' But we couldn't catch him!

Mind you, broken legs weren't exactly a laughing matter in our family. In 1954, my son Frank went down the mine. To be honest, neither Nellie or I wanted him to do it, but just as it had been with me, so it was with him. He was sixteen, and all his mates were going down, so he decided he had to as well. That summer, he was due to leave for his holidays, and just before that was the Whit Saturday. Frank said he wanted to work that day.

'Not on a holiday,' said Nellie. 'Even your Dad doesn't work on a holiday.'

'Aye, but I want to earn some money for my holidays,' said Frank.

'Well,' said Nellie, 'if you really want to work, then that's your money. I don't want it.'

So down he went, and the next thing we knew was that he'd had a bad accident. He was a haulage hand, and some tubs had run away out of control. He'd got jammed in between them, and one of them had run over his leg. They took him to Wigan Infirmary, and he had that leg in plaster for sixteen weeks.

I reckon that put him off mining for a bit, because in 1956 he came to us and asked if it was all right if he joined up in the army. We said: 'If that's what you want to do, it's up to you, but if you're going to do it, be sure and join a regiment where you can learn a trade.' So he went into the Grenadier Guards for three years. When he came out they had really straightened him up, and he started work in the building trade.

Then one day he was in a team knocking down some houses near Duke Street in Ashton. He came home, but didn't come through the door. Instead, he started taking his clothes off outside. Nellie saw him and shouted: 'What *have* you been doing?'

'I'm undressing outside here, mother,' he said.

'Why, what's up?'

'I'll not tell you, but I'll undress here,' he insisted.

'Why, where have you been?' asked Nellie, getting more and more suspicious by the moment.

Well, then he told her that he'd been in a certain house, and she understood right enough, because that particular house was renowned in the area for having bedbugs and God knows what. So she told him: 'Get down to the shed, and I'll throw you a towel there.' He had that bath down in the shed, and he finished there and then.

After that he went to the silk mill for a few weeks, but the money wasn't too good, and finally he found his way back down the mine, and, I'm proud to say, in my footsteps, because before I retired I was to see him as one of the delegates to the annual conference of the Western Area of the NUM.

It was late in 1957 that I first joined the NEC, and in that same year I was elected President of the union branch at Bold Colliery—being on the NEC of the Union meant that I was ex-officio on the Area Executive, and could no longer be a delegate—so it looked as though a career in the union had been signed and sealed for me, even though, in that same year, I was elected back on to Ashton Urban District Council as a member for the West Ward. But Chance, Fate, call it what you will, had one more card to play in my personal tug-of-war between union and politics.

I should say at this point that my socialism was always a gut belief. It was almost automatic, after the way that I had grown up. It certainly had nothing to do with books, or intellectual arguments. The books I've read on socialism wouldn't make a pile more than an inch and a half thick. No, you could say that my socialism was virtually bred into me.

Our political heroes in the early days were the MPs of the area, all of whom were miners' MPs, and at least once a year they'd all find their way to our house—and Nellie's, though I didn't know it at the time—because of our mothers' involvement in the women's section of the local Labour Party. Not that my mother ever did any political teaching or preaching at me—I suppose she didn't think it was necessary, believing that the political needs of people in our situation would speak for themselves.

Ashton was in the Ince constituency, and for years the MP had been Tom Brown. He eventually retired in 1964, at the age of about seventy-five, but if he had decided to go at the previous election, in 1959, the chances were very strong that I would have been selected to follow him at Ince, and I might well have been sitting for that constituency today. As it was, two other safe Labour seats in Lancashire became vacant, Wigan and Burnley—Wigan because of the death of the previous MP, Ronald Williams, in March 1958, and Burnley because the sitting member, Wilfred Burke, announced that he would be retiring at the next General Election. The miners put up candidates for both of them, Alan Fitch for Wigan, and myself for Burnley.

Alan won the Wigan nomination, and the seat, and still has it today. Burnley, though, was another matter. It had never been a miners' seat, and in fact I don't think we'd ever tried for it before. My rival nominee, who had been put up by another union, was Danny Jones; he won the nomination by three votes, and is still Burnley's MP. But I knew for certain that I could have won the nomination if I had been prepared to tell a few lies at the selection meeting. There was at the time a strong feeling in the constituency in favour of CND, with which I didn't agree then, and I was as sure as I could be that if I had indicated some measure of support for the Campaign, or even sat on the fence about it, I could have won.

But I didn't, and the Burnley miners were horrified at my defeat. More than simply horrified, they even threatened to withdraw their affiliation fees from the Party. A real local crisis was brewing, so I had to go to see them, and told them: 'This is stupid. This fellow's been democratically elected. You can't start threatening to withdraw, and stuff like that, because you'll weaken the Party, and the Party's more important than any individual.'

I'm glad to say that was enough to make them give up their threats, but I still hadn't given up my ambition of becoming an MP. That was finally to go a year later, in 1960, when Teddy Hall announced that he was retiring as secretary of the Lancashire area of the NUM, now the North-Western area. To be an area secretary was to hold one of the key posts in the union, and when I was nominated by Bold Colliery to run for the post, it was too good a chance to turn down.

In all, there were six candidates for the job, and it was extremely important to have the support of the outgoing secretary, in this case Teddy Hall. Now, I was on the NUM Executive with Teddy, and he was telling me all along that he was supporting me. But he turned out to be a bit of a fly one, did Teddy, and it was only through a pure fluke that I found out what was really happening.

In the middle of all the electioneering, there was an NUM Annual Conference at Llandudno, and as usual I took Nellie with me. On one of the conference days I had business elsewhere, and had to leave her behind, and that evening she had a drink with Sammy Watson, the leader of the Durham miners, a very respected man, and by then the longest-serving member of the Labour Party's National Executive. Nellie later told me what happened.

Sammy said to her: 'I want a quiet word with you. I want you to come for a walk with me.' Now Nellie has always had pretty fair looks, and she admits that, even with Sammy's reputation for being an upright sort of person, more than one kind of thought crossed her mind. It can be like that at conferences. But anyway, she figured, she was well able to take care of herself, and she agreed to go for a stroll.

Once they got outside, Sammy said: 'Joe's putting in for area secretary. Does he know what's going on?'

'What do you mean?' she asked.

'Teddy Hall is not behind Joe.'

Nellie was dumbfounded. 'What do you mean 'he's not behind Joe'?'

'I'm telling you now,' said Sammy, 'he's not behind Joe. I've had a whisper, and he's going for Arthur Bubbins. He's putting his name forward.'

'But Arthur's not in the running,' said Nellie. 'He doesn't know the first thing about it.'

'I'm telling you now, warn Joe.'

And warn me she did, of course, the moment I got back. It didn't take me long to figure out why it was happening. It was true that Arthur, who later became the superintendent of the miners' convalescent home in Blackpool, knew little about what the job would entail, but that was the whole point. Teddy, although he was retiring, wanted to keep the reins of power, and he knew that with Arthur elected he would still be able to manipulate what went on.

But he had made a big miscalculation. I knew that my only real rival was a man called Jim Hammond, a leading Communist. Hammond was a big man, who used to wear a wide felt hat, and who loved adopting a sort of pose where he stood, feet apart, fists on hips holding his coat open, like some Chicago mobster of the Thirties. He liked to organise things a bit that way, too, and his election would have been a disaster for the area.

So I phoned Teddy up the night before the ballot, and told him what I'd heard. 'If you think your man can win, Teddy, I'm afraid you're mistaken,' I said. 'It can only result in Jimmy Hammond walking away with the election, if you try to support Arthur. You'll not get the support you need. Well, if Jimmy getting in is what you want, that's what you'll get. It's entirely up to you, but I don't like two-timing. You've been telling me you were supporting me, and I was taking that for granted, but now I find you're telling other people you're supporting someone else.'

Teddy started to waver, and said he'd think about it, so I told him: 'You'd better get busy, because you're going to lose out on this one.'

The conversation had its effect, and Teddy withdrew his support for Arthur. As usual, the votes were counted at the Lancashire Miners' Bolton headquarters by members of the Area Executive, and I came top of the poll. So that was it—I was now the Lancashire Area Secretary of the NUM. But that *wasn't* it. Immediately, the Communist members of the Area Executive started kicking up a fuss and making allegations of ballot-rigging.

Meanwhile, the Union had paid for Teddy Hall and his wife to go on a world cruise, as thanks for all his years of service, but as soon as the trouble started we sent for him to come back—he had got as far as America—in order to investigate the allegations, since he had been the returning officer. But, whatever the results of that investigation were going to be, I knew there was only one course for me to take: I resigned, and called for a new ballot, in spite of the fact that Teddy had decided that no irregularities had occurred.

The non-Communist members of our area executive all said that I
must be out of my mind, but I told them: 'Hammond has started this. I
think it's just sour grapes, but now it's been started we'll finish it.' And
part of the finishing process involved telephoning Bill Paynter, who was
then the National Secretary, down in London, and himself a member of
the Communist Party.

'You'd better get on to the phone to your lads up here and tell them to
call off this bloody witch-hunt,' I told him, 'or Joe Gormley's going to
open his mouth a little bit.' It was no empty threat, and he knew it,
because I'd been involved in a couple of national ballots and had seen
the tactics used in some areas. 'Bill,' I said, 'I might be wanting to tell
people how perhaps some other people were elected. So you'd better call
them off.'

'You wouldn't do that, would you, Joe?'

'I bloody well would, mate. So don't kid me,' I told him. I'm not a
very pleasant gentleman when the chips are down, and I know how to
put the boot in as well as anybody.

I announced my resignation at a special area conference I had called,
and told them I was demanding a new ballot to clear the air: 'The name
of the union's too good to have this stigma on it.' Immediately after the
conference, we went down to the pub, where there were a lot of my
supporters and a lot of Jim Hammond's. I was talking to a delegate from
Wigan, who had always backed me, when Hammond came across to us
and started calling me a twister.

As I said earlier, he was a big man, a lot larger than me, but I turned
to him and said: 'Jimmy, if you don't shut your bloody din, mate, I'm
going to thump you one. Don't call me a bloody twister. I've never
twisted anything in my life. So don't start.'

Well, he kept on and on, and nothing would stop him, so I had no
alternative. I simply stuck one big punch into his gut, and I can see him
to this day, skidding away across the floor and under the tables. I was in
pretty good shape then, and my father's bits of training had stood me in
good stead. Of course, my supporters all then lined up, and his
supporters lined up facing us, and it looked for a moment as though
there'd be a real punch-up, but then the landlord came across and said:
'I'm glad somebody did that, Joe. I've been wanting to do it for years.'

I just said: 'That's it. It's finished.' And they all went back to their
drinking.

After I'd resigned, I returned to Bold Colliery, where the branch
elected me back again as their President, and, since the Secretary was ill,
I had to do that job as well. This lasted for three months, until, in
January of 1961, we held the new ballot I had demanded. I wasn't
worried about the outcome, or whether resigning would hurt my

position. I knew that it would have cleared the air, and make me stronger as a result.

At this second ballot, all the other candidates, except for Jim Hammond, withdrew. But instead of their being counted at our headquarters in Bolton, I insisted that the votes should go straight to the Electoral Reform Society. We'd never done that before, but it has been done ever since, I'm glad to say, because it lessens the possibility of any skulduggery.

Sure enough, in spite of the fact that Hammond was an area agent, I beat him by a majority of 10,585 votes to 7,351. I had won hands down, and the first one in our area executive committee to move that we accept the results of the second ballot was none other than Jim Hammond himself.

At the age of forty-three, I was well and truly ensconced as the Secretary of the Lancashire Area, and now finally there was no going back. My career was to be with the Union.

Perhaps I should explain at this point that the National Union of Mineworkers is really a national federation. Each Area, for instance, has quite considerable funds of its own, and in all the Areas the contributions which members make to Area funds are in fact larger than they make to the national fund.

Then again, in some Areas the Secretary is the official spokesman, whereas in others it is the President. We've always felt that it was better to let these old systems carry on, rather than try to force the same on everyone. It can be complicated for outsiders to understand, but it works within the organisation, which is what matters. And, even though we still regard the NUM as a national federation, it provides a unity which doesn't exist in many other unions. It's very much a matter of tradition, in the same way that, whereas the President of the NUM is the spokesman for the Union as a whole, in the case of other unions, like the TGWU, the General Secretary is the leader. In yet other cases, it's very much a matter of the President and the General Secretary slogging it out to see who emerges on top.

Well, in the case of Lancashire, the Secretary was the leader, and as such I was expected to move to Bolton, to be near the Area headquarters. So I resigned my seat on Ashton Council, and Nellie and I found ourselves on the move again.

My first act as Area Secretary was to look at the duties of our four agents, and I immediately found enormous discrepancies. Little Sammy Foster was looking after between eleven and twelve thousand members. Leo Crossley, who was also the Area President, looked after the north-eastern part of the area, together with a couple of pits in Wigan, totalling about nine thousand miners. Sammy Unsworth had about eight and a half thousand members in his care. And Jim Hammond, the fourth agent? He had the rest, which added up to between two and a half and three thousand men. I thought to myself, 'It's no wonder he has plenty of time to get involved in political machinations.'

So I reorganised the pits into different groups, in such a way that each agent would have about eight thousand men to look after. I took my plan to our first executive meeting, and they agreed. Among the pits I had allocated to Jimmy Hammond was Mosley Common, and although I couldn't know it at the time, Mosley Common was to be the very epitome of all that went wrong with the mining industry in the Sixties.

There were two main factors involved, on a national scale. The first was that we had an embarrassment of manpower, partly because, up until 1959, we had no compulsory retirement age, and therefore no payment for it—hence my father's readiness to work till he was seventy-five, if he had lived that long. But in 1959, as a member of the Union's NEC, I was at a conference in Scarborough. One evening I got Sir James Bowman, then Chairman of the Coal Board, into a corner in the hotel, and we stayed up talking till two in the morning about the question of compulsory retirement. As a result, I was able to get him to offer a lump sum, which would enable our men to accept the idea of compulsory retirement at sixty-five.

The figure then was only £200, but in 1959, with wages only a few pounds a week, it was a lot of money, nearly half a year's wages, and the vast majority of the lads had never seen a hundred quid in their lives. Even so, it would obviously take years before the winnowing effect of compulsory retirement could lead to a natural depletion of our surplus manpower, and this was without taking into account the second great factor of the Sixties—pit closures.

The problem was very simple. Oil. Cheap oil. Lots of cheap oil. Oil giving industry cheaper energy than we could afford to supply. Not surprisingly, industry started converting to oil, and doing so with the government's blessing. Nor was it a politically one-sided policy. At the start of the decade we were dealing with first the Macmillan Government, and then that of Sir Alec Douglas-Home, but even when Labour got back under Wilson in 1964, the trend was not reversed. In my view, it caused drastic long-term damage to Britain, and nowhere was the tragedy more clearly to be seen than in what happened at Mosley Common, the greatest fiasco of the Sixties.

Mosley Common was just on the outskirts of Manchester. It was the biggest single colliery in Britain, employing five thousand men. But it had continual industrial relations problems, and it seemed the men were on strike every other day; it was known as a trouble pit from well before my election as Area Secretary. The branch was led by so-called 'militants', though as far as I knew they were politically a mixed bag.

Well, two or three months after my election, there was yet more trouble. The men were out of work for most of one week, and then when they got that settled, some other problem came up. So I went down there on the Monday morning to sort it all out, and as soon as I'd examined the situation I knew I could settle it that morning. I knew where and how it could be settled, and I knew that the settlement I had in mind would be acceptable to the men.

But at least the lads were working while I negotiated, and I thought to myself, 'If I settle this problem immediately, another one will arise tomorrow, and there'll be another excuse for the lads not to be working.' So I kept them hanging on, day after day, until finally, on the Friday morning, I settled on behalf of the men. For the first time for ages, the lads knew what it was to do a full week's work, and I reckoned that would prove to them that it was possible to negotiate while still working, rather than have a walk-out first and negotiate later.

Most of the trouble at the pit was imaginary anyway, and after the settlement I had a meeting with the branch and gave them a warning. 'I want to tell you quite openly,' I said, 'that if you carry on like this there'll be pressure to close this pit.' The truth was that there was a running antipathy, not only between the men and the Mosley Common management, but also between that management and its own higher management. And I soon understood why.

That Friday, as it happened, I had been invited to have lunch with the NCB's Area Director, Jimmy Anderton. He was the man who invented the Anderton Shearer Disc, from which all modern coal-cutting equipment has evolved. Incidentally, I was the coal-cutter who first introduced this machine on a production face. It was more or less a courtesy invitation, to mark my election, and after settling the problem at Mosley, I drove over to Wigan to meet him. With me was my Area President, Leo Crossley, and Jimmy Anderton had with him Laurence Plover, who was the Industrial Relations Director.

We exchanged the normal greetings, and then just as we were sitting down to start lunch the subject of Mosley Common came up. I naturally mentioned that I had spent all week there, and that we had settled that very morning, whereupon Anderton said one of the most disgusting things I've ever heard in my life.

'Joe,' he said, 'I couldn't care less if they never work again. Because Mosley Common is costing us money when the men are working, so when they're on strike we're saving money.'

I was enraged. I put down my fork, pushed the plate away, stood up, and told him: 'Well, if that's your bloody outlook on life, you and I are not going to see so very much eye to eye. If that's the way you're going to encourage men to produce coal in a good pit . . . if that's your feeling, no wonder there's bloody trouble at the pit, and to hell with your lunch. I've spent all blinding week keeping the men at work, and this is your attitude? Well, to hell with you! I don't want any of your bloody luncheon. You can stick it, and don't invite me again.' And with that I walked straight out and got into my car.

Leo came out and tried to calm me down, but I was so furious I even told him, 'Get to hell out of it'—and drove off. Later that afternoon they came round to apologise, but I just said: 'It's too bloody late to apologise. That's not my way of doing things.' It was to be quite a while before we were able to come around to talking sensibly to each other.

And the trouble at Mosley Common persisted. I warned the lads again: 'If you don't ease up, your actions are going to close this pit, sure as Christ made taters.' But they kept saying: 'Ah no, Joe, they've spent nine million quid on this pit, re-organising it, and modernising it, and God knows what. So they'll not be keen to shut it.'

My reply was: 'Don't be so bloody stupid. If you're losing them a million quid a year'—which they were—'and if that's after they've spent their nine million on it, then from their point of view they ought to stop the pit, because in theory they'll get their own money back in nine years. They'll be able to write it off as a loss.'

It was a headache for everyone. Only about eighteen months after I had re-allotted the agents' responsibilities, Jimmy Hammond's wife came to me and said: 'God in heaven, Joe, why don't you take Mosley Common off him? It's killing him.'

'Oh, aye?' I replied. 'Well, you never bothered when it was killing little Sammy Foster before, did you? He had that and about a dozen other pits. You can't have your cake and eat it too, and since Jimmy always gets the votes of Mosley Common, he might as well have the work attached to it.'

It was a marvellous pit, too, with nine seams of good quality coal. But, by 1963, the Coal Board had had enough. They came along and told me: 'Well, we're afraid we've carried on long enough with this. We can't go on any longer, and we intend to close Mosley Common.'

As soon as the news got out, the branch officials from Mosley came to see me. They begged and prayed me to go down to London to see if, through the NEC, I could arrange a meeting between the national officials and the Coal Board to get the closure stopped. I said I would do everything I could, and having got the support of my area executive I took it to the NEC, who also gave their support. So down to London I went, together with Jimmy Hammond and Mick Weaver, the Mosley Common branch secretary, who happened to be a member of the Executive Committee of the Communist Party.

Bill Paynter, the NUM's General Secretary, and Sid Ford, the President, were there, and sitting opposite, in Room 16 of the Coal Board, was Alf Robens, the Chairman, and Bill Shepherd his Deputy. Alf had come from politics to the Coal Board, and in his last couple of years in the job became very unpopular, when he went up to Yorkshire and called the lads 'layabouts', which didn't make them very happy. In his first few years, though, he could charm the sparrows off the bloody trees—as indeed he *must* have been able to do, since he was winnng standing ovations at our conferences at the same time that he was cutting the Industry in half.

Bill Paynter started things off by saying to me: 'Well, Joe, it's your case, so you'd better put it.'

'Oh, no, no, no,' I said, indicating Jimmy Hammond and Mick Weaver. '*They're* here to put the case. I've simply arranged the meeting. Now it's for them to make their arguments.' I did that because it was their pit, their jobs which were at risk, and I wanted them to take some responsibility and be totally involved.

So, in turn, they put their case. They were *pleading* with the Board. I've never known two people be so much on their knees when arguing against a pit closure. When they had finished, I just added: 'Well, I'm not pleading, but I'm simply telling you that this is a damned good pit. There's some good seams of coal at that colliery, good calorific value coal, good coal for British industry. It's second to none in that area, and it should be a real winner. I'm sure if you give them a chance, that's what it will turn out to be.'

Well, in the face of all the pleading and the argument, the Board relented. They gave us twelve months in which to try to pull the pit into shape. The first thing I did was to take all Jimmy Hammond's other responsibilities away from him, leaving him Mosley Common on its own. 'Jimmy,' I said, 'that pit is yours. You're the agent, and you've nowt to do but only look after the one pit.' To Mick Weaver I said: 'Mick, you're the full-time branch Secretary. And you've a branch President who's nearly full-time, too. Now the three of you have got the job, day in and day out, of watching what's going on. If anything goes wrong, try and put it right straight away, so that it doesn't hinder production. And keep me informed of what's going on, day or night.'

I even had my own private secretary in the area office doing their branch books, so that they didn't even have that to worry about. And sure enough, for the first two weeks after our return from London, the coal absolutely *poured* out of that pit. But then it started to fall back again, week after week, back and back and back. There was no apparent reason; all I knew was that, instead of those three men I'd left in charge ringing me to keep me informed, as I'd told them, I would have to ring them myself, incessantly, asking to be told what was happening.

This went on for about four months, during which it became clear that the branch officials were unable to fulfil the promises they had made in order to get the twelve-month reprieve. I'd already heard the first rumblings of disaster, when Coal Board officials told me privately: 'Joe, you can't win unless, or until, the attitude changes, even though it's a damn good pit.'

So it was no surprise to me when, at the end of the four months, the Coal Board said: 'Joe, we're afraid it's a loser. This exercise is no good— the promises aren't being lived up to, and we're not getting the coal we know we can get, which was proved by what happened in the first two weeks. So we're going to have to cut our losses and foreclose on the twelve months. No doubt it will affect some of the other pits in your area, but we're just going to have to close it.'

Once more, the branch officials came to see me, and prevailed upon me to go to London to argue the case yet again. But, before I could go, I happened to hear that a special meeting of Mosley Common workers had been called for a Sunday morning. Mosley was the centre of three or four different villages, and they used to hold their meetings in different places; I wasn't told officially, but I learned that this meeting was to be held at Atherton Labour Club.

My first thought was, 'They must be trying to get all the men together to tell them how important it is to increase production, or at least stop it falling off, and keep the pit going.' But I was still curious, and at eleven o'clock that Sunday morning I decided to go along, even though I hadn't been invited, and find out what it was all about.

Well, I walked in about five minutes after the meeting opened, and it was packed. I walked the length of that room, down the centre, to the stage, and you could have heard the proverbial pin drop. Jim Hammond was there, Mick Weaver, the President, and the Chairman of the branch. All in dead silence. No one said a thing. So I just said to the Chairman: 'Well, what's on the agenda for the meeting?'

'Oh,' he said, 'we're just discussing the effects of the Redundancy Payments Act.'

'You what!' I said. 'Is that the only business you're discussing this morning, the effects of the Redundancy Payments Act?'

He simply nodded.

'Well,' I said, 'if that's the case, then all I can presume is that you've accepted that the pit's closed, and any of our exercises in trying to keep it open are a bloody dead loss.' I was almost blind with anger. I turned to the main body of the men and told them: 'To hell with the lot of you. I'm wiping my bloody hands of the lot of you, if that's the way you're going to work things.'

I strode off back down the room past the men, among whom was my own son Frank, and as I went I repeated: 'To hell with the bloody lot of you. You're asking me to fight like holy hell to keep the pit open, and you bloody well close it yourselves.'

Yet, in spite of all that, they still had the nerve to come to the Area Executive again the following week, asking me to go to London to try to save the pit. I told the Executive: 'It's a bloody forlorn hope, after what happened on Sunday. But I don't mind. I'll go down and argue the case. But I don't think there's a cat in hell's chance, in the face of that attitude and the failure to take the opportunities they've been given.'

So I set off for London, as they'd asked, but as I feared the whole thing was doomed. In fact, before I left, the Board had already told me privately: 'You can come, Joe, but it makes no mite of difference, because you're not changing our mind this time. There's no feeling to keep the pit open.'

And nor there was, and closed it was, and never has there been a bigger single tragedy for our industry.

There are millions upon millions of tons of coal in Mosley Common, which are simply stagnating there. It's very unlikely that that coal will ever be produced, because they have built a huge motorway junction—all the connections with the M6, the M61 and the M62—over the top of it. In any case, once a pit is closed, you can usually say that it's closed for good, because you get build-ups of water, collapses in the roadways and so on. Nor can you treat it as a brand new mine, because, as I have described, mining is a continuous process, and you can't carry on normally if you're suddenly likely to be confronted by an area which has already been mined.

The facilities at Mosley were unequalled in Britain. The average height of the nine seams was between four feet six and five feet nine, which is an excellent working height. Once it had been modernised, we cut the manpower down from the initial five thousand, first to four thousand, then to two thousand, in our efforts to resurrect it and make it economic. Finally, we cut the work force to one thousand five hundred men. But nothing worked.

Instead of losing £1 million a year, there was no reason on earth why that pit should not have been making a profit of one or two million a year. What's more, as the Coal Board had hinted to me, the tragedy was compounded, because once Mosley had closed they also had to close two or three other pits, as a result of the area as a whole losing so much money. Those were pits which, taken on their own, could rightly be regarded as uneconomic, but which, with the backing of a profitable Mosley, could have been kept open.

But it was the miners themselves who closed that pit, and I'll never forgive the people responsible, the NUM leadership there. Ah yes, the so-called militants, the fighters for this, that, and the other. Well, they fought all right, but all they succeeded in doing was to close a bloody good pit.

Not that we always fought against pit closures. On occasions, we would have to persuade the men to accept them. There was one little pit at Wigan, called the Dairy Colliery, where the men were working in atrocious conditions. There was a great deal of underground water, and it was very, very wet down there. We examined the situation, and found that there was a build-up of water in the shafts of various other pits nearby which had been closed.

Those water levels were higher than the bottom of the shaft at Dairy Colliery, so there was a real risk that there could have been an underground surge, which would have trapped the lads at Dairy. So Jimmy Hammond, who was the agent for the colliery—this was before I gave him Mosley on its own—came down there with me. We called a meeting of all the men, and explained to them how important it was to close the pit, not for any overall policy reasons, but simply for their own safety. We had all the maps and the technical information with us, but in spite of that we met complete opposition to the idea of closure.

They even called us 'the gravediggers', because we wanted to close it, and we had to point out that it wasn't either in their interests, or in the union's interests, to have men working in a potential death trap. In the end I had to say: 'Irrespective of your feelings, the union will demand that this pit be closed.' It was only then, when they saw how determined we were, that they finally came round to our point of view, and in the end they agreed to it.

Not long after that, the Board told me that they wanted to close a small pit in the Accrington area. So I went to see it, and found that there was quite a lot of good coal within a stone's throw of the pit bottom. My reaction was to tell the Board: 'You can't close this pit.' My executive backed me, and we even got support from some of the Board's area officials and higher management people.

The pit employed about 400 men, and when we went to a meeting with them I think every man jack must have been there, even those who should have been working that Sunday morning. Leo Crossley, who was the agent, opened the discussion, and I followed him and told them that we should fight to keep the pit open, and that we had an unanswerable case.

When I had finished, one fellow stood up and said: 'Mr Gormley, can I have a word?'

'Aye.'

'I think we ought to shut this pit,' he said.

'Oh aye? What do you mean?' I asked him.

'I just think we ought to shut it, and let's all get our redundancy pay.'

'You *what?t*' I said, almost dumbfounded.

At that, they all stood up and said: 'Aye, let 'em close it, Joe.'

That, taken with what had happened at Dairy Colliery, taught me once and for all, if I hadn't known it already, that as a union leader you have to be prepared to face in all directions at once. Arguments that seem cut and dried often turn out not to be that way at all.

Chapter Five

In Place of Strife

The decade of the Sixties was a chapter in the history of British mining which will never be repeated. The industry was under terrific pressure. In fact, it could hardly have been under greater pressure, since various government policies had actually given people the idea that they didn't need a British Coal Industry at all.

Up until 1958, ever since the end of the War, there had been no need to go out and sell coal, because all the coal produced was allocated - effectively, it was rationed. Then in 1958, by which time I was on the NEC of the union, the Coal Board came to us with their plans for the industry. Those plans envisaged that, by 1965, Britain's energy needs would have risen to the equivalent of 365 million tons of coal, of which the mining industry was to provide some 280 million tons of actual coal.

At the time the plans were put to us, we were producing about 220 million tons, and by the end of the year there were very few stocks on the ground, so it was obvious that the industry would need to gear itself up to producing a great deal more. And that's precisely what we started to do.

But then, in 1959, the powers that be made a discovery. After oil has been refined, to produce petrol and all the other by-products, a residue is left, which at that time was thought to be useless and was dumped. Now they found that in fact it *could* be used in certain types of engine, providing what appeared to be an almost inexhaustible supply of cheap energy, sold off to industry at just a few pounds a ton.

The plans were promptly changed. People forgot the part that the coal industry had played during the War. They forgot the years since the War, when we had provided the energy for the recovery of British industry. Much of that industry is powered by boilers, which have only a certain length of useful life, and as factories came to replace their boilers, they were encouraged to switch to types which used the new, cheap, oil residue.

They were all gearing themselves to what they called 'the economic sources of energy', in the crazy belief that 'economy' is synonymous with 'price'. They conveniently forgot another little factor, which is called 'security of supply'. We warned them, of course. The NUM records show that we pointed out both to the TUC and to the Labour Party that this was a course of economic suicide, putting us in hock to the oil producers. We warned them that the day would come when the country would rue the decisions then being taken, and it was a source of no delight when, more than a decade later, our prophecies were borne out to the letter.

Some changes, of course, were inevitable, like the phasing out of steam trains, which at their peak burned about 25 million tons of coal a year. In most cases, the switch was to diesel, which was a loss to us, though when it was a case of electrification it didn't make much difference - electricity is only coal on a wire.

But, in most cases, it was a free decision, a choice between two fuels. They took no heed of our warnings, they made the wrong choice, and suddenly the policy was that, rather than expand, the coal industry would have to contract. All our plans for extra production had suddenly to be turned around, and the effect was just as dramatic as if a car, accelerating towards sixty miles an hour, were thrown into reverse gear.

The attack on the coal industry had begun.

At the start of the Sixties, when I became the Lancashire Area secretary, there were 38,000 miners in Lancashire. By the end of the decade, that number had fallen to between twelve and thirteen thousand. We weren't alone. In Durham, too, they lost two-thirds of their jobs; in South Wales, nearly half. Scotland, Cumberland and North Wales also suffered badly, and although there were some areas, like Yorkshire, Derbyshire, Nottingham, Leicester and Kent, which did not have to face so many closures, the industry as a whole lost two-thirds of its jobs in that period.

True, some of those pits might have been closed anyway, because they were old and worn out, but many others went just because they were deemed uneconomic. In the North-East, for instance, some of the pits had very thin seams, and were closed for that reason, but some of those thin seams contain excellent coking coal.

While the national targets for the industry were being downgraded year by year, it seemed that nobody in industry gave a damn. Nor did we get much support from the TUC and the Labour Party. Of course, they passed resolutions at the congresses and conferences, but it didn't add up to anything. To me, they were talking with their tongues in their cheeks, and I got the impression that many people were glad to see a decline in the strength of the miners. They were still worried in the backs of their minds about what had happened in 1926.

To be fair, the NUM itself didn't fight as hard as it might. We kept passing resolutions opposing pit closures, but that was as far as it went. A lot of the Executive were so-called militants, but they still seemed to accept and acquiesce in what was happening. What's more, we seemed to be happy to accept a few pence, or a few shillings, as the normal yearly increase, so we were losing out in both directions. And it was against this background that one of the main arms of my philosophy was formed.

I became quite a disciple of John L. Lewis, who was President of the American Miners for forty years. His theory was that it wasn't his job to decide the size of the industry, but that it *was* his job to fight like hell for the best wages and conditions for those who worked in it. I said at the time: 'There's a good deal of sense in what he says, because the fact is we're *not* able to decide the size of our industry. It's being decided by pressures from outside. We can't say it will be any bigger than other people are allowing it to be. So we should be concentrating on getting the right wages.'

I took the argument to the NEC. Bill Paynter was the Secretary, and I told him: 'We must all be out of our sweet minds. Here we are, accepting pence or shillings for our members, simply because we're afraid of pit closures. But we're not *stopping* any pit closures. We've not even been able to *defer* many pit closures. Most of them have happened exactly as Alf Robens has planned them.'

To this day I remember Bill's reply. 'Well, Joe, if we take that line, it means accepting the Board's and the Government's plans for the coal industry.'

'Bill,' I said, 'I don't give a damn *what* it means accepting, but our job is to fight for a good standard of living for those people who *are* going to work in this industry.'

But there was one snag to the John L. Lewis theory. As long as he got good wages for those who were working, he didn't give a damn about those who were made redundant. He just forgot about them. That we couldn't do. But here again there were problems. I think I was the first to raise the issue that mining was being treated differently to other industries, in that, when a pit was closed, the first aim was to transfer the men to other pits. They would offer men the same category of work, and provide transport.

In my view, a colliery is a self-contained unit. When a pit closed, everyone should have been offered redundancy pay, and then, if a man wanted to work elsewhere, he could sign on and get the rate for the job he was offered. But what was happening was that men were being transferred without being made redundant, and that meant that they kept their previous rates for a certain length of time, while the receiving colliery tried to fix them up in their own grades. Now, that wasn't so easy, when you had a multitude of pits closing down, and only a few pits for the men to go to, and there were very many cases where two men would be working alongside each other at completely different rates, simply because one of them had brought his transfer rate with him.

It's not surprising that that caused a lot of bad feeling and bitterness, compounded by the fact that some men were becoming like gypsies, moving to perhaps five or six different pits during the decade, shuttlecocks on the Coal Board's badminton court. Those feelings were not helped by the fact that the union was, and to an extent still is, split between its desire to fight for a bigger industry and its desire for better conditions and wages. The seeds of what was to come, at the start of the Seventies, were being well and truly sown.

Looking back at those years, I often wonder how Alf Robens got away with it. I'll never know, although, as I mentioned earlier, I do remember how, when he came to our annual conference during his early years, he certainly had the knack of charming the delegates. Perhaps he was helped by the fact that we, as a union, were not as united as we should have been, since some areas were getting off much more lightly than others. Perhaps he was helped by the apparent apathy of the TUC and the Labour Party—apathy and, on occasion, some pretty half-baked ideas.

At one Labour Party conference, Frank Chapple of the ETU actually suggested that we should cocoon the pits which were being closed. I had to point out that you can't put a pit in mothballs, as you can a battleship, or even a power station. A pit is a live thing, and has to keep working to stay alive. I don't know of one pit which, once closed, has been able to be re-opened.

So Robens had a lot working for him. I got on with him all right as a fellow, but he was, after all, a politician, and in my view was not cut out to be Chairman of the Coal Board. I believe it was a miracle that he didn't have to face a conflagration during those years.

Now, as I mentioned earlier, one of my great friends and allies at that time was Sam Watson. For more than twenty-five years he had been General Secretary of the Durham Miners' Association, and for more than twenty he had been on the NEC of the Labour Party, making him the longest-serving member. He was the most honest and straightforward of men, with those clear blue Durham miner's eyes of his, and at the same time was, as they say in the North East, a very canny leader.

There were very few matters on which we didn't see eye to eye, and so it seemed in the natural course of events that, when he retired in 1963, I got the support of the areas to become his successor, as the NUM nominee. I was opposed, of course, just as Sammy had always been, and just as I was to be in the years which followed, but I won fairly comfortably, and this effectively meant being elected, because it was unthinkable then, and still is, that the miners should not have one of those seats on the NEC of the Labour Party.

There are twelve trade union seats in all, and they are voted for at the Labour Party Conference. This may seem a strange way of going about things, but the fact is that the TUC is not a political body in itself—it's just a collection of trade unions meeting under one umbrella, and by no means all of them are affiliated to the Labour Party.

So we came to the Conference that Autumn, and I was duly elected. In fact, I was never to be out of the first two places in the voting, and here again I was following in Sammy's footsteps. He was nearly always in the first two or three, except for one year, when he came bottom of the twelve. The reason was simple—he had infuriated Frank Cousins about something or other, and when it came to the voting Frank acted like a big girl and denied Sammy the support of the TGWU. When he realised the implications of what he had done, he actually went to the rostrum and apologised and said there had been a mistake. Well, there wasn't any mistake, but I think he was feeling a bit self-conscious, because it was a fact of life that most of the big unions used to support each other's nominees, knowing that if it came to a pitched battle every year, they wouldn't all win a seat.

The union block votes at the Labour Party Conference, I should point out, are only according to the number of members they have affiliated to the Party. The TGWU, for example, might have nearly two million votes at the TUC, but only about a million at the Labour Conference. The reason, of course, is that affiliation costs money - so much for each member—and quite a number of unions, like the AUEW, only affiliate a percentage of their members. The miners, I'm proud to say, have always affiliated on a hundred percent of their membership.

Parallel to the Labour Party, of course, there was the TUC, with important seats to be won on the General Council. For these seats, unions are divided up into different industrial groups, and the seats allotted according to the number of members in each group. At the start of the Sixties, the Mines and Quarries section had three seats. People tend to think of the mining industry solely in terms of the NUM, but there are other unions in it, like the National Association of Colliery Overmen, Deputies, and Shotfirers (NACODS). Members of the NUM join that association once they have achieved their certificates and have moved to a new grade in the industry.

Then there is BACM, the British Association of Colliery Management, to join which you must not only have passed the necessary exams, but also have had at least five years' practical experience in the pits, meaning, of course, that you must previously have been a member of the NUM. And there is COSA, the Colliery Officials Staffs Association, an integral part of the NUM, which in its time has had a profound influence on the way the industry has moved.

Now, all these groups are entitled to put up nominations for the General Council of the TUC, and there is just as much political bargaining and in-fighting for those seats as there ever was for the NEC of the Labour Party.

For example, Bill Paynter, Lawrence Daly's predecessor as General Secretary of the NUM, was on the General Council for just one year, 1960-61, the year of the fiasco over the expulsion of the ETU. When the vote on that issue came up, Bill abstained from voting, presumably because of his loyalties to the Communist Party, in spite of the fact that he knew, from what had been proved in the courts about ballot-rigging and the rest of it, that it was inevitable that the TUC should do something about the ETU leadership.

That was a mistake on Bill's part, and the following year he was defeated for his Mines and Quarries seat by the NACODS representative, Joe Crawford, as a result, I'm sure, of his abstention and of a general anti-Left Wing feeling in the TUC. After the vote, Bill swore: 'I shall never allow myself to be nominated again. I'm not going to be the shuttlecock.' And that decision had an important influence on a choice I had to make about my own life ten years later.

I was sorry that happened to Bill. He was a fine committee member, and in my opinion made a great contribution to the TUC during the year that he was on the General Council. He came from South Wales, the same area which produced his predecessor Arthur Horner, who had been the first General Secretary when the NUM was founded, in 1945, from what had been the Miners' Federation of Great Britain.

It's true that Bill was a member of the Communist Party, whereas I had been a member of the Labour Party all my life, but I found him a good man and very much a realist. He was a far-seeing man, too, and in both debates and committees he was progressive—very much a contrast to the negative views I was to experience in his political colleagues in later years. We opposed each other politically, but during all the years that we were together on the NEC of the Union, when it came to industrial matters we were closer together than any other two members.

The one exception to that was a vital exception, which came to a head in 1966, and that was the issue of the National Power-Loading Agreement. Bill had always supported the idea. I was dead against it. And I lost.

It was a strange incident which needs to be put in context. Since the War, I had seen very many changes in the pits. The coal-cutting systems, the transport systems, the haulage systems—they were all changing, and changing rapidly. The one thing that didn't change was the system of price lists, under which, as I described earlier, the miners' agent for the area would negotiate a rate for each job that came along.

That contract could not be altered until the teams moved to a new coal face.

But, of course, there was a great disparity between the rates paid for the different jobs underground. The colliers would have one price list, the coal-cutters another, the conveyors, the borers, the packers and so on and so on. There was clearly a great deal of unfairness about this, since, as I had demonstrated in my early days, the haulage hands are just as capable of stopping the flow of coal as are the colliers.

What's more, there was a vast disparity between the prices being fixed in different parts of the country. I already knew, from my brief stay in Staffordshire, that there were differences, but until we started to look deeply into the matter in the early Sixties neither I nor anyone else had the faintest idea how great the disparity actually was. Nottingham and Kent were way out at the top of the league, followed by Lancashire and Derbyshire, who were about equal, and then on down the list until we came to South Wales, Scotland, Durham and Cumberland, right at the bottom. It was simply a question of what the local areas had been able to achieve by negotiation, and in Lancashire, for instance, we had always had good negotiators and therefore damn good price lists. In fact I used to say that, if Lancashire lads had been filling the same amounts of coal per manshift as they did in Nottingham, they wouldn't have been able to take the money home on a barrow.

There is no question but that it was a jungle, a jungle where dog ate dog and man ate man. And the aim of the National Power-Loading Agreement was to sweep the whole system away. So why did I oppose it? For two basic reasons. The first was that I , and others who thought like me, knew that it was inevitably bound to affect the amount of coal which would be produced. The second was that it put a level on earnings—a man would no longer have the chance to earn more if he wanted to work extra hard—in effect, it would kill the necessary incentive.

In 1966, we came to the point where a decision had to be made, and the industry was very evenly split for and against. In the end, the agreement scraped through with the support of COSA, the clerical section. Even though they knew they couldn't benefit from it in any way, it was their vote which got the agreement signed, and it makes me sad that they should have been so maligned, in the years which followed, by the very people who *did* benefit.

Naturally, it couldn't all happen at once. The Agreement could only apply where a pit was fully mechanised, and by no means all of them were—in fact, coal was still being produced on piece work in some pits almost till the end of the decade. But, where it did operate, it meant that everyone was now on a day wage, and the pan-shifter now earned the same as the coal-cutter, the rippers as the colliers. But it gave no benefit to men working away from the face.

Not that even the day wage could, at the start, be uniform throughout the country, in view of the previous disparities. There were actually about seven different rates. An immediate rise of several shillings a day brought those on the bottom rates up to about 65 shillings a day, while at the top end of the scale Nottinghamshire miners were getting about 84 shillings. Clearly they weren't going to accept a drop to achieve parity. Equally, the NCB couldn't afford to increase everyone straight away to bring them up to that level. So, for several years, the lads from Nottingham, Kent, Lancashire, and Derby had to be satisfied with increases of a few pence while they could see the others getting bigger rises every year.It took a lot of swallowing, and was to lead to much of the frustration which finally erupted in the early Seventies.

The advantage of the agreement was to come later, at the start of the Seventies, when the whole country finally went on to the same rate. Then we were in a position to negotiate production bonus schemes which would benefit everybody, rather than just the select few.

Not that everyone accepted the position immediately the die was cast. At the very end of 1966, I was forced to say: 'I am not in a position to congratulate our members for any increased productivity. In spite of getting nearer to the end of the closure programme, it would seem that many men have not got the faith necessary to get this industry of ours in its rightful position.'

The truth is that the NUM, which includes a number of the old craft organisations, is fairly conservative. Members' ideas are not easily changed. For example, during the mid-Sixties I went on a holiday to Majorca. It was then far less commercialised than it is today, and at a village outside Palma I saw a large number of acres which were going very cheap. I made enquiries about them, and found that it would have been possible, for about a quarter of a million pounds, to build a miners' convalescent home on that land.

Now, in Lancashire, we had, and still have, a big miners' convalescent home. It's on the North Shore at Blackpool, a windswept and fairly bleak place, and one of the positions I held at the time was that of Secretary of the home. So, when I came back, I suggested that it would be a wonderful idea if we sold the Blackpool building and built a new home in Majorca, where the sun would be shining for ten or eleven months out of every twelve. I said Majorca, simply because I had been there and seen it, but it could just as well have been Malta, or anywhere similar on the Mediterranean.

I even did research into the transport position, and found out that it would be possible to take a whole plane, fully loaded out and back, for a cost of about £7 a person, at a time when it was costing nearly that to send some of our lads to Blackpool.

So I then put the idea forward as a serious plan, but sadly the majority of my colleagues pooh-poohed it, and it was abandoned. Within a few years, they had all changed their minds, and they wanted to go into it again. But by then the cost of land and the cost of labour had rocketed, and it just wasn't possible. They said:'By God, Joe, that was a marvellous idea. We wish we'd taken you up on it.' And I answered:'Well, that's the difference, you see. I try to look years ahead, and see what's likely to happen a few years in front, rather than what's just going to happen today or tomorrow. Because, you know, there are a lot of other tomorrows after.' But it was too late, anyway, and we're left with a convalescent home up there, costing us a lot of money, and which, although it has been modernised, remains, and will always remain, an old-fashioned building—in the wind and the rain.

In the autumn of 1966, following the Labour Party Conference, and just two years after Labour had returned to power under Harold Wilson, I was elected Chairman of the Party's Organisation Sub-committee, one of the most influential positions in the Party. It meant dealing with the staff, dealing with the rules, vetting the names of Parliamentary candidates, handling arrangements for the Party Conference, and generally being responsible for the Party organisation in the country.

One of my biggest efforts was in pushing for a national agents' scheme. I believed, and still believe, that it is ludicrous, in a Party like ours, for the agents to have to spend more time organising efforts to raise their own salaries than in political organisation on behalf of the Party. Unfortunately, it is still the case, and it's wrong, and the sooner it's put right the better.

The problem will be to find ways and means of financing them. As it is, of course, the bulk of the Party's funds come from the unions anyway, and unless and until alternative arrangements can be made, this is the way it will have to stay. That's why I consider it unfair when people attack the unions for the influence they have on the Party. For a start, we don't put pressure on to nearly the extent that some would believe. But, in any case, it is unreasonable not to expect those who are paying the piper not to want to call a little of the tune from time to time.

This is why, even when I had been elected to the Chairmanship of that committee, I still regarded myself as, and took the role of, an industrial leader rather than a politician. And being on the NEC itself was made extra tricky by the fact that Labour were in power. I remember Sammy Watson once saying to me: 'The problem with being a member of the NEC, Joe, is that when your Party is in power, you should be spending half your time protecting them.' At the time he said it, he was absolutely right. The accepted view was that the Party should protect its own Government, and give them all the support possible, refraining from unnecessary criticism. How *that* view has changed!

But at least, I believed, my place on the NEC would allow the voice of the miners to have a say in shaping political trends, and I frequently argued as much. Today, looking back on it, I think I was wrong. It doesn't happen, particularly when the Party is in power, and it certainly didn't help us over the issue of pit closures and our constant demands for an overall energy plan, not just a theoretical plan, but one which would be put into effect.

In the autumn of 1967, feeling among miners over the closures was starting to run pretty high, and we put a resolution to the Party Conference which not only called for a national energy plan but also urged the Government to underwrite the industry and assume the total social costs of reorganisation during the transitional period. Well, the NEC accepted it, and the Party Conference accepted it, but the only result was an ineffective meeting between the Party's Home Policy sub-committee and the Minister of Power, Dick Marsh. I duly attacked Government policy, and he duly trotted out a defence of that policy. In the face of the white-heat of Wilson's technological revolution we were getting precisely nowhere, in spite of the fact that the Six-Day War in the Middle East, and the resulting Arab oil embargo, had shown just how fragile our supplies of that fuel could be.

It's true that at a private meeting with Wilson the Executive Committee of the NUM managed to wring from him the promise that he would postpone some of the pit closures. But it was only a temporary reprieve, and it seemed a poor reward for the years of loyalty that the miners had shown to the Party, especially in supporting the Labour Government's Prices and Incomes policy. After all, harking back to the John L. Lewis theory, once we could see that we were unable to determine the size of our own industry, at least we should have been able to take comfort from the fact that now our efforts would not be divided. It should have been the moment to go all out for better wages and conditions. Instead, we backed the official policy of wage restraint.

It was here that Will Paynter once again demonstrated his capability of far-sightedness. I well remember him saying to us on the Union's Executive at that time that he realised the inevitability of government and unions getting involved in matters of industrial relations. Whatever the colour of the government, he said, there was no question but that it would come to intervene more and more, even on the question of wages, and that the unions would have to learn to respond, and, equally important, be *seen* to respond, in a reasonable manner. Little could he have known that within five years that prophecy would be borne out with a vengeance.

Meanwhile, after a lifetime in mining, I now found myself flung in at the deep end in a completely different industry—shipbuilding. The Government had set up a Board to try to reorganise shipbuilding in Britain, and they asked me to sit on it. The Chairman was Bill Swallow—Sir William to give him his title—and for three years I became totally immersed in the subject, conversant with every reach of all the waters of Britain, to such an extent that I ended up knowing almost as much about shipbuilding as about mining. Sad to say, my two overwhelming memories of that period both concerned tragedies.

The first arose from a visit we made to Northern Ireland. As a result, a scheme was drawn up to build the biggest dry dock in the world at the Harland and Wolff yard, created out of a natural bay that they had there. It would turn Belfast into the focal point of British shipbuilding, allowing them to build three ships at a time in that dock. The cost was £38 million. Supported by Bill Swallow, with whom I saw very much eye to eye on all the implications of the plan—not least, the creation of between six and eight thousand new jobs—I persuaded the Board to accept the scheme. This was in 1969. And in due course we got the Government to put up the money for it.

Well, about three years later that dry dock was finally completed, but within a few months they'd ousted the chief convenor, whom we had met, and whom I thought an excellent fellow, just because he was a Catholic. A Protestant took his place, naturally, and almost immediately led them all out on strike to march the streets of Belfast in support of Ian Paisley. My thought, when that happened, was, 'What the hell have I helped to create here?' My only interest, and hope, had been that by creating jobs we might help to stabilise the position in Northern Ireland. The reverse seemed to have happened.

The second tragedy was the Upper Clyde fiasco. In order to make the Clyde shipyards more efficient, we recommended that they should be split into two groups—the Lower Clyde and the Upper Clyde. The latter was to be composed of five or six yards, but there was just one of those yards whose managing director was in no way interested in co-operating. He simply didn't want to join. So he was told that, unless he did join, he wouldn't get any orders from the Navy.

His response was, to my mind, diabolical. It was my firm belief then, and still is, that some accountant was manipulating the figures. They showed losses of £2 million for the current year. Funnily enough, I liked the fellow, but I told him: 'You bugger, you. I know this is wrong, but I cannot get at you.' I never mind if someone beats me in an argument, but on this occasion I knew they were running rings round me, and I had no way of getting at them, even though I was quite clear in my own mind that the following year they would have had to show not a loss, but a *profit* of £2 million.

The implications were clear. If that yard were forced to join the rest, there was no way they could carry the burden of a £2 million loss, and the whole lot would be declared insolvent. Once that happened, the creditors would come crowding in, and liquidation would follow.

So I took Harold Lever, who was then the Paymaster-General, up there with me, and we talked to a few hundred shop stewards of the Boilermakers Union—Harold, I don't think, had ever seen a shop steward in his life—and had to explain to them why it was necessary that we exclude this particular yard from the consortium. That wasn't too easy, because they knew as well as I did that the whole thing was a bloody fiddle, but I think we persuaded them.

All that was actually required was a £10 million injection of capital by the Government to tide the whole group over the initial period, to eliminate the risk of insolvency—and Harold Lever in fact said to me: 'Hell, why don't we give them the money?' That was just before the election of June 1970. But then the election intervened, Heath got in, and John Davies, the Minister for Industry, determined not to support any 'lame ducks', said in effect, 'Oh well, that's it then, we're not having them any more.'

So the creditors came swarming in, and in the end it cost the Tories £30 odd million for the same rescue operation that £10 million would have achieved just a little earlier. What's more, it threw up leaders previously unknown. When we were up there, the chief shop steward was Jimmy Airlie, a good man who fought all he could to save the Upper Clyde. Jimmy Reid, for example, wasn't even a prominent official. So not only need the whole fiasco never have happened, but Jimmy Reid need never have happened, either.

But shipbuilding was only a tangent, albeit a sizeable one, off the main course of my career. And there was plenty else to worry about. By 1967, I was getting extremely worried about the way that the Trade Union Movement was losing control of the Labour Party. After all, the unions had set up the Party in order to give themselves a voice for their aspirations in the House of Commons. And as I pointed out earlier, we were, and are, the paymasters of the Party, and in many ways its custodians. So, as far as I was concerned, the unions had to be seen to be in control of the Party.

Now, on the one hand that was becoming less and less the case, and on the other many people were attacking us for having too great a say in Party policy. It was an attack that had happened before, and has happened since, but this time there were many different organisations putting on pressure to water down any control that we still exercised.

It was clear that the Labour Government, and in particular Barbara Castle, was not exactly out of sympathy with these pressures, so much so that I said publicly during 1967 that if this were the case, then the Trade Union Movement would have to form another political party, functioning in exactly the same way, and with exactly the same objectives, as was the case when the Labour Party was first formed. It caused quite a stir, but it was no more than a blunt statement of an obvious truth—the Union Movement *must* have a voice in Parliament, able to push for legislation to further its aims, and if the Labour Party was no longer prepared to be that voice, then it would have to be somebody else.

The warning wasn't heeded. As we went into 1968, it became more and more apparent that the Labour Party was bent on some form of legislation to curb the power of the unions. And it was because of that that Chance, once again, took a hand in deciding the course of my life.

Will Paynter was due to retire from the General Secretaryship of the NUM, the post which he had held since 1959, in December of that year. He had served with two Presidents, Ernie Jones and Sid Ford. Now, at the top of the NUM, the President and the General Secretary are of equal status. They get the same salary, and the same terms and conditions. But, although the NEC always accepts the President as the one who talks official policy on behalf of the Union, it's the stronger one of the two who is actually regarded as leader.

Ernie Jones had been well-known. He had been a powerful member of the TUC General Council. And he was very much the leader of the NUM. But, with the arrival of Sid Ford, things changed. He was a good chairman of meetings, but he wasn't a strong character. It wasn't in his nature to go out on to the streets and the hustings and preach the gospel about mining. At conferences he was never the great haranguer which it is sometimes necessary to be in order to impress upon people the importance of what you are saying.

So Will Paynter emerged as the stronger individual, and therefore the 'natural' leader of the miners. To succeed him, two people were nominated, Lawrence Daly and myself, each of us put forward by seven areas.

I was regarded as the odds-on certainty. Lawrence had only been Secretary of the Scottish area for four years, and not very long on the Union's NEC. He certainly wasn't regarded as being among the national leadership. He had been a Communist, but had left them in 1956, as did many others, over the issue of Hungary.

I, on the other hand, seemed to have everything going for me. I had been the first pitman ever to go straight from the coalface to the Lancashire Secretary's chair in Bolton. I had been one of the few rank-and-file miners to win a seat on the NEC. As I said at the time:'Those of us termed moderates, I feel, are nearer to the lads at the pits.' What's more, I had the great advantage of being on the NEC of the Labour Party. The great advantage? The great disadvantage, as it turned out.

We just had no idea how deep and bitter was the feeling that had grown against the Labour Party. Like Johnny Boyd of the AUEW, who suffered in the same way, I was clearly tarnished in the minds of the miners by my association with the Party. They couldn't know that, within the NEC of the Party, we were arguing against the introduction of any legislation even more strongly than was the case in the TUC.

The ballot took place at the pits between the 3rd and 10th of November 1968. There was a seventy percent poll, and when it was counted Lawrence had won by 115,531 votes to 105,501.

Needless to say, I was pretty shattered by the result, but it didn't take me long to realise why it had happened. So when, within two months, on January 16 1969, Barbara Castle finally published her infamous document, 'In Place of Strife', as a White Paper, I doubt if any politician or trade union leader was more furious than I.

It was happening as Will Paynter had forecast, but even he could not have guessed that a government would be prepared to go so far. It was an attempt to shackle the unions by bringing legislation into the field of industrial relations. What was worse, it proposed to back up that legislation with the threat of punishment by the courts. And, since by no means all the workers in Britain belong to trade unions, its effect would be to make certain relationships compulsory for some sections of the working population while entirely omitting others. As I said at the time: 'It must affect everybody or nobody. But in any case you can't legislate for these things. Industrial relations have to be on a voluntary basis if they are to be any good at all.'

The extraordinary thing was that Barbara Castle should have chosen to put this plan forward only a few months after a resolution at the Labour Party Conference which had rejected 'any further legislation, the aim of which would be to curtail basic trade union rights'. God knows who advised her, but to my mind she was utterly stupid, and on top of that, backed by Harold Wilson, utterly adamant.

But she soon got a shock. On March 26, we had a meeting of the Party's NEC to discuss the White Paper. At that meeting I said: 'For God's sake will you realise that you're souring the very voters that you're going to have to rely on, the very supporters you need to win an election. Unless you get away from this, you'll never win an election. You might get your balance of payments right, but you'll not be in power long enough to enjoy it.'

At the end of the discussion, Jim Callaghan, who was then Home Secretary as well as being the Party Treasurer, moved a resolution,

which I seconded, which stated that the NEC could not 'accept
legislation based on all of the proposals in the White Paper'. That
resolution was carried by 16 votes to 5, and what was particularly
embarrassing for Wilson and Castle was that Jim Callaghan was by no
means the only member of the Government who voted for it.

But they still wouldn't change their minds. They wouldn't listen to
the advice of those like myself who knew the feelings of people in the
streets. They made the same mistake that the Labour Government had
made after the War, when, it is my firm belief, they kept rationing on too
long and lost the election of 1950 as a result. They forgot that the Labour
Party relies for its votes primarily on members of the affiliated trade
unions and their families. When you take the seven million-odd
affiliated trade unionists, and add in the voting members of their
families, you are talking about some twelve million people, which is
roughly the vote that you can normally guarantee that Labour will get.
So I argued that it was suicide to introduce legislation which hit at those
very people.

The argument raged on. Eventually, after a head-on battle with the
TUC, they withdrew 'In Place of Strife' before it ever came to
Parliament. But the withdrawal was, to say the least, ungracious, and I
use that word quite deliberately. They made it clear that they were only
doing it because they had been forced to do it, not because they had been
convinced by the arguments.

A few months later, in the spring of 1970, Harold Wilson came to me,
in my capacity as Chairman of the Organisation Sub-committee, to tell
me that he wanted to call a General Election. This is something the
Leader has to do, because he needs to know how well geared up the
Party machinery is in the country, and so on.

Now, after the narrow Labour victory in 1964, he had held another
election in March 1966, which had given him a very comfortable
majority. So there was no need for him to call an election for another
year, and I told him so. What's more, I knew it could only end in defeat.

'The scars of your industrial relations policy haven't healed yet,' I told
him. 'We're not ready. You've soured your supporters, and we don't have
the activists on the ground. We don't have the people willing to work in the
constituencies. In Lancashire, even, where I used to be able to get three or
four hundred miners out on to the streets and the hustings—well, I'd be
hard pushed to it to rake up a dozen at the moment.'

But he wasn't going to be put off. He gave me a number of arguments
for the General Election, including the fact that Roy Jenkins had finally
got his balance of payments right. 'That may be so,' I said,'but the fact is
you've hurt that trade union support. You have an election, and I'm
telling you you'll lose it.'

Well, I lost the argument, and he went ahead. We did all we could, of course, but it was a losing battle, in spite of one curious aspect of the campaign. In May, I was asked to go to the Prime Minister's room at the House of Commons. It was all very clandestine, and I had no idea what it was all about. When I got there, I found that George Brown, Harry Nicholas, Alice Bacon and Judith Hart had also been invited, and when we were all present the publicity people we'd hired brought in these cake-boxes.

It crossed my mind that a tea party wasn't going to win the election, but then they brought out these models of the Tory leaders, made by the artist Alan Aldridge, and told us that the campaign was going to be based on the theme of 'Yesterday's Men', asking the electorate why, after a few years of Labour government, they should want to change back to people who had had their chance.

We were being asked to approve the idea of the campaign, and we did. My attitude at the time was that, although the idea seemed a bit bloody ludicrous, there was no point in destroying the enthusiasm of the people we'd hired to help us. Looking back on it, I think we must have been cockeyed to believe that that portrayal would attract many serious-minded votes. It wasn't really treating politics seriously, and I think in the end it rebounded against us.

It was then, and still is, very fashionable to talk about PR men selling an image. But the only person who can really sell an image is that person himself. You can spend all the money in the world on PR experts, but in the end the nitty-gritty has to be portrayed by men or women showing the real image of themselves. Try creating a false image, and the public will eventually see through it.

As far as I'm concerned, if we as a party can't project our own image, how can we expect others to do it for us? And we've wasted a lot of money on PR campaigns, not least up in the North-East, where Dan Smith ran a big exercise for us. Now, if we ever needed any propaganda in the North-East we should have been ashamed of ourselves, because over the years it had been nearly solid Labour. But that didn't stop us spending a fortune up there.

The Election took place in June 1970, and sure enough my worst fears were realised. The Tories under Heath swept in, getting almost a million votes more than Labour, and 43 seats more than us in the Commons. And the greatest irony was to be that the ideas which had cost us the election were to be the platform on which the Tories built their industrial relations policies.

That autumn, the long-brewing discontent among the miners began to surface. The Coal Board had made us an offer of an average £2.50p a week increase, which the NEC finally decided to accept. Many disagreed with us, and 103,000 of our 292,000 members went on unofficial strike. There were some unpleasant scenes at picket lines, which were widely reported in the Press, and when we went down to London for an NEC meeting in November we experienced that unpleasantness at first hand.

About 500 miners were picketing our headquarters in the Euston Road, which wasn't a surprise, because we'd been expecting some lads from Scotland and South Wales. What we *didn't* expect was that Sid Schofield, the Vice-President, would be roughed up, Albert Martin, who was just behind me, got kicked, and I got hit.

What annoyed me most of all was that it happened just as we were going into the building, and as I swung round to see who had hit me, there were so many of them that I couldn't tell who it was, and therefore couldn't hit back. He didn't hit me enough to hurt me, but enough to hurt my dignity; I was brought up in a rough school, and if people want it rough I don't mind, as long as I can hit back!

What I said to the Press was:'My only regret was that I couldn't hit back. It seems that the allegations being made about hooliganism by pickets must be a fact. If we allow this to happen, there'll be no union left. We intend to stop it.'

What I said privately occurred when I got into the waiting lounge and found Mick McGahey and another lad from Scotland called Bill McLean sitting there. I played all holy hell with the pair of them. 'If you want to bring pickets down, you bring pickets down,' I said, 'but you bloody well keep control of them, because if you don't there's going to be a row in this bloody union.'

They claimed that they were not responsible, but I told them:'You're responsible when you bring people down, my mates. I'm speaking now as a member of the NEC from Lancashire, and I'm telling you, if it happens again I'll bring a few dozen Lancashire lads down and we'll sort the bloody lot of you out.'

It was a skirmish, if you like, before the real battle with Mick, which was to come six months later. Early in 1971, our President, Sir Sidney Ford, announced that he was going to retire for reasons of ill-health. Sid was only sixty-one, so everyone had expected he would stay for a few more years. When I had lost the election against Lawrence, I certainly didn't envisage that there would be another chance of becoming a National Official for many years.

There were only two nominations for the job, myself and Mick, who was then forty-six. The mainspring of my support, as before, came from the lads in Lancashire, only this time, if it was possible, they pulled out the stops even more than before.

The rules in NUM elections are pretty flexible. For example, you are allowed to canvass by issuing statements and documents, which the rules say are supposed to be vetted, though it never seems to happen that way. Then again, you're not really supposed to go stumping round the country, into other areas, but it's expected that your supporters will find their way around and spread the gospel on your behalf. And, if your area is truly behind you, it's quite proper for them to use some of the area's funds to help your campaign.

Well, Lancashire couldn't have been more loyal to me. It was expected that they would spend some of their funds in sending people round to canvass for me, and the Area Executive and Conference agreed to donate a generous amount. The lads found their way into nearly all the first time round taught us a few lessons about how to succeed at the second attempt.

The ballot took place during the week of May 24 to 28, with each lodge or branch voting within a defined twenty-four-hour period. When the votes were counted, I had 117,663 to Mick's 92,883, a fairly overwhelming majority of 24,780. There could have been many reasons for it. Perhaps Lancashire put more effort into the election than Scotland. Perhaps the lads didn't like the idea of having two Scotsmen at the top. Perhaps there was some reaction from the previous ballot.

But, whatever the reason, I was declared President with effect from June 10, 1971. In exactly forty years, I had come all the way from the pit bottom to the very top.

Chapter Six

222 Euston Road

I could hardly have taken office at a more critical period in the history of the miners. At the start of the Sixties, the NUM had had approximately 700,000 members. Now, that membership had fallen to less than 290,000. From being near the top of the wages league, we had fallen to seventeenth position, with the face workers, the highest earners in the industry, getting a paltry £27 a week.

Within a month I had the chance to indicate the sort of leadership I intended to give, when we held our annual conference. When I took Sammy Watson's place on the NEC of the Labour Party, in 1968, I had had to make it clear that I was not Sammy but Joe Gormley, with my own way of saying and doing things, characterised by the fact that I'm a blunt-spoken Lancastrian, rather than a soft-spoken Durham man. Now, once again, I had to create—or perhaps 'demonstrate' is a better word—my own image, following as I did Sid Ford, who had started out as a clerk in the National Office, and had never been an actual working miner. That was something I had been for thirty years. I was proud of it, and I determined to show the union that I was proud of it—in the place of a clerk, they were now dealing with a rough miner, who had roughed it every bit as much as they had, and who was still willing to rough it if that was the way they wanted it.

I also wanted to show that not only was I the President, but I intended to be the leader. As I wrote earlier, the President and the Secretary of the NUM are of equal status, so it was a question of who would be the stronger, and I've never played second fiddle in the whole of my life. It has always seemed to turn out that I should be the leader or the spokesman for any group I've been involved with, starting way back from that time when, as a young lad, I became the leader of the haulage hands at Stones Garswood.

Why that should have been, I don't really know. Perhaps I'm a bit of a bully! Equally, Lawrence Daly is not an extrovert. On his day he's a good speaker, but I think that in many ways he's more of a political dreamer than I. I'm a realist, and as a trade union leader you *have* to be a realist, as well as an idealist.

I had many misgivings about that first conference. Although I had been President of my local branch, and had chaired many committees,

I had never been an area President, and therefore had never had to chair a really big meeting. I had just three weeks to brush up on all the rules and make sure I could run the conference properly and control things.

I needn't have worried. The delegates, knowing that I was a new boy, were first class, and the tone was set by my rival for the job, Mick McGahey. Since the conference was being held in Aberdeen, it fell to him to give the welcoming address from the Scottish Area, in which he made a point of saying: 'I hope the Conference will be successful, and may I take this opportunity of extending a very special welcome to our new President, Joe Gormley.' As Maurice Rowe, an NEC member, said a little later: 'I think the whole of this conference will pay tribute to the comradely and sporting manner in which Mick McGahey accepted his defeat in the election.'

For me, the date of that opening day of the Conference was yet another of life's coincidences. It was July 5, my fifty-fourth birthday. And the best present I received was the reception the delegates gave to my Presidential address.

I started by referring to the terrible run-down the industry had suffered in the previous decade, and went on: 'This has inevitably resulted in a very great lowering of morale within the workforce, because of the uncertainty of the future, but I believe this attitude is now changing because Britain's energy position has changed dramatically since last Conference. Swinging from the position of excess coal production and large stocks in 1968-69, fuel policy mis-management led to a critical fuel shortage as the winter of 1970-71 approached. The creation of new smokeless zones was halted, with many existing orders being lifted, and coal imports were allowed, all in an effort to prevent Britain's industry drawing to a halt because of a coal shortage.

'The mildest winter in living memory, the power workers' work to rule, and the current economic recession eased the position, and now that we are in the summer months, stocks of coal are beginning to build up towards a level commensurate with the normal fluctuations in coal demand. But, as the figures show, coal consumption is still exceeding production, and the NCB is faced with the necessity to expand production. Their aim is to produce 150 million tons by 1975, but already there are signs that this will not be enough, as a world-wide shortage of oil appears to be becoming permanent and the more modern energy forms (e.g.nuclear energy) fail to come up to expectations.'

To this, I added the simple lesson: 'The NUM has insisted for years that a fuel policy which ignores the coal industry is doomed to failure. Now, under the pressure of the events predicted by the Union, this view is becoming accepted by most fuel economists.'

I went on to remind the Conference that, although our productivity had consistently been going up, actual coal production was falling—by twenty-eight million tons over the previous three years—and that coal stocks had fallen by five million tons in twelve months. 'Had it not been for a mild winter and the other outside influences,' I said, 'this country would have been facing a fuel shortage such as has not been faced since the days of coal rationing. If that had happened, no one in the country could have laid the blame on the Mineworkers. It could only have been placed at the feet of successive Governments accepting Fuel Policies based on half-baked assumptions from so-called economic experts.'

To meet the need for increased production, I said that we should press for mechanisation in *all* pits, and added: 'To me it is degrading that in the 1970s we are asking miners to fill twenty-five to thirty tons of coal in a shift or remove the debris of a big ripping, all by hand filling. We must continue our pressure in this direction if we are going to encourage the young men of Britain to feel that this is an industry which has a great future and is worth working in.

'I know the present manpower trends are favourable, but I am not quite as optimistic as some people about our ability to attract the right people. Too often have I seen the pattern emerging, whereby the Mining Industry is only able to attract sufficient manpower for its requirements when either there is a War on (when men are directed to the Pits) or when a general recession is hitting outside industries and causing long dole queues. The latter position now facing the country may be easing our manpower problems.

'This inability in normal circumstances to attract manpower in the right numbers should indicate that many people regard mining yet as a dirty, dangerous job, and of course they are right. So, to combat this feeling, we have to do two things. First, create a wage pattern which makes miners able to be regarded as the highest paid industrial workers in Britain, and second, put pressure on the Coal Board to ensure that the best possible working conditions are created.'

To underline the dangers—not that the delegates needed reminding —I then had the sad duty of reporting that, between January 1970 and May 1971, 124 men had been killed in the pits, and 912 seriously injured. The public, of course, only tends to hear of major pit disasters, but the fact is that, even today, with all our efforts to improve safety, there are still fatalities week in and week out, often through nobody's fault. Mining is a very dangerous game.

Nor is it just a question of accidents. There are the occupational diseases. As I told my audience: 'The report on the 1969 results for the Periodic Chest X-Ray Scheme shows a slowing down in the fall in the prevalence of pneumoconiosis in the last five-year period. This indicates a gradual increase in dust exposure of the miners employed below ground, particularly face workers, and that dust suppression has not kept pace with the increase in productivity. God forbid that there should be an upsurge in this dreadful disease! No coal is worth this much! The health of our men must not be imperilled by conditions of work just for the sake of production. We must not rest until we obliterate from the pits the scourge of silicosis and pneumoconiosis, just as we obliterated the former scourge of nystagmus.'

I couldn't know, as I spoke, that within three years I myself would be diagnosed as having slight pneumoconiosis—or, as miners call it, 'the dust'.

Then I went on to talk about what the Tories under Heath were trying to do to us. 'In trying to deal with the Trade Union Movement,' I said, 'the Government are seeking to put on the Statute Book the well-known 'Industrial Relations Bill', an unexpurgated copy of the previous White Paper 'In Place of Strife'. In my opinion, although unlike its predecessor the Industrial Relatons Bill will become law, it will prove to be completely unnecessary and unworkable.'

And I ended by giving my views about the role of the trade unions in politics, starting with the way the previous Labour Government had failed. 'In their desires to create a strong financial position,' I said, 'they adopted policies which created unemployment, and they decided to try to have a showdown with their own supporters, the Trade Unions. Many of us warned them of the consequences of their actions, which were creating a split in the Movement, and I for one will never forgive some of the people involved, for in my opinion they handed the Government of this country to the Tories on a plate.'

In order to defeat the Tories, I said, 'I believe that the Trade Union Movement have got a big responsibility. Instead of being passive and being regarded just as a means of finance to the Party, we have got to be the activists also at all levels.' I was greatly in faour of giving political training to trade unionists, and I added: 'I shall never rest content until it can be shown that the whole of the Cabinet in some future Labour Government started their careers in the ranks of the Trade Union Movement. The language of Socialism is in my view the language of the Trade Union Movement, and there must be a complete marrying of the so-called two wings of the Movement. We must, in the future, be determined that all factions in our Party are completely welded.'

Now, as things had worked out, I wasn't the only new boy present at that Conference. Only two days earlier, on July 3, Derek Ezra had become Chairman of the National Coal Board. We were happy enough to see him there. He had worked his way up through the ranks of the Board, becoming Director General of Marketing, and then Deputy-

Chairman, so at least, unlike previous Chairmen, he was a man who was thoroughly steeped in knowledge of the industry.

It is the custom for the Chairman of the Board to be invited to speak at our conferences, and on the third day he made a good speech, much of which echoed what I had been saying about the industry. He saw the future success of the industry as being dependent on 'greater safety and better health, improved efficiency (by which he meant the best and most reliable mechanisation), reduced costs and overheads, and concentrated marketing and sales efforts'.

Then he came to wages, which he knew we had already discussed. 'You clearly have the right and the duty to your members,' he said, 'to put forward such claims as you consider to be in their best interest...we in the Board have always accepted that proper rewards for those who work in the industry are not only essential to its health but a real priority responsibility.'

But he went on to give what was really a polite warning: 'I hope, however, that I can also ask you to recognise that the Board as managers of the industry have obligations as well. And our overriding obligation is to secure the continued and successful operation of the industry. This we have to do not only for the benefit of those at present serving in the industry, not only for the benefit of those who will be serving in subsequent years, but also for the benefit of those who depend upon our product to keep their factories going and to warm their homes.

'I hope, therefore, that when we eventually meet to discuss the claims that you will be putting forward, there can be a fair recognition of all these interests and obligations; and that we shall be able to negotiate in an atmosphere of mutual understanding.'

At the end of his speech, I presented him with a three-volume history of the miners, and said I hoped they would be read 'because it does depict some of the struggles the miners have had in achieving things over the years, and no doubt in the years ahead some of the lessons in these books you can learn if you read them, because no doubt we shall be having some struggles in the years ahead between us'.

Said Derek, after thanking me: 'I hope all these struggles you mention will be struggles together in the interest of our industry.'

With benefit of hindsight, and knowing what was to come within six months, this exchange looks like the courteous diplomatic niceties of two ambassadors talking shortly before their respective countries engage on all-out war with each other.

And, in a sense, the battle lines had already been drawn, because on the previous day the conference had unanimously supported the following composite resolution:

'This conference of the National Union of Mineworkers calls upon the National Executive Committee to submit a claim for a substantial increase in the wages of all its members and to seek to establish a minimum wage on the surface of £26 per week, a minimum wage of £28 per week underground and a minimum NPLA rate of £35 per week.

'Further it should negotiate all differentials in order to establish a realistic measure of job values, and seek a simultaneous date for the operation of wage settlements for all sections coming under the Coal Mining Industry Wages and Conditions.

'In the event of an unsatisfactory response from the National Coal Board the National Executive Committee to consult the membership with regard to various forms of industrial action.'

Derek Ezra could have been in no doubt that the struggles we both had mentioned would be real ones, because his Industrial Relations Director, Cliff Shephard, had been sitting listening to the wages debate, and must have realised the absolute determination in our ranks.

On July 20, that determination was expressed in writing, when we sent the Board a letter setting out our claim. This, if met, would represent an increase in basic pay of £5 a week for face workers, £9 for other underground workers, and £8 for surface workers. It may seem strange to those who don't follow these matters closely that our smallest claim was for those who did the hardest and most dangerous job, the face workers. So I should explain that it was yet another example of how the miners tend to stick together and act for the common good. It was felt in the Union that, now that the National Power-Loading Agreement was operating at an equal level throughout the country, the gap between their wages and those of the other miners had become too great— particularly when one remembered that many of the underground and surface workers had originally been at the face, but had had to leave it through injury or ill-health.

Our claim was based not only on the 9.4 percent increase in the cost of living over the previous year, but also on the comparative wage increases in other industries over several years, which had left the miners way down the wages league.

Then, on September 14, we met the Board face to face in the industry's Joint National Negotiating Committee, a body which meets regularly to iron out problems in the industry. It is a large committee, composed at that time of sixteen representatives from each side, and the meeting was held, as usual, in Room 16 at the Board's headquarters, Hobart House in London's Grosvenor Place.

We used the meeting to repeat our claim, and to put further arguments in its support. One was that, unlike many other industries, the newly-agreed wages structure in mining meant that basic minimum wages often tended to be *the* wages. The only way our men could increase their earnings was by overtime, and for many of them this just wasn't available. We were also able to give concrete individual examples, showing that men were taking home net wages ranging from £11.10p to £15, in cases where they were having to find between £3 and £5 a week for rent alone.

What was more, we pointed out, recent pay increases in other industries included £4 a week at the London Brick Company, up to £7 a week for some brewery workers, and the 30 percent increase that arbitration had awarded to the staff of the General and Municipal Workers' Union.

This mention of a percentage was, as both we and the Board clearly understood, a vital one, since the Heath Government had imposed a ceiling of 8 percent on pay increases, and in the case of the underground workers our claim represented an increase of just over 47 percent. But, as we pointed out, it was generally agreed that the two toughest industries were trawling and coalmining, and the Grimsby trawlermen had recently been given a £5 a week increase, bringing them to a minimum rate of £28. Coalminers working underground, we said, certainly shouldn't get any *less* than that.

Finally, we asked for a quick reply, so that any offer could be discussed at our NEC meeting due to take place on October 14, and this was agreed. But, the Board said, they would be less than frank if they let us leave thinking that they could in any way measure up to the high claim we had made. On the other hand, they did understand that the claim was for a substantial increase, and they would consider it most carefully in the light of what we had said.

Exactly four weeks later, on October 12, we all gathered again in Room 16. Before giving their reply, the Board outlined some of their problems, which included stagnant productivity, increased competition as a result of the Government removing import restrictions, the advent of natural gas from the North Sea, which was forcing the Electricity Industry to peg its prices, and a general loss of customers, including ICI, because of the recent price increases for coal. What was more, coal stocks on the ground were rising sharply, and this was costing them a great deal in interest charges.

Indeed, they said, if they were to look at the industry's books on a strictly commercial basis, they'd have to say that there was no money available at all to meet any wage claims. They were, however, hopeful that with the union's promised co-operation they would be able to achieve a productivity increase of 1 hundredweight per manshift, and they thought that now might be the time to close a few of the very high-cost, and high-loss, pits which had been kept going because of the previous high demand. In these circumstances, they thought they would be able to find a total of £25 million to meet our claim.

This, they said, represented an increase to all grades in the industry of £1.60p a week, and that was their offer.

Well, we didn't need to hold any caucus meetings to decide what we thought of *that!*

We told them: 'All that we've heard has been most interesting, but it's basically the same theme that's been heard in previous years. In fact, this pattern has been repeated in dealing with wage claims ever since 1947. You're always optimistic at the start of the year, but when it gets near to wage negotiation time you're always able to find adverse factors.'

'Our membership isn't just going to be disappointed,' we continued, 'but they're going to be angry and insulted at this shabby treatment, in view of the facts we presented at the last meeting. We've had many telegrams from all over the coalfields urging us to take industrial action if the full claim isn't met.'

And we told them what they must have known before we started: 'The offer's completely unsatisfactory, and if that's the best you can do, it will only lead to trouble in the coalfields. On this basis, negotiations will be quite impossible. We've offered to sit jointly with you to discuss productivity, and if you hope to create the right atmosphere for that you should make a realistic wages offer.'

After that there was a bit of to-ing and fro-ing in the argument, but then we came to what, in the end, proved to be the crunch question. There had been a newspaper article that very morning, an exclusive interview with John Davies, the Minister for Trade and Industry. He was reported as saying that, although the Government hadn't interfered, it had expressed its views on our claim. So we asked the Board: 'Have the Government in fact interfered with your offer?'

Their reply, in effect, was: 'Because we're a public corporation we often have to discuss matters of all sorts with various Ministries. But this offer is our own assessment of what the industry can afford.' So we suggested that they ask the Government for assistance to improve their offer, but they claimed that they were already borrowing from the Government to maintain coal stocks, and if they borrowed more it would cost them more in interest.

We didn't exactly seem to be racing towards a settlement, so at that point we had an adjournment, and the union lads and I went off to another room to discuss the offer. Not that there was much to be gained from *that*. Obviously, none of the negotiating team thought the offer acceptable, and we went back in and told the Board so. In fact, we said, we couldn't even recommend it to our NEC as a basis for negotiation, because the Union had to carry the majority of the members with it, and for this to happen, the offer would have to be considerably improved. 'We know the situation is serious from your point of view,' we said, 'but you must also realise the difficulties we face.'

So we had another adjournment, this time for them to go out and see what they could come up with. The answer was—a pittance. Given our co-operation on improving productivity, they said, and by mortgaging the gains that would come from that, they could offer an increase of £1.80p for the minimum surface grades, and £1.75p for the rest, an average overall increase of 7 percent. It was throwing down the gauntlet, and I can't believe they didn't know it.

In fact, privately they had every reason to know it. As it happened, Derek Ezra wasn't at that meeting, but only shortly before that I had met him by chance at some social gathering. We were having a quiet drink together in a corner, and naturally the subject of our forthcoming wage claim came up—I say 'naturally', because by then he knew all about the militant talk that had gone on at our conference.

'So, what's the position, Joe?' he asked me. 'What is the sort of figure at which your men will settle?' And, unknown to any of my members, even my Executive, even Lawrence Daly, I told him. 'The figure you will have to settle at is in the region of three and a half quid.'

Understandably, he was a bit shaken. '*How* much, Joe? You know that's impossible.'

'Why is it impossible?' I said. 'In any case, whether it's impossible or not in your mind, that's the figure which in my mind you'll have to come to if there's to be a majority on my Executive Committee. What's more, since you've asked me the question, I've got to say that if you don't heed what I'm telling you, it'll get harder and harder to settle the dispute, and it'll become more and more expensive for you every day and every week.'

And so, of course, it was to prove. That figure was a good deal less than we finally achieved, though the achieving of it was to cost our members a lot, too.

'You must be out of your mind, Joe,' he said.

'I'm not out of my mind,' I replied, 'and I'm telling you - that's the figure.'

In fact, it was a figure I had already made up my mind about immediately after our annual conference. I was convinced that, given all the circumstances, it was logical. But at that time, if I had mentioned it to my colleagues, it might have shocked even some of *them*. They might have thought it was too ambitious, being far in advance of anything we'd ever got before. Equally, if I'd said what I had in mind, some of the so-called militants might have started making trouble. You can't be too careful in negotiations, and sometimes it pays to be a bit secretive even with your own side. Apart from Derek Ezra, the only person I mentioned that figure to was Peter Walker.

All my life I had been a negotiator, first on my own behalf, then for others, and once I was elected President I was determined that negotiate was what I would do. The trouble was, as rapidly became apparent to me during that meeting on September 14, we weren't negotiating with the right people. The NCB were the people chosen to run the coal industry, and to negotiate with the workers in that industry. But they weren't being allowed to exercise those functions. Whatever the Board might say, it was quite clear, almost from the outset, that they were being completely hamstrung by the dictates of the Heath policies.

So, when they came back into Room 16 with their miserly improved offer, we just told them that we were sorry, but it didn't help; in fact, it didn't even reach a level which could provide a platform for further negotiations. We would continue the meeting on our own, we said, to decide what to recommend to the National Executive.

What we did recommend was:

1. That the Board's offer be rejected.

2. That a Special Conference should be called on Thursday, October 21, 1971, for the purpose of presenting a full report.

Two days later, on October 14, the NEC met at our headquarters at 222 Euston Road. There was special anger at the Board's suggestion that money to pay for wage increases could come as a result of more pit closures. For once, the word 'militant' would be accurate in describing the mood of the meeting. The minutes record in more sober language what went on:

'The National Officials suggested that the National Executive Committee should recommend to the (Special) Conference that an overtime ban should be imposed as soon as it could be approved by an Area vote, and simultaneously a Ballot Vote should be conducted on the question of a National Strike. Approaches should then be made to the Trade Union Congress and individual Trade Unions to elicit support in the event of there being a call for a strike.

'It was generally accepted that in calling for a strike it should be made clear that no strike pay would be paid from the National Funds. It was essential that there was complete unity in this fight and that no action was taken by any section or individuals other than that nationally agreed. Therefore, no Areas should seek to take decisions or to hold meetings before the Special Conference took place, but must await the Special Conference and then hold meetings to facilitate a proper decision.'

After dealing with the date of the conference, the minutes continue: 'It was then proposed that as a manifest of the Union's complete disgust with the attitude of the Board there should be a complete withdrawal at all levels from the Consultative Machinery. It was also clearly understood that if the overtime ban which could be imposed almost immediately had the necessary effect no strike need take place, but it was essential that the National Executive Committee had the authority to call a strike as and when necessary.'

For once, there was unanimous agreement on that committee. And our disillusion with the Board was compounded by what seemed to us a piece of pettiness which had come up at the end of the meeting. Some time before, in discussions with them, we had raised the question of a national agreement on subsidised transport for those miners who had to travel a distance to work. The Board had promised, verbally, to put forward some kind of offer.

Now, it appeared, they had written saying that they had not promised to do any such thing. As the minutes of our meeting record: 'Strong exception was taken to the Board's reply, and the National Officials made it clear that they had been convinced from conversations with representatives of the Board that an offer on a new Subsidised Transport Agreement would have been forthcoming. It was obvious that the Board had now changed its mind. It was clear that the Union could no longer put any reliance on verbal communications from the Board, and in future would have to insist on everything being put in writing.'

By comparison with the major battle being fought, this transport question was obviously only a minor skirmish. But I include it as an indication of the degree of bitterness and distrust that was growing daily. The Board and the Union were, and are, partners in a nationalised industry. For years, particularly in our co-operation over pit closures during the Sixties, that partnership had worked through informal discussions and negotiations just as much as through formal channels. Now, it seemed, we could neither negotiate with them properly, nor, which was worse, could we trust them.

That unanimous vote in the NEC was virtually unique in the history of the NUM. There was always before, and has been always since, a block who would vote against anything, on principle. But this time I told them: 'In the light of the interference by the Government, in the light of the impossibility to negotiate, we've got to be completely united. If you go into a battle divided, you've lost. And if you go into a battle, you've got to go under the assumption that you're going to win. You can't go into a battle thinking that you **might** win.' So we stuck together, and throughout the dispute the votes remained unanimous.

A week after that meeting, on October 21, we held the Special Conference, at Congress House, the TUC's London headquarters. Again, there was complete unanimity. They endorsed our recommendations that there should be a ban on overtime as from November 1, that from the same date we would withdraw from the consultative machinery, and that we should ballot the membership, seeking authority for the NEC to call a national strike if necessary.

We were in no doubt whatsoever that the implications of the action we wanted to take went far wider than just the coal industry. Lawrence Daly, as General Secretary, had put the NEC's view to the delegates, and in summing up his long, detailed, and blunt speech had said: 'Finally, we have all to remember that the entire Trade Union Movement has its eyes on the Miners today. We are in the vanguard, because a whole number of other Unions, large and small, are awaiting the outcome of the Miners' struggle and the Miners' settlement, because they know if we cannot break through Conservative wages policy that they may be left to be isolated and beaten down as the Postal Workers were earlier this year.

'So we are fighting not only for the interests of the Miners and their families, we are fighting for the rest of the Trade Union Movement, and on the basis of our struggle I believe it is possible to create a broad unity in the Trade Union Movement that will smash Conservative economic policy and help to pave the way for the defeat of the Tory Government and return a Labour Government which will introduce economic policies that can receive the full support of the Trade Union Movement.'

Reflecting on the way the previous Labour Government had behaved, I thought his last point a bit optimistic. And, as regards bringing the Government down, I had always made it plain that I thought that was a very dangerous attitude. A strike, if it was necessary, should always be on industrial, and never on political, grounds. But, in what he had to say about our relationship with the Trade Union Movement in general, he was absolutely right. We knew that where we led, others would be able to follow.

Four weeks later, during the week of November 22, the ballot was held, and on December 2 the Electoral Reform Society gave us the results. 86 percent of our members had voted, with 145,482 for rejecting the offer and for taking strike action, and 101,910 against. In percentage terms, that was 58.8 percent against 41.2 percent.

Only a year before, when the Rules demanded a two-thirds majority for strike action, that wouldn't have been enough. But we had just changed that rule at our Annual Conference, making a 55 percent majority sufficient. I believe that the size of the minority vote convinced a lot of the powers that be that we were on a loser, and that a strike, if it came, would not be united. Doubtless many remembered the way the miners had been defeated, even crushed, in 1926, and thought we wouldn't dare risk a repetition. It was a big mistake. I knew that there would always be a sizeable chunk against strike action, for the simple reason that, knowing there would be no strike pay, and with hire-purchase and other commitments to keep up, many men would reason that they just couldn't afford it. But I also knew in my bones that, with the NEC clearly united as it was, the decision, once it was taken, would have total support, and that it would probably be those who didn't want to strike who would fight hardest when the time came, if only to win as quickly as possible.

The NEC met on December 9. We had had no further offer from the Board, but it was felt that the overtime ban, which we had estimated would cut production by about 15 percent, was having a considerable effect. This was of double importance. First, it might still force the NCB to come to the negotiating table with a decent offer before any strike took place. Secondly, if it did come to a strike, we would have reduced the stocks of coal on the ground. And they were considerable. As Lawrence Daly had reported at our Special Conference, the Coal Board had 32 million tons of coal on the ground, of which 22 million tons were distributed.

It was clear that they had been quietly preparing for a fight. Indeed, as Lawrence had gone on to report: 'What they did not say to us is that for the past six months the C.E.G.B. has been pushing coal into every hole and corner it can find in preparation for a possible miners' strike. Indeed, the increase compared with last year in distributed stocks happens to be five million tons. Last year the C.E.G.B. had twelve million tons of stock. This year it has got sixteen and a half million tons. The C.E.G.B. alone is almost entirely responsible for the increase in distributed stocks that have taken place, and of course, if there is no strike they will go back to normal.'

And in fighting mood he had added: 'If there is a strike we will put them back to normal a lot quicker than they estimate, or if there is an overtime ban as we recommend.'

So the news that the overtime ban was beginning to bite was good. But we still had to have the strike weapon available if it were required. Some members suggested that we delay strike notice until we had had another meeting with the Board, but it was pointed out that, since we were determined to do everything absolutely legally, we had to give the correct strike notice, and that meant giving the longest period of notice required for any of our members, which was one month.

The decision was taken. We agreed 'that the National Coal Board be given formal notice on behalf of all the members that they would officially be on strike as from the 9th January, 1972, unless there was a satisfactory solution to the Union's wage claim'.

A few days later, Lawrence and I went to meet the Board, at their request. They started off with a new offer, of £2 a week increase for men

swald's Junior School,
ton. Sixty years on, an
Old Boy returns

Duke Street — the family mansion!

. . I threw my books into that brook and watched
them sail merrily away.'

Cutting a dash with Nellie at a holiday camp
in 1948

Our Winifred and our Frank — after the War,
we took them to Torquay a couple of times

d to wear a number of different hats in
his was on my first visit to Moscow, in
1963 . . .

nd this at a New Year's Eve party in
an, Nellie at my side

Photo: J.-L. Deb

Brussels mini-Summit. Roy Jenkins was President of the EEC, and I of the ECSC. The handshake was slightly less than hearty!

At a memorial service in Yorkshire with Tony Benn, then Energy Minister. Soon after, he offered me the Chairmanship of the NCB

Photo: National Coal B

The things one suffers in the line of duty! A visit to Japan in the mid-70s. By coincidence, the head geisha was the same as when I went there five years previously with the Shipbuilding Board. I never forget a pretty face!

Not quite such pretty faces. In 1979, a deputation of trade union leaders visited 'Silicon-chip Valley' in California. I seem to have got pole position, though students of form will easily pick out Bill Sirs, Frank Chapple, Clive Jenkins, David Basnett, and Ken Gill

SRI INTERNATIONAL BUILDING

Photo: Francis Grimshaw

A Lancashire Area Secretary and his agents. From the left, Jimmy Hammond, who looked after Wigan, Sammy Unsworth from St Helens, myself without a drink, and Leo Crossley, who handled Burnley and was also Area President

By 1962, Jimmy Hammond had become Area President. I was at his right hand during this visit by a delegation of Russian miners to Parkside Colliery. Jimmy still stood like a Chicago gangster, but he wasn't calling me a twister any more

Photo: National Coal Board

Photo: Brian Duff, Daily Express

71, a month before the election for President, maybe wondering what Mick McGahey was up to

Photo: Brian Duff, Daily Exp

June 10th, the day I took office. Six grandchildren helped me celebrate

A Lancashire Miners' Gala at Leigh. They were always good fun . . .

. . . and all sorts of people dropped in, though Jim Callaghan looks as if he had another appointment to keep

'All sorts of hats.' But this is the one that matters. 'And a hard life it is.'

ou could tell Roy Mason was the Energy Minister at the time — he was the one in the suit. I was still Area Secretary, taking him on a pit visit

o to South Wales in 1979. Emlyn Williams, Area President, is on the far right — of the picture, that is

Members of the Executive leave Downing Street. The 1974 strike was settled. From the left, Mick McGahey, myself, Lawrence Daly, Arthur Scargill, Joe Whelan, and Peter Tait. The policeman's politics are not recorded — the rest are!

Photo: Terry Kirk, Financial Times

Some people were regular visitors to our Conferences. Len Murray seems happy to have a chat with Mick . . .

. . . Derek Ezra less so!

Friends of Israel dinner, 1974. Wilson was back in power, and I was furious with him. I doubt Gold
Meir realised the irony of the seating plan

In Covent Garden, at the opening of a Trades Union Workshop. Jack Jones trying to prove he cou
make the buses run on time, with a little help from Clive Jenkins and myself

The NUM officials at a TUC Conference. Lawrence already seems to have decided to stand the Social Contract on its head

Photo: Terry Kirk, Financial Times

November 1981. Delegates from Egypt and Tunisia at the International Miners' Conference on P
and Detente in Newcastle. 'I finally brought that dream of mine to reality.'

at the face and for surface workers, and £1.85p for all the rest. We told them straight away that that wasn't enough. So they went out, and came back with yet another offer, this time of £2 a week for surface workers, and £1.90p for the rest. There was also an indication that they might be prepared to think about another week's annual holiday, but only starting two years from then, in 1973.

But the offer was made conditional upon the NEC recommending its acceptance, and I was certain they wouldn't get it. Sure enough, at our next NEC meeting on December 16, the offer was rejected, and the decision taken to seek an early meeting between the NEC and the Board. That duly took place on December 21.

It was a forlorn hope. We have a saying in Lancashire that negotiations consist of you and the other fellow starting to walk towards each other, and it's a question of who walks faster. But, as far as we were concerned, the Board, obviously inhibited by the Government in the background, weren't walking at all any more. They had come to a standstill, as they proved when they repeated their last offer.

We clearly weren't going to accept it, nor did we see any point in restating all our previous arguments. But we did throw in a couple more for the Board to chew over. We pointed out that, between 1958 and 1968, productivity had increased by 66 percent, but with no gain for our members. We compared the fact that, since October 1951, average earnings in Industry had increased by 218 percent as against 164 percent for the miners. We referred them to the 38 percent rise that MPs were to enjoy in two weeks' time, on January 1, 1972. And we brought up the fact that many mineworkers were now getting so little take-home pay that they were at the level for claiming Family Income Supplement.

But it was all to no avail. And, when we finally asked them point-blank whether their sticking to an offer of about 7 percent was because of Government influence, they replied that in devising their latest package offer 'they had, of course, to take account of what was happening externally', though they still insisted that 'the main factor influencing their decision was the financial state of the industry'.

'We'll discuss it,' we said, 'but we can't see any reason for calling off the threatened strike.'

I can't say it was all that happy a Christmas, nor New Year come to that. We didn't *want* to strike. We were all perfectly well aware that any gains as a result of a strike would be offset by loss of wages while it was going on. What's more, we were novices at the strike business—in the quarter century since the NUM was formed, we'd never *had* a national strike. But, as far as we were concerned, we had an absolutely just case, a case in which we had the support of many other unions. And, if striking was the only way to get that case answered, then so be it.

On January 5, the NEC had a final meeting with the Board to see if anything could be done to avert the showdown. Lawrence and I had previously had informal talks with them. They had hinted that they might be able to improve their cash offer very slightly, although it would still be well below the increase of the year before. But they said that any such offer would be dependent on us saying that the NEC would recommend acceptance of it, or would undertake to convey the offer to our members.

'We can't give you any such assurance,' I said. Then they had started talking about productivity schemes, and indicated that they might be able to move a bit towards us on the question of holidays, but I had to tell them: 'If you can't make us a cash offer substantially bigger than you've offered so far, we can't see any hope of a settlement.'

Following those talks, we had a letter from them saying that in the circumstances they proposed referring our claim to the National Tribunal for arbitration. As far as that was concerned, our NEC was having none of it, knowing from past experience how much tribunals were influenced by Government policy. And, as for the hint of an improved offer, the NEC clearly couldn't come to any decision on that unless they knew what it was. So at that point we invited the Board's officials, waiting outside our conference room at Euston Road, to join us.

They came in with their new offer, but it was no more than a nudge in the right direction. The cash was basically the same, but would be back-dated to November 1. Then they talked about productivity schemes. Their idea was that if, between that January and October, the output per man shift improved by 3 hundredweight over what had been achieved in 1971, there would be a back-dated bonus. And they moved a bit towards us on holidays, saying that they were now prepared to offer an extra week's holiday as from May, but that it would have to be taken as a series of individual one-day holidays, rather than a solid week, in order to keep the pits running.

It was a long meeting, with a great number of questions and answers, ranging from what the relative arrangements would be in the cases of the Cokeworkers and the canteen staff, to what was to be done with uneconomic pits. But when, at the end of a tiring session, the Board's officials retired, it was immediately clear to me that none of my Executive thought it an offer worth accepting.

For a start, the cash simply wasn't enough. It didn't even keep pace with the increase in the cost of living. As regards the holidays, this was a claim the Union had been pressing for some years. Most of British industry already enjoyed a three-week holiday, to such an extent that the TUC were already starting to push for four. We were on two, and just wanted three to keep up with the rest.

As for productivity, the offer meant that we would have to wait until October to know whether it would be worth anything or not. What's more, productivity very much depended on the efficiency of the machinery in the mines, and we knew perfectly well that far too much time was being lost through mechanical breakdowns. Any increase would mostly depend on the extra sweat of the lads underground.

Even so, yes, it *was* possible, but it could only be done with the co-operation of the Board, and that, first and foremost, had to come in their demonstration that they trusted the miners and appreciated their efforts. The way to do *that* was to offer them a significant increase in cash. And that was just what the Board had not done.

As far as we were concerned, there was no alternative to going ahead and pushing the button. So we voted, again unanimously, to reject the revised offer, to go ahead with the strike as planned, to instruct the Areas that no strike pay should be made from National or Area funds, and that the proposal to submit the claim to a Tribunal should be rejected 'because Government interference had resulted in complete loss of confidence and faith in arbitration'.

We also decided to instruct the Areas to hold special branch meetings, at which votes would be taken, so that we could know the extent to which our decisions were supported by the rank and file.

If the die was cast, I've got to say it wasn't without some trepidation among us. Apart from anything else, the Tories' Industrial Relations Bill had become law on January 1, and nobody was very certain what its effects would be, except that the immediate effect was to give a whole lot of work to the lawyers, it was such a clumsy mess. Among its provisions was a sixty-day cooling-off period, and it wasn't certain whether that would apply to us since we had given our strike notice before it became law.

I have gone into some detail about all the meetings and the arguments which preceded the strike, because I think it is important in people's minds, even now, to realise that we weren't plunging in helter-skelter. In fact, at a private meeting with Ted Heath I had said: 'It'll be a crime if you allow this strike to happen, because we shall win it, you know. There's no doubt in our minds about that. And when we have won, this will become the pattern for industrial relations for the next decade.' How true *those* words have proved!

We really did try to negotiate our way out of the situation. Perhaps if Derek Ezra had taken me seriously right at the beginning, when I mentioned the figure of £3.50p to him, he would have offered that and I could have persuaded our members to accept it. Maybe he *did* want to offer it, but was prevented from doing so by Government interference. In fact, months later, a Cabinet minister quoted Peter Walker to me as having said: 'I wish to hell we'd taken Joe's advice.' And Walker, to whom I had told the figure, was a close friend and colleague of Heath's.

Whatever the truth, at midnight on Saturday, January 8, 1972, the National Union of Mineworkers embarked on the first national strike in its history.

Chapter Seven

Strike

It is something of a cliché that any law which doesn't have the support of the majority is bad law. I think it's probably also true that a national strike which doesn't enjoy similar support, among the population in general, is likely to be an unsuccessful strike.

From Day One, Sunday, January 9, we knew we had that support, and it was to grow and grow throughout the strike. To back that up, we received the results of the Area voting, which showed 293 votes in favour of the action we had taken, and only 22 against. And even those 22 followed the Union's tradition of loyalty, because from the moment the strike started, it was one hundred percent effective. I knew that we had to win.

We set up our strike headquarters in the canteen in the basement at Euston Road, and at every pit and in every Area there were liaison committees, representative of all the workers including the craftsmen and the clerks, the members of COSA. This was very important, because we had to make certain that some of those clerks *did* work, so that our men could get any back pay due to them, as well as income tax refunds and so on. So united were we, that it was often hard to get them to do so. They took the view 'one out, all out', even though they were losing the chance of continuing to earn wages.

In addition, we had to issue precise instructions to make sure that members of NACODS, together with essential safety men from our own union, were allowed to go down the pits to maintain safety cover. After all, we wanted jobs to come back to when it was all over, and it's all too easy to get an explosive build-up of gas, or water levels which will weaken the roof supports.

Where we did instruct men to work, we left it up to them as to whether they kept their wages or not. We had always taken the view that if a man works he's entitled to be paid, but in a great number of cases they made substantial donations to their area funds, simply because they wanted to be a part of what was going on. As for ourselves—the National and Area Officials—we declined to accept any salary during the strike, on the obvious grounds that, although the strike meant far more work for us than normal—I would get in at about six in the morning, and seldom left the office before midnight—we should be seen to be suffering along with everyone else.

The reason we had told the men there would be no strike pay was simple. We couldn't afford it. We had no strike fund, and there was only about £1 million in the Union's kitty. Since we had more than a quarter of a million members, that meant we had enough to give them each £4 for a week, and after that we'd be bankrupt. There obviously wasn't much future in trying to fight a battle like that from the bankruptcy courts.

But we did start to receive a flood of financial help from outside the Union, from rank and file trade unionists, ordinary members of the public, even the traditional widows' mites. And that meant that we were able to pay £2 a day expenses to those pickets who travelled away from home. This in turn brought forward even more volunteers for picket duty, so that very shortly we had more than 60,000 men picketing up and down the country.

On Day Two of the strike, that picketing received a welcome piece of support from the TUC, whose General Secretary then was Victor Feather. They put out a statement saying: 'At a special meeting of the TUC Finance and General Purposes Committee this morning to consider the dispute in the coal mining industry, it was evident that there was great sympathy with the mineworkers' case.

'It was also evident that, as the NUM had already been in direct consultation with unions whose members are engaged in handling coal supplies, there was no necessity for the TUC to arrange a meeting of those unions, whose members will understand that, in accordance with normal trade union practice, they should not cross picket lines set up by the NUM.'

Ah yes, but where were those picket lines going to be? This is what I believe shook the Coal Board and the Government from the outset. They thought that we would merely be picketing the pits, to make sure that there was no production of coal. But we took the view that we should not need to picket pits, and anyway that would only lead to a long drawn-out struggle, and from the point of view of the miners, the industry, and the country at large, we were determined to make the battle as short and sharp as possible.

So, with that backing from the TUC, we decided not only to stop production of coal, but to stop movement of coal as well. We sent pickets to all major power stations, ports, coal depots, and steel works. The only coal we would allow to be moved was that for hospitals, schools, old age pensioners, and the infirm, and we worked out a system of priority certificates, issued by doctors or social service departments, to make sure that it went to the right people and places.

This blocking of coal movement was vital, because, in spite of our overtime ban, there were still almost 19 million tons of coal held in stock by customers, and nearly 10 million tons held by the NCB. Of the former, nearly 13 million tons belonged to the CEGB, but a lot of that was kept at some distance from the actual power stations, and, with the co-operation of other unions like the TGWU and the rail unions, we were able to stop it being transferred.

And now we were doubly certain that we would get that co-operation, because on the morning of the third day, Tuesday, January 11, Vic Feather came down to Euston Road to see Lawrence Daly and myself, and repeated in person the assurance that trade union members would be firmly instructed not to cross such picket lines 'in any circumstances'. I thanked him, naturally, and told him the results of our Area voting. But I also had to tell him something else.

The previous Friday, Derek Ezra had announced that, if the strike went ahead, 'an entirely new situation will arise, and we shall be bound to withdraw all offers'. Vic, of course, knew this, but I told him:'As fas as we're concerned, Vic, that was a bloody provocative thing to say. And I can tell you this, from what we're getting in from the Areas, the lads' attitude is hardening by the minute, and it won't have been helped by what Derek had to say.'

It's a complicated thing to run, a coal strike. For example, on the following day, Wednesday the 12th, we had a meeting of our Finance and General Purposes sub-Committee, which was acting as the strike committee. The first thing we heard was that the Inland Revenue had said they couldn't man special centres to pay our men tax rebates if the COSA members went on all out strike. COSA in turn had told us that to do what we wanted, 35 percent of clerical staff would be needed, and that the selection of that 35 percent was bound to cause aggravation. From down there in our London basement, all we could do was repeat that the minimum necessary number of COSA members should go to work.

Then there were problems about safety cover to be ironed out. And what to do about the pit ponies? 'Bring 'em out if possible,' we said, 'but, failing that, the handlers should attend for work.' And schools—we'd omitted schools from our original list of places which should continue to be supplied, because our information had been that they had sufficient stocks. But now we had Press reports of schools having to close, after only three days of the strike.

We agreed: 'That reports of schools closing on account of a coal shortage had grossly overstressed the early effect of the strike on supplies of coal to schools. However, in the interests of public relations it was agreed that schools be added to the list of places to which coal can be delivered during the strike, and pickets should allow coal to move for that purpose.'

Public relations were very important. We knew we had started off with a lot of goodwill—on the very first day, for example, the *Observer* had come out with a feature in its Business Section showing how badly the miners had fared over the years, and much of the Press was also well-disposed, but we knew there would also be those who would want to exaggerate anything against us.

On a personal level, I soon found out what people really thought. Nellie and I had just moved south. Originally, we had intended to keep the bungalow we were buying in Bolton, but I had soon found out that it was impossible, as President, to commute from there, so I sold it, for the same price I had paid for it, which in terms of inflation actually represented a loss.

From the people we knew, in Bolton, we moved to people we definitely didn't know, at Hurst Park, near Hampton Court, which is not exactly renowned as being an area which supports the Labour Party. For once, one evening, I'd got home in reasonable time, and I said to Nellie: 'What the hell, let's go out and have a drink.' So we went to this pub, and when we got in I saw they were responding to calls to save energy—there were candles everywhere, even for serving the beer.

'Bloody hell,' I thought,'what's the reception going to be like in here? Ah well, why worry?' So we walked to the bar, and you could have heard a pin drop. Suddenly somebody said:'Good God, look who's here. Joe Gormley! What are *you* doing here?'

'Like you, I want a pint of beer,' I said.

'Well, when are we going to have these lights on, Joe?'

'As soon as the buggers decide to pay us!'

All of a sudden there was a great roar of laughter, and people came over to us, and congratulated us, and slapped my back—for Hampton Court it was quite unbelievable. I turned to Nellie and said: 'Bloody hell, mate, if this is an example of how the people of Britain think, we cannot lose.'

Mind you, it wasn't *all* sweetness and light. Nellie had found a hairdresser's in Molesey, and of course they soon found out who she was. Soon after the strike began, she went for an appointment, and after they'd rolled her hair up, some old lady came in and started calling me everything in the farmyard but a duck. 'We were having sherry last night,' she said,' and discussing it, and that thing from Hurst Park, I know what I'd do with him.' Nellie just sat there, furious. Mind you, the old lady didn't know who she was.

But the proprietress knew, and then she joined in: 'Yes, I know what I'd do with him—I'd dump him in the Thames and leave him there.' Well, they kept poor Nellie sitting there four and a half hours for her shampoo and set, while they pulled me to bits, and normally she'd have stood up and let them have half a dozen pieces of her mind. But she was so conscious that it would go straight into the papers that she said nothing. When she finally got out, she was so shaking with rage that she couldn't drive the car for half an hour.

When she did manage to get home, she phoned our son Frank to tell him what had happened. 'Well, mother, *you've* altered,' he said. 'No,' she said, 'I was only thinking about him and what it would do to him.'

Luckily, that sort of personal loyalty wasn't put to the test too often. In fact, a story appeared in the local paper quoting the local supermarket as saying what they'd do if I went into their store, and how they would give me a ticking-off and refuse to serve me. Well, it turned out it must have been one of the young assistants shooting his mouth off, because in the very next issue there was an apology from the manager, saying that 'Mr Gormley is welcome to come into the shop at any time'. As it happens, there's not much I like less than going shopping, but it was nice of him anyhow.

In general, the public response was overwhelming, and this was especially helpful when it came to the pickets. Obviously, £2 a day wasn't going to get them bedrooms at the Ritz, but the offers from the public of beds and shelter and meals was more than we needed, even in remote areas where there had never been any history of mining. And where there weren't even any houses, in places like Lincolnshire, people lent them the materials to build what were like small Nissen huts, and they'd have their fires by the roadside and do their picketing.

In fact, it was only six years later that I learned that Dr David Owen, later to become Foreign Secretary, had four miners staying with him and his wife for the whole length of the dispute. He told me: 'I've never met four better-mannered lads in my life.' And apparently those lads didn't forget the meaning of gratitude, either, because for years they sent the Owens presents at Christmas.

In many ways, I think that was typical. Many people who hadn't known miners, but who became involved with them over the strike, grew to be their admirers. They found that miners weren't all uncouth, and swearing, and rough, and drunk. They found out that miners are dedicated, well-mannered men, for the most part, and that they were capable of putting over a good case on their own behalf.

Running that strike was very much a day to day affair. We were learning all the time. One early problem came up at our NEC meeting on the first Thursday, January 13. It appeared that the Derbyshire Area were paying their men £4 a week strike pay from their Area funds. Now, this was a dilemma. As I have pointed out, the NUM is still very much a federation, with each Area having its own funds and its own rules. And the Derbyshire Area rules said that they had to make this payment. On the other hand, we had ordered that there should be no payments. So we had an impasse, and I had to make a decision. I ruled that where there was a conflict between Area Rules and National Rules, the latter would have to take precedence. I suppose it could be said to have been a dictatorial decision, but it was one which had to be made in the cause of unity.

During the second or third week of the strike, it became clear to us that we had a real problem, one with a good deal of irony in it. Many of the power stations were dual-fired—that is, they could burn either oil or coal. The fact that they were so was very much due to our insistence, especially during the Sixties, when the availability of cheap oil was tempting people to build stations for oil-burning alone. Now, it seemed, that was rebounding on us, because although we were being successful in stopping the movement of coal, the stations were saving their coal and burning extra oil.

Well, at between six and seven in the morning, late on in the week, the phone went in my office. It was Ray Buckton, General Secretary of ASLEF, the locomen's union. 'Joe,' he said, 'there's a lot of oil flowing out of Thames Haven, more than normal. My men are telling me about the flow of oil increasing as against coal.'

'What are you saying, Ray?' I said. 'Are you telling me that if we tried to stop the flow of oil we'd get your co-operation?'

'Yes.'

'Right, I'll get back to you in a bit.'

I rang down to the picketing office in the basement, and got two of the men from Kent to come up to my office. They were Joe Holmes and Terry Harrison, both of them damn good lads.

'Listen,' I said,'I've just had word from ASLEF that, if we start picketing oil distribution, we'll get their co-operation, particularly the oil depots where it's coming in from the sea. It seems to me that Thames Haven is an ideal place. We ought to put a picket line outside there.'

'But, Joe,' they said,'it's a main railway line!'

'Well,' I said,'so what? I'll leave it to you. I'm sure you'll think up something. But I'm telling you, if we can get a picket line outside Thames Haven, the loco drivers will not pass it. Now, how you do it I'm leaving to your own ingenuity. I don't know the area.'

So off they went, and when the strike committee met at ten o'clock I told them what I'd done.

All I can remember of what the others said was a chorus of 'Joe?!!!'

'Aye,' I said,'when you're in a battle, you've got to fight to win. There's no use being namby-pamby about things. Now that we're rolling, we've got to do something that's going to make it shorter rather than longer. We've got to apply the pressure points. As I see it, in conjunction with ASLEF, we'll put the pressure on here, and stop the oil flowing. And now's the time to make the decision, because nobody's bloody well moving, and we've got to shift 'em.'

Then I forgot all about it, because there was so much else going on, but at about eleven o'clock the phone rang. It was Ray Buckton again, and for the first half-minute he couldn't say a thing, he was laughing so much.

'What's happening, Ray?' I asked him.

'Well,' he said, 'I've just had the manager from Thames Haven on to me, going mad. He's jumping in his boots. He told me, "The train load of oil that went out of the sidings this morning has just rattled back again." It seems the driver told him, "There's a miners' picket line up yonder, and we're not going to pass it." You know what your lads have done? They've got a poster and they've printed on it "Miners' Picket Line. Don't Pass". And they've hung it over the parapet of a bridge, on the main railway line. As soon as the driver got to it, he stopped dead, and went back to the sidings again.'

It was the first really hard turn of the screw that we had been able to apply, and in my opinion it was that sort of co-operation which in the end won the strike—co-operation which was even to lead to ASLEF being threatened with legal action.

Nor was ASLEF alone in the help it gave. Up and down the country, hundreds of our picket lines were given a waiting-room, warmth, food and accommodation by fellow trade unionists. What's more, their local shop stewards gave us a flow of valuable information, and in most cases we only needed to mount a token picket on power stations, since local trade unionists had promised to warn us of any impending movements of fuel.

With movements of coal and oil by rail having been stopped, the only way of moving fuel was coal by road. Here the TGWU came to our aid, with their drivers refusing to cross our picket lines, so that the only movement possible was by non-union members, who frequently did so with police escorts.

With all this assistance, it wasn't hard for our pickets to comply with our repeated instructions, written and verbal, that picketing should be peaceful, and throughout the seven weeks of the strike, with more than a thousand picket lines in operation, there were no more than a dozen reported instances of violence.

The majority of those I believed then, and still believe, were engineered—contrived for the benefit of television crews or freelance photographers. Typical of these was an incident at six in the morning in Doncaster, outside an office where half the girls were members of Apex. The television crews were there, and a few of our lads were jeering at these girls, and then some man claimed that a picket had spat at his daughter. As far as I could establish, it was a load of tripe.

I found out about a slightly more sinister incident one day, when our picketing office in the basement rang up to say: 'Joe, there's a bloke on the phone on about a camera.' So I got them to put him through to my office.

'Oh, Mr Gormley,' he said, 'what are you going to do about this? A cameraman of mine has had his camera smashed by your men, and I want to know what compensation you'll be giving.'

I told him to call me back in an hour, after I had made enquiries. It turned out this firm had sent this freelance photographer, with two or three others, down to our picketing line at Battersea Power Station. They had got out of their taxi, and started getting their cameras out, when our lads, about six in all, said: 'You don't need your cameras, bugger off.'

Then the other men started jostling our lads, while this freelance bloke took pictures, making it look as though there was a pitched battle with a miners' picket line. Not unnaturally, one of our lads decided there was nought to do but take the camera off him and smash it, which he did, and then told them: 'Bugger off if you don't want them all smashed.'

So when the man who'd phoned with the complaint got back to me and asked what I was going to do about it, I said: 'Nothing.'

'Well,' he said, 'if that's so, we'll have to make a case . . .'

'You can make any case you want out of it, mate. Your lads had no right and no authority to go down and interfere with our picketing line. I can only tell you they were bloody lucky they weren't thrown in the river. If you'll take advice from me, you'll just keep them away in future. And, as far as your camera is concerned, you can just wish it goodbye and claim it from your insurance, because that's all you're going to get.'

I never heard another thing about it from him. Of course I knew that NUJ members also had a job to do, but it was the jostling that made me take the attitude I did, more than the photography, although anyone has a right to say he doesn't want his picture taken. Besides, I doubt if that cameraman was even an NUJ member, because we found out later that he was from an organisation which was out for some cheap publicity to use against the unions.

But they needed more than cheap publicity to defeat us. We were quickly learning how to make the strike as effective as possible. For example, lorries were allowed out of coal depots if they could show that they were delivering to a school, a hospital, or whatever. But, if the pickets were suspicious, they'd send a car to follow the lorry, and if it turned out, as sometimes happened, that he had been using a false pass, and wasn't going to a school at all but to some small yard, or works, he would be turned back and not allowed to take any load out again.

Above all, we were determined to remain within the law, and on January 19, following some reports in the media of picket line disturbances, Lawrence Daly, as General Secretary, wrote to all our Area Secretaries under the heading 'Peaceful Picketing'.

The note said: 'Reports have appeared in the Press and on Television about disturbances involving NUM pickets and workmen who attempt to cross the picket line. Having regard for the size of the exercise which has been undertaken by the Union, such incidents are minimal, but unfortunately they attract maximum publicity, particularly when people are injured.

'In addition to the discomfort suffered by the unfortunate individual, there is the damage which such incidents inflict upon the good name of the Union and its members, and that we cannot afford if we intend to keep public sympathy on our side.

'Will you, therefore, impress upon the members who volunteer for picket duty that they are engaged on *Peaceful* Picketing, and that *physical contact with persons who attempt to pass through the line is illegal*, and should be avoided, regardless of any provocation which our members may have to endure.'

In fact, the only real tragedy in all the picketing—and that was with more than 60,000 men on picket duty—was the death of one of our own members, on February 3. Fred Matthews had come from Hatfield Main Pit to join the picket line at Cadeby Power Station. Well, as I said, most of the drivers acceded to our requests, and turned back from the lines, but you always get odd bods, and there was one of them at the wheel of a big articulated lorry coming out of the gates. The pickets tried to stop him, to talk to him, but he just drove straight through, the back end of his lorry swung round on to the pavement, and it caught Fred Matthews and killed him. Unfortunately, we had no redress, because it could always be argued that Fred, and the others, had acted illegally by trying to obstruct the traffic.

There's no doubt, though, that the news of his death, which spread through the members faster than even the papers could get it out, hardened the attitude of a lot of pickets, and as a result a number were arrested, forty-eight in the first four weeks of the strike.

And there's no doubt at all that the membership as a whole became more and more determined and unified as the strike went on. I visited most parts of the country during those weeks, and I was amazed to see the solidarity, even among the wives, who of course were having a hard time. They could claim social security for themselves and their children, but that had to spread across the whole family, because after the first couple of weeks the men would have exhausted anything they had to come in the form of tax rebates and the like. Even so, at all the meetings Lawrence and I addressed, we found nothing less than total support.

Support came from abroad, too. On January 20, the Bureau of the Miners' International Federation, which had been meeting in Vienna, put out the statement that the Bureau 'having received at first hand from Lawrence Daly, Secretary of the National Union of Mineworkers, a report on the strike of the British miners, assures the British miners of the wholehearted support of the Miners' International Federation in their struggle for an adequate level of wages, and calls upon the affiliates to do all in their power—and in conjunction with the transport workers of their country—to prevent exports of coal to Britain during the strike'.

The day before, while Lawrence was in Vienna, Sid Schofield, the Vice-President, and I had gone to talks at the TUC at Vic Feather's invitation. The Board were there, too, but there was no resolving to be done. It was one of those meetings which are talks about the possibility of talks, and once Vic had established that no productive talks were likely to be forthcoming, he told us that in view of the national importance of the dispute he intended to seek a meeting with Robert Carr, the Secretary of State for Employment, to see what else could be done.

By the end of January, the strike was starting to have a deep effect. Up till then, the Government had been fortunate in that it had been an exceptionally mild winter. But then, from January 30 to February 1, there was a very cold spell, which caused major power reductions, which continued throughout the following week. Many power stations had exhausted their coal supplies, and twelve closed at the start of February. At those still functioning, stocks varied between a few days and a few weeks, but we had now realised that by preventing the supply of flashing oil—essential to the operation of the coal-fired stations—we had a neat way of rendering even those stocks useless very quickly.

Several steel works, as well as other industries, cotton in particular, had been forced to close through fuel shortages, and domestic supplies were becoming very short throughout the land. And *still* the public supported us. Not only were letters of support and individual donations continuing to flood in, but members of the public were even reporting movements of coal to us, enabling us to tie up all the loose ends.

One such was a very large loose end indeed. During the fifth week, the strike office got on to me and told me that they had discovered that at the Saltley Depot, down in Warwickshire, there was a huge dump of about 100,000 tons of coke which was being used.

'You *what?!*' I said. Straight away I got on to the Midlands Area and told them: 'Get some bloody pickets down there as soon as you can.'

Immediately they started arguing about finance for the pickets, but there wasn't any time for that, and I said: 'We'll deal with that later, but for now I'm telling you to get those pickets in position.'

But, before they could get there, it turned out that Arthur Scargill, who was in charge of picketing lines in South Yorkshire, had also heard about Saltley, and he'd taken a couple of busloads of Yorkshire miners down there. Now Saltley was on the outskirts of Birmingham, and as soon as Birmingham Trades Council heard what was happening, they saw it as a wonderful opportunity to show full solidarity with the miners. So *they* joined in, too. It became a huge national story, but the net result was that, because of the pressure of opinion in the area, the police themselves were forced to close and lock the gates.

On February 3, John Davies, the Minister for Industry, told a Cabinet meeting that the situation was getting worse. He put it down not only to our effective picketing, but also to the fact that the way we had done it was so unexpected—what would come to be called 'secondary picketing', which, although maybe distasteful to some people, was perfectly legal. And legality was something we were having to be extra careful about, since the picketing regulations of the Industrial Relations Act had come into force on January 31, and Lawrence had had to circularise the Areas again.

'These [the regulations] provide that *peaceful picketing is permitted,*' he wrote, 'and we must make sure that is is peaceful and that we are not under any circumstances provoked into acts of aggression.'

Indeed, I knew that even the Government recognised that we were doing everything by the book, because, through Vic Feather's intercession, we and the Board had had our first, separate, meetings with Bob Carr down at the Department of Employment in St James's Square. And, although nothing came of these meetings, at least I had the satisfaction of Carr telling me: 'The trouble is, Joe, that you're doing everything legally. I can't find any way of getting at you.' He was quite open about it, and I thought that, considering we had found ways and means of bringing the country to a virtual standstill, it was a great tribute.

It was because of our success that John Davies, at that meeting on February 3, asked the Cabinet to declare a State of Emergency, but they turned him down. In retrospect, that seems a curious decision. Either they were prepared to consider giving way to us, or they weren't, and if they weren't, from their point of view, they might as well have had it sooner than later.

After all, they knew we had solid backing by now, because following that first meeting with Carr the TUC had issued a Press statement saying: 'The General Council took the view that the reasons why the meetings with the Secretary of State had not yielded any productive results, and indeed the reasons why the dispute had escalated to a stoppage of work, were largely to be found in the Government's negative attitude. This derived from its attempts to impose rigid restrictions on collective bargaining in the public sector, and from the extent to which the Government had undermined the confidence of trade unionists in the machinery of independent arbitration.

'The General Council recognised that in the present deadlock there was little likelihood that the NUM and the NCB would find a mutually satisfactory basis for a settlement unless the Government itself accepted its share of responsibility for creating a more flexible situation. The General Council considered that the first essential was for the Government to recognise that the mineworkers have a strong case which must be examined on its own merits, not by reference to doctrinaire considerations.'

It was a pretty strong statement, especially as they went on to announce that they were inviting all unions to subscribe to a fund to help us. If the Government had ever entertained the notion that they could get the Miners, or the Movement as a whole, to break ranks, they surely knew now that they could forget it.

By February 5, coal supplies at those power stations still operating were down to an average of three weeks, and the strike was estimated to be costing the Board £3 million each week. And on February 8, the Government, finally forced to concede that they were losing, declared their State of Emergency. This gave them wide powers, including the use of troops if necessary. But it was too late. It would have been in practical terms impossible to use the troops, because fellow trade unionists had successfully 'blacked' those supplies which, under police escort, had managed to break through our lines. And there was no doubt that any further attempts to break through the lines would have resulted in much wider industrial action.

The following morning, February 9, Sid, Lawrence and I went down to St James's Square to see Robert Carr, at his invitation. He told us that he had been talking to the Board, and that, despite the industry's financial difficulties, some more money might be made available to us, provided we were prepared to discuss the agreement lasting longer than the normal twelve months. In addition, he asked whether, if the miners were treated as a special case, the TUC would be prepared to accept that they shouldn't use our settlement as an argument in negotiations with other employers.

'No way, we're not having any of that,' I said. 'We're here to talk about miners' wages and conditions and nothing else. What anybody else negotiates within their own industry is up to them.' To me, that's what free collective bargaining is all about, and in any case I had consistently argued, within both the TUC and the Labour Party's National Executive, that I didn't want the miners treated as a 'special case'. I simply wanted our claim dealt with on its own merits.

Then he brought up again the question of arbitration, and the possibility of a Court of Inquiry. We said we weren't too keen on either, but that we'd talk to anybody provided there was money available to offer us a substantial increase above the Board's 'final offer', the one which Derek Ezra had later withdrawn.

'Well,' he said, 'I'm still very anxious for you at least to have exploratory talks with the Board, provided your Executive agree.'

So back we went to Euston Road, and reported to the Executive, who were waiting to hear the outcome, and they agreed we should meet the Board, and make it clear that we were in a position to negotiate. And that we did, meeting at St James's Square, with one of Bob Carr's officials in the chair.

The offer was a complicated one, so, rather than go into a mass of detail, I'll stick to the one example of the surface workers, who were the lowest paid. The Board were now offering them an increase of £3 a week on their £18 minimum wage, but with the guarantee that for a normal five-day week they wouldn't get less than £22, an effective increase of £4. The point of *calling* it £21 was that this was the rate on which any overtime would be calculated. This offer compared with our original claim for £8 a week, and their 'final offer' of £2 a week.

But there was a big catch to it. They wanted the offer to run for eighteen months from the resumption of work, rather than for twelve months from the previous November 1. So, in place of an offer worth £32 million over a twelve-month period, they were now making a £48 million offer which would effectively cover a period of *twenty-two* months from November 1, thus putting a very different complexion on the whole thing.

The following morning, Thursday, February 10, we reported back to the NEC. It was what the Press call a 'crunch' meeting, because I went into it certain that there would be some members who would want to accept the offer. And so it turned out. Someone even moved that we accept it. But by then I was becoming a bit bloody-minded. Our lads had already lost more than a month's wages. We had had to drag the Board along, penny by penny, with repeated statements from them that this was the 'final offer'.

So I told the Executive: 'No, no, it's not enough. I don't think we've reached the right figure, and I believe that there *is* more money available if we continue to negotiate. So I urge you not to force a vote on it, because I want us to remain completely unified.'

I must say that I was relieved when the motion was withdrawn, because although I don't think the majority wanted to accept, there would undoubtedly have been a split vote, and we would have gone back weaker to the negotiating table. Of course, they could have insisted on a vote, which was their right, but I suppose they were convinced by my arguments. It's equally true that, if there *had* been a vote, it would soon have become public, because it's difficult enough keeping secrets even in Cabinet, let alone the NEC of the NUM, with so many political factions all wanting to blow their own trumpet.

We ended up with unanimous agreement that the offer was completely unacceptable, but with the Executive authorising us yet again to go back to talk to the Board. So back to St James's Square we went. The Board were furious. They said we apparently didn't appreciate their efforts to improve the lot of the lowest paid men. In fact, we had great difficulty in keeping them at the table. The only move they then made was to ask whether the deal would be acceptable if they back-dated it to November 1.

'Well,' I said, 'we're expecting that anyway. But you still haven't offered us enough cash.'

'All right,' they said, 'well, you just tell us what it *is* that you want.'

'If you want serious negotiations,' I said, 'you'll have to be thinking along the lines of a £6 increase for the surface men, and £7 underground. And of course there'll have to be a corresponding increase for the face workers.'

All around that table I could see eyebrows go up and faces fall. They went off to another room to talk about it, but when they came back they said: 'You're making demands which you know we can't concede. So, as far as we're concerned, you're acting irresponsibly. It seems you don't care either about the Industry, or the nation as a whole.'

'It's funny *you* should say that,' I said, 'because we had rather got the impression that this whole situation is something which *you* have contrived to bring about.'

It was an obvious stalemate, and at that point Bob Carr asked to see us. 'It's clear there's such a wide gap between you,' he said, 'that I've decided to appoint a Court of Inquiry. Now I'm suggesting that your men return to work on the basis of the present offer, but on the clear understanding that if the Court of Inquiry recommends more, that will be back-dated to the day work restarts.'

'I'll put it to my Executive,' I said, 'but I'll tell you here and now that it's not a practicable suggestion.'

Following that meeting, he told the Press that any increase in wages would result in a considerable increase in the price of coal, and that that in turn would have an adverse effect on the economy as a whole. Well, that statement had an adverse effect on the Executive, when we reported to them the following morning, because it was felt to be a sign that the Court of Inquiry would be subjected to Government pressure. Certainly, we agreed, there could be no provisional return to work. And, although we also agreed to give evidence to the Court of Inquiry, we were not going to be bound to accept its findings.

That day, February 11, was a crucial date in the strike. John Davies decided to make use of the special powers he had been given four days earlier under the State of Emergency. He imposed a three-day week on all industrial production, and announced massive power cuts, including 15 percent reductions for domestic use. During the following week, 1,600,000 men were to be laid off work. This, we thought, was the moment that we would start to lose public sympathy, but the strange thing was, it didn't happen. The letters of support, and the contributions, came in unabated.

On the same day, Bob Carr announced the composition of his Court of Inquiry. It was to be chaired by Lord Wilberforce, a Lord of Appeal, and his colleagues were to be John Garnett, Director of the Industrial Society, and Laurance Hunter, Professor of Economics at Glasgow University. The Court was to start its proceedings, in public, on the 15th, and our research and industrial relations department, led by Trevor Bell, set to, working night and day, to prepare all the facts and figures and arguments which Lawrence Daly, as General Secretary, was going to put to them on our behalf.

In addition, we called in Professor Hugh Clegg, well-known for his expertise in problems of industrial relations. This was because we realised full well that the arguments did not relate to ourselves alone, however much we insisted that we were simply arguing our own case. We knew we stood for millions of other workers in the public sector who were being frustrated in their aim of free collective bargaining, and we wanted Professor Clegg to argue for a more reasoned approach, not only to our own case, but also to similar 'special cases' in the future.

What's more, since we as a Union had made our priority the situation of our lower-paid workers, and since they in a sense represented millions more in the same boat, we called in Michael Meacher, M.P., who had become he country's leading expert in the so-called 'poverty trap'. We also had the support of the Trade Union Research Unit of Ruskin College.

The Inquiry sat for two days, on February 15 and 16. I will not here go into detail about what went on. After it was all over, an excellent book was prepared for us, and published, called *A Special Case? Social Justice and the Miners*. But I have to pay tribute to the three members of that Court, who conducted it in a far more impartial way than we could have dared to hope, especially since, as I learned later from talking to them, they were all subjected to pressures from both the Right and the Left.

It was clear, during those two days, that the Court was frequenty astonished by what we had to tell the, with the help of witnsses from among our own membership. For example, there was Jack Collins, from Kent, who was working in a pit so hot that, as he told the Court, the men worked naked. In 1963 he had been earning £5.50p a shift. Now, nearly ten years later, he was down to £5 a shift. There was sixty-two-year-old James O'Connor, from Maltby, who had worked in the pits since he was fifteen, and whose wages had dropped by £5 a week from what he had earned five years previously. And there was Alan Carter, from the Rhondda, having to keep a wife and four children on a basic wage of £18 a week, and with virtually no chance of overtime. The only way he could keep going, he told the Court, was by claiming means-tested social security benefits. He could earn an extra 45p a week when he was put to driving a heavy pit lorry, a job for which men in other industries were getting between £30 and £35 a week.

And so it went on. From time to time it seemed that the Court found it almost unbelievable that we could have got the miners to accept this situation for so long. We proved to them beyond doubt that not only had the miners fallen dramatically in the wages league, but also that, in the light of inflation, their real standard of living had suffered a large cutback. And we demonstrated to them how, during the Sixties, the Union had given full co-operation over pit closures, and at the same time had so improved productivity that each miner was producing 150 tons of coal more per year than he had been in 1960.

There were witnesses from the other side, of course. Bill Campbell Adamson, Director-General of the CBI, found himself forced to agree with us more than he disagreed. Various members of the Coal Board came and went and were, I can say without any prejudice, well and truly rebuffed. And there was a marvellous moment when Derek Ezra tried to cast doubt on our figures by pointing out that miners enjoyed various benefits in kind, like concessionary coal.

'In our estimation,' he said,'those amount to £2.30p. That is the cost to the Coal Board. Of course, if these benefits in kind were not made available to the members of the National Union of Mineworkers, they would cost them a good deal more, and I would like to know whether those have been taken into account in this computation?'

Said Lawrence: 'When I made references, as I have done in the last two or three weeks, to your salary of £20,000 per year, I was by no means taking into account, either for you or the other members of the Coal Board, the various 'perks' that you receive on your job.'

Well, he'd asked his question and he'd got his answer, but Lawrence went on to say: 'The same with mining. These figures vary. There are thousands of members who do not qualify for concessionary coal, the vast majority do not qualify for cheap rents, many of them live in CIHA (Coal Industry Housing Association) houses where the rent charged is the same as the rent charged by the local authority for similar accommodation, and for those who do have cheap rents they are generally nineteenth-century housing for which no one would expect to be paying more than a few shillings in these days.'

In fact, Lord Wilberforce then came to our aid, by eliciting the fact that in the comparative tables we had put forward, showing our relative positions in 1967 and 1971, no side benefits had been included in either table, so that our argument still applied.

That Court of Inquiry must have broken all records for the speed with which it reported. It finished taking evidence on Wednesday the 16th, and on the morning of Friday the 18th we were summoned to St James's Square to hear its conclusions.

To our delight—though perhaps not entirely to our surprise, since we had seen the way that the Court had been conducted—the report was a total vindication of our arguments, and a defeat for the Government's policies, as a few examples will serve to show.

'Working conditions in coal mines,' they wrote,'are certainly among the toughest and least attractive, and we agree that miners' pay levels should recognise this. In addition, as many underground workers have to be redeployed on surface work (which attracts comparatively lower pay than underground work) because their health has been adversely affected by working conditions underground, we think that equity requires that pay levels for surface work need also to be improved.

'The British coalmining community is in some ways quite unique. Coalminers and their families often live in poor housing in isolated communities where coalmining is a traditional and sometimes the only way of life. There is a strong egalitarian feeling among the men, which manifests itself in their concern for the lower paid men in the industry. One example of this is the industry's long standing arrangement that holiday pay is not calculated on an individual worker's usual earnings, but on the average pay of the workforce. The miner's concern for his fellow men has been reflected in the role which his Union has played in attempting to resolve the many difficult problems which have faced his industry since nationalisation.'

They went on to talk about the pit closures and job losses of the Sixties, and remarked: 'This rundown, which was brought about with the co-operation of the miners and of their Union, is without parallel in British industry in terms of the social and economic costs it has inevitably entailed for the mining community as a whole.'

They accepted our argument that in mining the basic wage represented a far higher percentage of actual earnings than it did in most other industries. They accepted that we *had* declined both relative to other industries, and also in standards of living.

What's more, having discussed the new wages structure which, with our full co-operation, had gradually been phased into the industry since 1955, they wrote:'We agree with Professor Clegg when he said in relation to this situation that 'one consequence of the power-loading agreement was to hold back the pay of most faceworkers in relation to the rest of the industry, and to hold back the pay of some groups of faceworkers far more than others. It is, I believe, generally agreed by practitioners of industrial relations, that, when a new pay structure alters the relative pay of groups of workers in an industry or undertaking, there is need for generous overall increase to be injected, so that all, or all but a few of, the workers who suffer a relative setback should nevertheless receive a net advance. But over the last few years a large number of miners have been asked to take a reduction relative to the general level of miners' earnings at a time when that general level has been falling behind the movement of pay in the country as a whole." In our opinion, this is a special and powerful factor underlying the present unrest and calling for adjustment.'

As *The Times* commented: 'The Wilberforce Report conceded almost all the miners' case . . . It reads like a printed version of the arguments used by NUM leaders.'

Yes, 'almost all', but not quite all. Certainly they agreed with us, when discussing the Coal Board's ability to pay our claim, and the pit closures that might result, when they wrote: 'If, however, such a reduction in employment is quite unacceptable, then the Government will have to provide the necessary finance, because it is unreasonable to expect miners' wages to be held down to finance uneconomic operations.'

But then they came to the figures they suggested. In a nutshell, it was £5 for surface workers, £6 for underground workers, and £4.50p for the face workers, giving respective minimum rates of £23, £25, and £34.50p. And they recommended that the agreement should run from November 1 for sixteen months, rather than start a whole new round of pay talks within a few months.

Well, straight away, after receiving the Report, we held an NEC meeting in the Department's conference room, and the feeling was that, since the agreement was to last for sixteen months, the pay offer still wasn't enough, although it was now that we had the first split in the Executive during the whole dispute, the Report being rejected by 15 votes to 10. But the fact was that most of us knew in our heart of hearts that there wasn't a cat in hell's chance of getting more actual cash. No Government worth its salt could possibly have turned round and said, 'Well, we've set up this independent inquiry, but we don't think it has been generous enough, and therefore we propose to be more generous'—they wouldn't have lasted ten minutes.

On the other hand, many of us were getting pretty bloody-minded by now. We were at the end of the sixth week of the strike, a strike which had cost the Union and its individual members a great deal. Equally, we weren't so irresponsible as to ignore what it was doing to the country. Only the day before, John Davies had announced even fiercer power cuts, and had admitted that our picketing had succeeded in reducing coal stocks to a week and a half's supply—very near the precipice. Somehow, an agreement *had* to be worked out that day, a day which was to turn out, without exception, the longest and most exhausting of my life.

There was one way out of the apparent impasse. We made out a shopping list. It was as long as your arm. It consisted of all the minor, or in some cases not so minor, claims and fringe benefits and adjustments and allowances which we had been after for years—items which year after year had come up at our annual conferences, and which year after year had somehow either not reached discussion with the Board, or had been shelved for 'further discussion'—things like the payment of adult rates at the age of eighteen, the question of holidays, and so on.

So I told the NEC: 'It's my belief that although we can try, I don't reckon we're going to get any more cash out of them. But there are all these other things. Why don't you authorise us to go and see what we can do on those?' They agreed, and Lawrence, Sid and I went off to another room to see the Board's officials, and told them what we wanted to discuss. Then, to save time, we invited them to come back and join our meeting.

There, they listed certain issues which could be sent for discussion by working parties, and a further five on which agreement could be reached immediately. These last included accepting the recommendations of Wilberforce, whose opinion, they said, they accepted as fair, and one to which they could subscribe. It wasn't the time for recriminations, but I must say I thought to myself, 'If you're prepared to say it's fair now, why the bloody hell didn't you agree to the £3.50p I mentioned months ago, and save us all this?'

What they couldn't do, they said, was offer us any more cash, or reduce the sixteen-month period for which the agreement would operate. They were prepared to be flexible on everything else, they said, but not on those two items. Then they left the room for us to consider what they had said.

The general feeling on the NEC was that we were likely to get satisfaction on most of these extra points we had raised, but that we still wanted more cash. So the offer was rejected, and we, the National

Officials, were asked to go back to the Board on the basis that we would be prepared to recommend a return to work if we got increases of £6 on the surface, £7 underground, and £4.50 at the face, the last of which, of course, we had already won.

'No,' said the Board. 'That would make nonsense of any future arbitration. But, in order to try to get agreement, we'll make you an offer right now on some of these items which we were originally going to start discussing next week.'

There were seven of these items, ranging from the fact that they would increase piece rates, where they still applied, in line with the Wilberforce recommendations, to the staggering of arrears of rent. 'We're prepared to be as generous as we can,' they said,'but it has to be within the confines of Wilberforce.'

Well, things were obviously moving very fast. It was clear to me that the Board, too, had decided that there had to be a settlement that day, if disaster was to be avoided. But the NEC, to whom we reported back, decided once again that the Union should still press for more cash, and that the National Officials should meet the Secretary of State, Bob Carr.

That decision was taken at three in the afternoon. I had gone along with it, but I knew I was walking the proverbial tightrope. Because , as I have said, that morning, when we first saw the Wilberforce Report, there had been the first split vote during the whole dispute, 15 to 10 against acceptance. And by now, with the concessions which the Board had just made, I knew that if I went for acceptance I could have swung some of the moderates with me and won the vote. In fact, earlier in the day, one or two of the members who had voted against acceptance now told me on the side, 'Don't worry, Joe. There'll be no problem. You'll get the votes.'

Ah yes, I'd get them if I *put* it to the vote. But to myself I said 'To hell with them. They've made us suffer for six weeks, now they're going to suffer. I'm going to go for every last drop I can wring from them, because I'm going to teach them a lesson, the lesson that they'll have to start heeding advice in future.' I felt that the whole thing had happened because people hadn't listened to me. Derek Ezra and the Board hadn't listened, when I told them the sort of settlement that would be accepted. The Government hadn't listened when I told them that, if it came to a fight, it would be a fight to the finish, and that, whatever previous votes might indicate, the miners, when it came to it, would be completely united. The TUC, for all their support when the strike did come, had initially been sceptical. And even the NEC of the Labour Party, of which I was a member, and which I could therefore keep regularly informed, remained lukewarm in their belief that we could win. So I made up my mind to prove it, once and for all.

The meeting with Bob Carr achieved nothing. He told us that he had seen the Board, and that there was no change in their position, and that therefore he was now making arrangements for us to see the Prime Minister. So the whole caravan moved off to Downing Street, and the three of us went in to see Ted Heath.

'What's the position, then, Joe?' he asked.

'Well, if we're to recommend acceptance, we'll have to have an increase over and above Wilberforce,' I said,'and that's the truth of it.'

Bob Carr and Tony Barber, the Chancellor, were with him, and he said:'We've just had a Cabinet meeting, and we've decided that there's no possibility of increasing the amount. We set up the Inquiry, and announced that we would abide by its findings, so our hands are tied. We can't move on it at all.'

'In that case, we're in a bit of a cleft stick, Ted,' I said,'unless there are some other items we can negotiate with the Board.'

'Well, that's between you and them.'

'Are they in the building?'

'Yes, they are. Why don't you go and meet them and see what you can come up with.'

So, once again, we started on our shopping list. Lawrence, Sid and I were joined in the negotiations by Trevor Bell, the Union's head of industrial relations, and every now and then we would go back into the room where the Executive were waiting, to test the water on what we had been able to achieve. In addition, Vic Feather was waiting in yet another room, and every now and then we would pop in and tell him how things were going.

Finally, at about midnight, we had won agreement on no less than twenty items, many of them issues that we had unsuccessfully fought for years. Apart from being exhausted by the negotiations, the four of us were pretty vexed, because every time we went back to the room where the NEC were sitting, they had either just finished one lot of beer and sandwiches, or they were about to order another, so none of us got a bite to eat!

But still there was one more battle to win, and it was one of the most important of all.

It was a running sore which had been with us for more than twenty years, and it arose from the time when we negotiated the five-day working week in 1947. But we didn't want to lose money over it, and at the same time, with the fuel shortages, the Attlee Government wanted us to work to mine extra coal. So a bonus system had had to be devised. We would work a five-day week, but be paid for six, the last day being known as the bonus shift. But if a man only worked four days, because of sickness or whatever, he would only get four-fifths of the bonus shift. If he worked on the Saturday, naturally he got paid extra for that, but we had always regarded this bonus shift system as pernicious, especially since, if a day was lost through a dispute, there wouldn't be any bonus shift at all.

So, once again, I went back to the Executive, and I said:'Look, we've pretty well drained the barrel dry. We've skinned the kitty. I reckon we can move them on this, and get the bonus shift incorporated into the normal shift rate. But I can only do it if I know that you'll recommend acceptance if we get it. We can't go on for ever with this sort of a game.'

At that, a couple of the members said: 'Oh, no! Let's go home and come back tomorrow.'

'Not on your bloody life,' I said.'We've been negotiating all day while you've been sitting here enjoying beer and sandwiches. If anybody goes home tonight, he loses his bloody vote. We're having a settlement before we leave here tonight. So now let's have a vote on it.' The vote, as I expected, went 17 to 8 in favour of acceptance, provided we won on the bonus shift.

Back in the room where the Board were waiting, I told them the situation.

'What *is* this, Joe?' asked Derek Ezra. 'You keep backing away and backing away.'

'Listen, Derek,' I said,'we've never indicated so far that we'd be in a position to recommend acceptance. But I'm telling you now, if you accept our request on this issue, we'll recommend acceptance.'

'Is that right, Joe?'

'Yes, it is.'

Bill Shepherd, Deputy Chairman of the Board, was sitting next to Derek, and he practically exploded. 'Do you know what this will cost, Joe? It'll cost us eleven and a half million quid a year!'

'Bill,' I said, ' after all these negotiations, what's that between friends? We've been on strike for six weeks now, so what the hell are you miethering about for eleven and a half million quid?'

Well, they went out, and ten minutes later, and I suppose after consulting the Government and everybody else in sight, they came back and told us: 'Okay. On the understanding that you're now recommending acceptance, we'll give you that too.'

For the final time that day, we commuted back to the other room. 'Well, we've got it, lads,' I said, 'so now we've got to be big enough to keep our word and recommend acceptance.' Well, there were *still* those, among what I always called the 'antis', who didn't want to accept, and someone moved to that effect.

But I'll never forget Dai Francis, from South Wales, who had always been among the 'antis' and voted against everything, saying: 'Well, Mr

Chairman, I think you've done a wonderful job, and I shall be voting for acceptance.' I thought that might have persuaded one or two of the others. It didn't. But I still got a vote of 18 to 7 in favour of accepting.

The next move the 'antis' made was to say that we shouldn't have a ballot vote, but an Area vote. They knew they would still be defeated, but not as heavily as in a ballot vote.

'We *must* have a ballot vote,' I said. 'After a six-week strike we must ask every individual member of the Union what he thinks of what we have achieved.'

Then someone brought up the fact that normal ballot votes took two or three weeks, sometimes as many as five.

'It doesn't need to take that time,' I said. 'We can have the ballot papers out in two days, get them delivered to the pits, and have them ferried back to London straight away. We can know the result within a week.'

When I went out and told Ted Heath what had been decided, he asked: 'But do you *need* a ballot vote, Joe?'

'Well,' I said,'you need a ballot vote to make sure you get the right type of majority.' I think he took the point—but then he had to, because we were going to have a ballot vote anyway.

To me, it was very important. You may think you know in your mind that you've got it right, but once you've consulted the membership you're a damn sight surer. In Area voting, it's often possible for delegates to cast their votes without consulting their members. But a Union is no more nor less than its members, and it's vital that they should participate.

We left Downing Street at two in the morning, and as we got into our taxis, Vic Feather said he'd like to drop in and see me in the morning. 'I'll be in the office at eight,' I said, and that's when he was there. 'Joe,' he said, 'I don't know what the hell you did to Ted Heath, but you frightened me to bloody death!'

The ballot took place the following Wednesday, and on the Friday, February 25, we had the result. The vote against acceptance was 7,581. The voting for—210,039, no less than 96.5 percent. The 'antis' could judge the degree to which they were in touch with the membership. And the strike was over.

No one could say it had been other than a great victory. We won far, far more than even Wilberforce had suggested. All those extra items added up to more than the actual cash offer. Among them, apart from getting the bonus shift removed (which had an extra importance, since overtime is based on the daily wage, and that was now one fifth rather than one sixth of the weekly rate), we had won an extra week's holiday, and we had ensured that within two years the adult rate would be paid to everyone over eighteen, another long-fought issue.

It cost the Government maybe £200 million, including £100 million in the form of an emergency grant they had to make to the Coal Board, but it restored the miners' standard of living to what it had been five years previously, and we were back near the top of the industrial wages league. And the irony was that, on the very day the strike ended, February 28, the anti-strike provisions of the Industrial Relations Act came into force, provisions which would have made it far more difficult for us to achieve the effect we did.

Even so, looking back at it all, I'm not sure whether that strike performed a good service or a bad. It was good in that it united the lads, and showed them the strength which that unity could bring. On the other hand, its success led to an attitude of mind, prevalent today, where people, the moment they don't get what they want, think and talk immediately of strike action.

But it was a great exercise, and I wouldn't have been anywhere else.

Chapter Eight

Heath and Wilson

When I was first elected President of the NUM, many people expected me to leave the NEC of the Labour Party and seek a seat on the General Council of the TUC. I resisted the idea. I said publicly that in my view the General Council was nothing more than a 'talking shop'. That belief was doubtless reinforced by the fact that I very much enjoyed my work with the Party and being privy to its inner councils.

At the end of 1971, following the Labour Party Conference, my enjoyment was boosted by my election as Chairman of the Party's International Sub-Committee. I have always been a strong internationalist, and the eleven years of my Presidency were to see miners' representatives from all over the world invited to our Conferences. So it was a job I was really delighted to be given, compounded by the fact that I had aready been a member of the Socialist International Bureau for a few years.

I had served for ten years on that International Sub-Committee, and for the past eight of them Walter 'Padley had been Chairman, and a very good one at that. But he had had a very serious illness, and none of us really expected him to carry on. That was the only reason I even dreamed of opposing him. I thought I was doing the job pretty well, and when, a year later, the NEC again held its first post-Conference meeting, at which it elects its committees and their chairmen, there was no question in my mind but that I would be asked to continue in the post. Then came the vote, which was by a show of hands, and it was obvious straight away that the Tribune Group had been conducting a little private exercise of their own. I was defeated for the Chairmanship by Ian Mikardo, and was also ousted as a member of the Bureau.

It came as no surprise. Once I knew who else had been nominated, I could see the ploy, and realised exactly what was happening. I should have known it before, but I didn't, and that was perhaps what upset me as much as anything, because there were only three votes in it, and if I'd had any warning perhaps I could have done something about swaying a few of those votes. I was angry, and I was hurt by the way it had been done, and I said: 'Well, if that's the way you're playing at things, then I'm sorry I can't be with you any longer.'

I walked away from the meeting with Jim Callaghan, who was then Party Treasurer, and he said: 'Don't worry about it, Joe.'

'To hell with it,' I said. 'I'm leaving 'em this year. I shall get nominated for the TUC, and take my place on the General Council on behalf of the Miners' Union.'

Of course, it wasn't quite as simple as that. In fact, it was very complicated, but once again a set of coincidences combined to determine my line of action and made me do something which, on reflection, I think was right, but which otherwise I would not have wanted to do.

The story of miners' nominations to the General Council could almost make a book on its own. Suffice it to say, that up to the start of the Sixties the Mines and Quarries Section of the TUC was entitled to nominate three members. The entitlement depends on the number of members in the unions concerned.

Before the War, the miners had a monopoly of these seats, until 1939, when one of our nominees, Arthur Horner, our General Secretary, was defeated by a quarryman from North Wales. The explanation, simply, was that Arthur was a Communist. By the time that Will Paynter was elected, in 1960, the quarrymen's place had been taken by a NACODS representative, and that year the seat was taken for NACODs by Joe Crawford. A year later, as I have already described, Will Paynter was kicked off the General Council, which in itself was very unusual. As he wrote in his book *My Generation:* 'There was supposed to be an unwritten law that once on, the TUC would not put a member off, and certainly more than a few members could only have retained their seats by this rule, but that law, too, had very definite political limitations. I heard also that some NUM leaders, on the eve of the Congress, had made it known that two of their nominees were loyal members of the Labour Party, and that a Communist ought not to be given preference over them.'

Well, I knew nothing of those particular machinations and, although I've always been strongly anti-Communist, I thought that Will Paynter was an excellent man to speak on our behalf. And he was right when he said that, in the main, once on the General Council you stay on. So we had the position of Joe Crawford having one of the seats, and the NUM the other two. Then, following the run-down of the Industry in the Sixties, the massive drop in our membership led the TUC Congress of 1968 to decide that the representation of the Mining and Quarrying group should be reduced to two seats. That was to take effect when one of our three members either died, or decided to resign or retire.

That year, the NUM was represented by our President, Sir Sidney Ford, and by Albert Martin, while Joe Crawford still held the NACODS seat. But, in the year 1970-71, Sid Ford retired, and the seats were duly reduced to two. The following year, Lawrence Daly took Albert's place, but Joe Crawford was still there, and in fact became Chairman of Congress in 1972-73.

So there was no room for me, and although it was perfectly possible for the Union to nominate me, I would certainly have been defeated by Joe Crawford, and you can't afford to be nominated for a position like that and not get it. What the NEC of the Labour Party couldn't have known, but which I already knew, was that Joe Crawford had decided he was going to retire that year. Nobody could have guessed that. Joe was enjoying being on the General Council, and there was no reason for him to stand down. But I knew, and so there was already quite a battle going on in my mind, because I realised that here was a chance for the NUM to win back that second seat.

My mind was made up for me by what had happened in the NEC of the Party. I didn't want to leave the NEC. Even a straightforward defeat for the International Chairmanship wouldn't have made me go. It was the way it was done which decided me to make the move, because it was a deliberate exercise for no apparent reason, an exercise which as far as I could see didn't achieve anything towards improving the Party. I remember thinking to myself, 'Bloody hell! If people are spending all their time manoeuvring for positions rather than fighting on behalf of the Party, I must be wasting my time here.'

But I won't deny that I was sad, very sad, and that it was a wrench, because the NEC of the Party had been my life much more than the TUC. On the other hand, it was also true that the miners needed more of a voice at the TUC. Lawrence was on his own for the NUM, and Joe Crawford wasn't exactly the most vociferous of men in putting the case for the Coal Industry. The NUM needed to be brought back into the limelight, and its opinions heard when energy policies were being discussed.

Having made the decision, though, I still had to get the nomination, and here there was another snag. The NUM elects its nominees for the TUC and the NEC the year before they actually go forward. At our Conference in July 1972, I had been elected our nominee for the Labour Party NEC of 1973-74. And, at the same time, Lawrence Daly and Len Clarke were elected our nominees for the TUC General Council, their names being due to go forward at the Congress of 1973.

Now, you can't be nominated for both positions, so in the July of 1973 I dropped out as a contender for the NEC seat, and stood for the General Council nomination. The other two contenders were Lawrence and Mick McGahey. Lawrence was a certainty, being the sitting member, and got 278 votes. And I scraped in, it must be admitted, against Mick, with 146 votes to his 135.

But that, of course, was for 1974, and I wanted to leave the NEC that year, 1973. At our Executive meeting following Conference, the problem was solved for me. Len Clarke announced that, since he wasn't going to be the nominee for 1974, and in the interests of continuity, he felt that I should go forward immediately rather than wait a year. And the Executive therefore agreed that Lawrence and I should go forward for 1973. This left the question of who should take my place as nominee to the NEC of the Party, and we decided, along the same lines, that Sid Vincent, who had been elected for 1974, should also be nominated immediately.

That autumn, I was duly elected to the General Council. To be truthful, I still think it's a talking shop, though one with a bit more authority than it used to have. And on the whole I think the move has paid off. It's difficult to say which is more important, the NEC or the TUC. But it is true that the TUC and the Government of the day must know each other's thoughts, whether that Government be Labour, Tory, Liberal or Communist. And the TUC is always in a position to try to influence the policies of ministers, whereas the NEC of the Party can only have real influence when the Party is in power. So, all in all, that move, forced on me by a set of circumstances not of my making, proved to be the right one. I became, in every sense, a full-time union leader.

While all this was going on, the Coal Industry was lurching its way towards yet another battle. It was not one of our seeking, nor was it by any means inevitable. But it was clear from the start, this time, that our argument was not with the Coal Board, but the Government of Edward Heath, and its final outcome was to be the fall of that Government.

Under the agreements reached after Wilberforce, the wage settlement then achieved was to run until the end of February 1973. But, towards the end of 1972, the Government had introduced its Counter Inflation Bill, and while we were starting the new round of negotiations, Phase Two of that policy came into operation. This limited, by law, any increase to £1 plus 4 percent, and since our agreement had been running for sixteen months, this would not even take care of the increased cost of living over that period.

On January 10, 1973, we met the Board at our Joint National Negotiating Committee, and put our claim to them. We wanted £30 for surface workers, £32 for underground workers, and £40 for men at the face, representing increases of £7 for the first two, and £5.50p at the face. The Board responded as we expected they would. They offered the legal maximum of the £1 plus 4 percent, and we, as they in turn must have expected, rejected it.

Further meetings failed to break the deadlock, and on March 16 a meeting of our National Executive decided to ballot the membership, asking them to support our rejection of the offer, and also to give us the authority to call strike action. Well, they turned us down, by 143,006 votes to 82,631. Nobody could argue that that was other than a very conclusive decision, so we went ahead accordingly and accepted the offer, which gave the surface men £25.29p, the underground workers £27.29p, and the NPLA men at the face a basic wage of £36.79p.

Just why that vote went the way it did, nobody can be quite certain. One factor may have been the introduction, in December 1972, of the Coal Industry Bill, which was about to get the Royal Assent. It was brought out by Peter Walker, who, in November, had taken over from John Davies at the Department of Trade and Industry, and he described it as the biggest reforming Bill we had had since Nationalisation. Certainly it had brought big increases to the miners' pension scheme, and had reversed the policy of closing uneconomic pits. We had welcomed the Bill, even though we didn't think it went far enough, and our members may have taken it as a hopeful sign that a Government was at last prepared to think seriously about the British mining industry.

Then again, they may have trusted that their standard of living would be restored at the next wage settlement, due to be negotiated that autumn.

Equally, as I said in my address at our annual conference in Inverness at the beginning of July: 'Let nobody misunderstand the vote which took place this year. My own interpretation of the vote was quite simple. I don't think the miners had quite recovered from the wonderful fight they put up nine months previously. People have got to realise that when men have been on strike for seven weeks, they have created debts and those debts have got to be repaid.'

But I had also warned: 'There is no question of a voluntary agreement on wages whilst we are confronted by a Government such as the one we have which has been responsible for the biggest rise in the cost of living in any one single period of government in this last hundred years. It is impossible to get members of the NUM, and workers in general, to accept lower wage increases when they can see their cost of living, and their standard of living being eroded week in and week out.

'What with high rises in prices of food, rising rents, rising mortgages, rises in the costs of houses which our members are wanting to buy, all of these things, which are hitting at the standard of living of our members, will make it impossible for a voluntary moderate system to be applied. It's just not possible, and therefore no one should be under any misapprehension about the miners' attitude on these matters . . . when the chips are down, the miners will struggle for the right wage for the job, the wage which I have said previously must be the highest industrial wage in Britain, because the job warrants that wage.'

The delegates obviously agreed, because the resolution they carried said:'This Conference of the National Union of Mineworkers rejects the Tory Government's claim that inflation is caused by high wage increases and emphatically rejects its wages policy.

'Conference instructs the National Executive Committee to secure increases in wages/salaries of all members of the Union in order to establish minimum wages of £35 per week for surface workers, £40 per week for underground workers, and £45 per week under the NPLA. Appropriate differentials to be established for craftsmen, WPIS, and other grades. These improvements to take place so as to revert to the pre-Wilberforce negotiating period.

'The National Executive Committee to consult the membership in accordance with rule and precedent for their decision on any negotiated settlement or forms of industrial action.'

Across the board, this was an increase of nearly 35 percent. Not only was it far in excess of anything allowed under Phase Two of the Government's policy, but it would clearly run counter to Phase Three, which was due to be announced in the autumn. To the Government, it must have seemed that we were deliberately setting ourselves on a collision course with them. We weren't. We simply wanted the right wages to keep young men coming into the Industry. All the same, I wasn't too surprised when, having just got back to London, I got a call inviting me to an informal private chat with Ted Heath at Downing Street on July 16.

I should say at this point that on a personal level I got on perfectly all right with Heath. I found him neither stubborn nor unapproachable. He may have seemed a little aloof at times, but at least when I said what I had to say he would listen, and I knew he was listening, whereas Harold Wilson often gave the impression of being somehow detached, and not really listening at all.

What I do think is that Ted was badly advised, both at the time of the first strike, and again in 1973. Being immersed in the negotiations for entering Europe, which was his great ideal, he delegated to a great extent, and perhaps even he was a bit shaken by things like the Industrial Relations Act—which now had little credibility with anyone, even most Tories—which his ministers had come up with.

July 16 was a hot day, and so we sat and talked in the garden at Downing Street. It was absolutely secret. My Executive didn't know about it; the Cabinet didn't know about it. The only other person present was Sir William Armstrong, Head of the Civil Service, whom I didn't know, but who was the man most responsible for helping Ted Heath draw up his Incomes Policy.

'Well, Joe?' said the Prime Minister. 'What are the chances this year?'

'It's going to be tough, Ted,' I told him. 'In fact, it's going to be bloody tough. You know we've just carried this resolution at our conference. I fully support it, and you know what it says. So any policy you're talking about must give us a chance to reach those objectives.'

'I see. Well, in that case, things are going to be difficult.'

'I'm afraid that's it—difficult,' I said. 'But, of course, wages aren't the *only* things we'll be claiming from the Board. For example, we shall have a claim for an increase in payments for unsocial working hours.'

As far as I was concerned, I had given them the biggest possible hint as to how they could find a way round the problem. And I was convinced that they had both taken the hint, because they turned to each other and said: 'We never thought of that. We never thought of that at all!'

'Well,' I said, 'these are things for you to think about.' And I left that garden in a much more optimistic frame of mind than when I had entered it. I had shown them the loophole, which would allow them to pay the miners more, and yet retain their incomes policy, if that's what they were determined to do. And I was sure they would use that loophole to avoid a second confrontation.

On September 12, we put our claims to the Board at the Industry's Joint National Negotiating Committee. Apart from our main wage claims, we pressed strongly for an improvement in 'enhanced shift payments'—the extra money for unsocial working hours which I had mentioned privately to Ted Heath. We also told them that there was a strong feeling among the men that holiday pay should be at the NPLA rate. In spite of Lord Wilberforce's kind remarks about the way in which we had always averaged out the holiday payments, it did in fact mean that the NPLA men had to take a considerable drop for their paid holidays, and it also caused resentment on the grounds that it resulted in mineworkers getting paid less for their holidays than cokeworkers, who were also members of the NUM.

These, we told them, were the three main priorities in our claim, though there were a number of other items we would like to settle. They couldn't give us a reply straight away, but the one thing they did say was sufficient to show me how the wind was blowing. It was over the question of returning to our former settlement date of November 1. Wilberforce himself had said that he saw no reason why we shouldn't return to it at the end of our sixteen-month agreement. Well, the Board reminded us, which was true, that our agreement earlier in the year had been on the basis that it would run for eleven months. But in any case, they said, the Government's legislation would not allow a further settlement to be made at an earlier date. In other words, if we ever *did* return to November 1, it certainly wasn't going to be in 1973.

It was crystal clear. We weren't even faced with the pretence of negotiating with the Board. We were dealing with the Government direct. In my heart of hearts I felt sorry for Derek Ezra. My personal relationships with him have always been good, whatever our arguments. And I've always found he was someone with whom I could negotiate and argue.

Of course, you can never know a man so well that you can always be sure when he's bluffing, especially someone like Derek – you can never put your hand on your heart and say you can't push him a little farther, although I think that at times, perhaps, he knows how far he can push me. But then, I'm a different type of person – I tend not to hide my light under any bushels, and I usually know where I'm going and what I can legitimately fight for.

But Derek, even though he may not be a great extrovert, understands the industry. It has been his life. He was one of those who set up the Coal Commission in Europe after the War, and he speaks and fights for a bigger and better coal industry, whether it be with the TUC or the CBI or the government of the day. Now, however, he was virtually powerless. The decisions had been taken out of his hands, and he was not being allowed to do the job he had been appointed to do.

He obviously felt it strongly. Four years later, in a Thames Television programme about this period, he said: 'I think one of the things which went wrong...was that it moved into the Government sphere too soon. I think it's very important in negotiations of this sort that it should be left as long as possible, however important the enterprise—and of course mining is very important—between the negotiating teams. That is, the Union and the Employers.

'But in this case, it was very quickly taken up to Government level, and the NEC of the NUM had an early meeting quite soon after the rejection of our initial offer, with the Cabinet, or with Ministers, at any rate, in Downing Street, at which we were not present. And this was succeeded by further meetings between the Union and either the Prime Minister, or the Secretary of State for Employment, or other Ministers.

'And this, I must say, was a thread of confusion, as far as we were concerned, throughout the whole of that period. Because we weren't there, the Unions tended to tell us their view of what went on. We heard from Government Departments their view. And we were put in a somewhat difficult position.'

'Somewhat difficult'! That must be one of the understatements of the Seventies. They were put in an *impossible* position. But most of that was to come later. And in the month between that first meeting, and the meeting on October 10, at which they were due to make us that initial offer to which Derek referred, two crucial things happened.

On October 6, the Middle East exploded in what came to be known as the Yom Kippur War, and within a few days the Arab oil states announced that they were going to cut production drastically. They also announced that they were increasing the price of crude oil by a staggering 70 percent.

The implications, where our case was concerned, were clear enough for a child to see. At last our arguments, repeated over dozens of years, about the need for a national energy policy, and the maximising of our own resources, were coming home to roost.

Yet even *then* the Government, as individuals later admitted, were slow to react. Two days after the start of the War, they went ahead and published the White Paper giving details of Stage Three of their incomes policy, in spite of the fact that what was happening in the Middle East was bound to give a completely different complexion to the situation in Britain.

The new regulations had a number of clauses to them. The main provision, as regards wage increases, was that they would be limited to either 7 percent of the average pay of a group of workers over the previous twelve months, or £2.25p a week per head, subject to a limit of £350 a head.

But, to our astonishment, another provision stated that a premium payment could be introduced or increased for any hours worked between 8 pm and 6 am, provided that this premium wasn't more than a fifth of the basic time rates. In other words, the hint that I had given to Ted Heath and William Armstrong at Downing Street that day, as a way of getting round their difficulties with the miners, had been taken up, all right, but not for us alone. It applied to everybody. I must say that I wasn't best pleased. I had gone there to try to solve our problem, not to give them help in running the country as a whole. Whether it was through stupidity or deliberate policy I never knew, but they had effectively blocked a loophole by which our position, relative to the rest of industry, could have been restored.

Two days later, on October 10, we met to hear the Board's offer, knowing that now it was a pretty foregone conclusion. Sure enough, it was precisely within the limits of the new legislation.

There were six parts to their offer. 1. A wage increase of the 7 percent or the £2.25p, whichever was the higher. 2. They would improve the shift allowance for unsociable hours from 2.5p to 17p. 3. As allowed under Stage Three's 'flexibility' clause, they would make concessions in other areas costing a further 1 percent of the wages bill. 4. We could have an extra day's holiday. 5. They would make a productivity agreement with us giving, as Stage Three allowed, up to 50 percent of the wage increase. And finally they said they were prepared to enter into a 'threshold' agreement, giving us further increases if the cost of living rose beyond certain stated limits.

Our reply was to accept the 17p an hour for the unsociable hours, though we said we also wanted that to include the afternoon shift. We also accepted the extra day's holiday, although, since it was to be New Year's Day, and since the Government had made that an extra statutory holiday anyway, it didn't amount to much. And we went along with the idea of a threshold agreement. But when it came to the actual wage offer, our reply was an emphatic 'No'.

Six days later, in an effort to find some way round the problem, Lawrence and I, together with Mick McGahey, who had been elected Vice-President in succession to Sid Schofield, went to see Vic Feather at the TUC. It wasn't much help. The TUC had already declared its opposition to the Government's policy, so there was no way that they could act as intermediaries. In fact, one way and another, it was rapidly becoming clear that there was only one person who *could* do a deal with us, and that was the Prime Minister himself.

Accordingly, we wrote to him, asking for a meeting and suggesting some dates, and the result was that on October 23 the entire Union side of the JNNC trooped along to Downing Street. There, we explained our case to Ted Heath in detail, and, against the background of an oil crisis which was worsening daily, a pretty strong case we thought it was. Put simply, the country needed all the energy it could get, yet the current position was that 600 men a week were leaving the Coal Industry to go to more attractive and better-paid jobs elsewhere. There wasn't much that could be done about the unpleasant nature of mining, but there *was* something to be done about making wages good enough to attract recruits and keep miners in the mines.

Heath's reply was polite, but unbending. He said he would consider our comments along with those which the TUC and the CBI had made about the proposals contained in Phase Three, and he told us what he hoped to achieve by Phase Three. But any flexibility within Phase Three was a matter for us to negotiate with the Coal Board.

Well that, to use the current jargon, was a Catch 22 situation, since the Coal Board had already indicated that they couldn't move beyond what the Government allowed. To say I was disappointed by that meeting would be an understatement. My private meeting with Ted had persuaded me that he was prepared to be reasonable. Now, it seemed, Phase Three was an idol, or a dogma, to be worshipped regardless of any other consideration. If there'd been an earthquake in the middle of London, it appeared, relief work would have been limited to what Phase Three allowed!

It wasn't surprising that, at a special meeting of our NEC, held two days later on the Thursday, there was a mood of considerable frustration. On the other hand, there was a feeling that it was still too early to call for strike action. But a Special Conference of the Union had been arranged for the following day, and after a long discussion we agreed to put the following resolution to it:-

'This Special Conference of the National Union of Mineworkers having received a report from the NEC authorises the Committee to call a complete Overtime Ban (with the exclusion of Cokeworkers, who shall be entitled to work up to their contractual hours) if and when necessary, in the light of further negotiations which the NEC will undertake.'

That Friday the delegates met, discussed our Resolution and all its implications, and carried it unanimously. With this backing, we met the Board four days later, on October 30, and told them what had been decided, but that we were still prepared to negotiate. For example, we were prepared to sign a 'Cost of Living' threshold agreement. And we were prepared to talk about a productivity deal, though it would have to be on a national basis. But the fact remained that we still had to have a better wages offer. Catch 22 again. The Board were adamant that they must conform to the wretched Phase Three.

A week later, on November 7, we met the Board yet again, but this time we were in an even stronger position. There might previously have been a suspicion in their minds, and in those of Government ministers, that the anti-strike vote earlier in the year showed that the majority of miners were not in the mood for another fight. Now, they knew that wasn't the case, because, following the Special Conference, we had arranged an Area Ballot to test the feeling of the membership. It was utterly conclusive. Not one Area voted against our recommendations, which included, of course, the power to call an overtime ban.

The Coal Board, naturally, knew this, and had managed to inch their way forward – well, not so much an inch, but about half a millimetre. Apart from some financial juggling which would slightly improve holiday pay, they had managed to rearrange the figures allowable under Phase Three, and thus could improve the pay offer. This was now £2.30p for surface workers, and £2.57p for underground workers, increases over the previous offer of 5p and 7p respectively.

5p and 7p! Against our original claim, which was for nearly £7 and £9, they were still talking a completely different language, and we told them so. 'If you think that's enough to make us change our recommendations,' I said, 'I'm afraid you're very, very wrong.'

At a meeting the following day, members of our Executive thought so, too, and supported our rejection of the offer. A complete ban on overtime working was called, to start from the first production shift on November 12. The response from the lads at the pits, even though we hadn't called a pithead ballot (which, under the Rules, we didn't need to), was immediate and total. Overtime working stopped dead. The membership was one hundred percent behind us.

Now, people who don't understand the workings of a mine might think that wouldn't be too serious, and that it would just mean a bit of extra coal that wouldn't be produced. But it was far more serious than that. Most of the maintenance work in a pit is done at weekends, and that's overtime working. And for many reasons, most of all safety, you can't have men going down to the coal face until that maintenance work, and all the necessary repairs, have been done. And, if it hadn't been done at the weekend, it would have to be done during the normal working week. The net result was that within a few days, production had been cut by 40 percent.

We knew that would happen, the Board knew that would happen, and therefore the Government knew, too. This time, unlike their delays in 1972, they didn't hang about. They called a State of Emergency on November 13, the day after our ban started, saying they had to make sure they could keep industry going, together with electricity supplies and essential services. It wasn't surprising they were worried. The price of oil delivered to Britain was in the process of being doubled, there were long queues at the petrol stations, and now they could see themselves running short of the indigenous fuel, coal. But then, *that* had been the crux of our argument all along, not as a form of blackmail, but from the point of view that, if we needed that coal, we also needed men to mine it, and to get those men entailed paying them an attractive wage.

During the next fortnight, we had more meetings with the Board, at which they were able to make marginally improved offers, together with a number of promises and declarations of intent, but they were still not nearly enough to make us think of recommending acceptance. We were back to the position from which we had started, namely that the only person we could really deal with in the circumstances was Ted Heath himself. So, when he invited our entire Executive to meet him at Downing Street on November 28, I had hopes that at last something might be starting to move.

Not a bit of it. When we got there, he had most of the Cabinet with him, and he proceeded to give us a dissertation on the precise effects the Middle East War was having on the economy. He also went over the details of the Government's economic strategy, and said that in his view we stood to gain more than others under Phase Three.

Finally, he appealed to us to end our industrial action for the sake of the nation. 'If you accept the Board's offer,' he said, 'we will start a wide-ranging examination of the Coal Mining Industry, and of the position of miners in this new energy situation we find ourselves in. But for the moment, in our view, the offer which has been made to you will more than restore the relativity which you enjoyed after the Wilberforce Inquiry.'

I said little at that meeting. Years later, Sir William Armstrong, or Lord Armstrong as he was to become, gave it as his opinion that I was 'leading from behind'. The truth was that up to that point I had been in the forefront of negotiations, often alone, and I felt that the Government might have come to the impression that I was speaking for myself. I wanted them to see that our attitude was unanimous.

The only point at which I really interjected came when Mick McGahey, in answer to a remark or a question during the discussion, said words to the effect of 'Of course I want to change the Government, but I want to do it by democratic means, through the ballot box'.

At that, I interrupted and said to Ted Heath: 'I'm not here to talk about changing the Government. *We* are here as the NEC of the NUM, discussing the possibility of ending an industrial dispute, and trying to get the right wages for the men on the job. That's our position. When you go to the country, you go to the country. You'll decide that. And I shall decide to oppose you at that time, and I shall work like all holy hell to get you defeated at that time. But this strike is not about that. This strike is about wages, and that only.'

Unfortunately, the damage was done. Someone leaked Mick's remark to the Press, and it was reported inaccurately and out of context, so that it looked as if he was saying the strike was about bringing down the Government. That, of course, was marvellous propaganda for the Tories, and was to become almost the entire theme of their subsequent dealings with us.

But what the argument was *really* about was best summed up by one of the lads on the Executive who, after the discussion had been going on for a bit, said: 'Prime Minister, what I can't understand is this - you've told us that we've no option but to pay the Arabs the price they're demanding for their oil. Now, as far as I know, the Arabs never helped us in World War One, and they never helped us in World War Two.

'But we, the miners, *we* were in World War One and World War Two, and we flogged our guts out in all of that. Why can't you pay us for coal what you're willing to pay the Arabs for oil?'

It was spot on and, as Eric Morecambe would say, 'There was no answer to that one'. Certainly Ted Heath gave none. Nor had he given us any real reasons for changing our policy, because he wasn't prepared to change his, even in the face of representations from the Parliamentary Group of miners' MPs.

On December 13, Ted Heath announced that the country would go on a three-day week, starting on January 1. In a television broadcast he said: 'As Prime Minister, I want to speak to you simply and plainly about the grave emergency now facing our country. In the House of Commons this afternoon, I announced more severe restrictions on the use of electricity. You may already have heard the details of these. We are asking you to cut down to the absolute minimum the use of electricity for heating and for other purposes in your homes.

'We are limiting the use of electricity by almost all factories, shops, and offices, to three days a week. We are imposing other restrictions. For example, on late night television. Now I want to tell you why we have done this, and what else we are doing. The reason why is quite simple. At the moment, as a result of their ban on overtime, the coal miners are now sending to the power stations sixty tons of coal for every hundred they would normally do. So the stocks built up earlier in the year are falling.'

Ah, yes, but what he didn't say was that the stocks were enormous. They were at a record level, and, as was subsequently proved, there was absolutely no energy reason for that three-day week. But there was a political reason, which was to alienate public opinion from the miners, and so to isolate them. In my view, it was as crude as that.

Even *then* we were still prepared to try to find a way out of the impasse. At the beginning of December, Willie Whitelaw, who had been Secretary of State for Northern Ireland, moved to the Department of Employment, taking over from Robert Carr. He let it be known that he would appreciate a quiet chat with me, to find out exactly how matters stood from our point of view. I was certainly willing to do anything to avert disaster, and slipped down to Brown's Hotel for a meeting with him in a private room there, at which we had a general chat about the situation, and I outlined our position. He listened, I thought, with sympathy. Following that, on December 20, I went with Lawrence and Mick to see him at St James's Square. He started off by repeating much of what Ted Heath had already said to us, but he did seem to be in a conciliatory mood, and suggested that perhaps there was still more available under Phase Three than the Board and ourselves had been able to extract from it.

At that time, there was an IRA bombing campaign going on, and while we were in the middle of the meeting we got a message that a bomb had been planted in the building. So we all went outside and stood in the street for a bit, and then the lot of us decided to go off to a nearby Italian restaurant where we had a bottle of beer together. It was then that I played what I felt was my final card.

'You know,' I said, 'there *is* one chance, and that's if we can come up with something on waiting and bathing time.'

'How do you mean?' Whitelaw asked.

'Well, this is something we've been on about for years. When you're a miner working underground, it's not as simple as just clocking on as you would in a factory. You often have to spend a long time, after changing into work clothes, waiting around for the lifts to take you down. This is not paid for. And then at the other end of the shift there's the question of bathing. You probably get dirtier down a mine than at any other job, even a car mechanic. The dust gets right into your skin, and you get bloody filthy.

'So it's a natural consequence of the job that you have to have a bath as soon as you're finished. If we can get a proper time allowance for those two things, which apply to miners and nobody else, maybe that would be a solution.'

'Yes,' he said, 'I can see that. Well, if you can get the Coal Board to agree, there might be a good chance that the Pay Board would go along with it.'

He was quite obviously taking what I said very seriously, and I was convinced that we'd achieved the breakthrough, and that he was willing to do something about it. I went home confident, and a good deal happier.

The following morning, it so happened, I had arranged to meet Harold Wilson, then Leader of the Opposition, at his home in Lord North Street. There was nothing strange about that. It was natural that I should see him from time to time to keep him up to date with what was happening.

I got there at about nine, and after we had chatted for a while about the situation, he said: 'Well, there seems to be no hope then, Joe?'

'Oh yes, I think there *is* hope,' I said. 'I think there's a possibility that we might resolve it today, as a result of the soundings we made with Whitelaw yesterday. The feeling we got was that the Government sees our point of view, at last, and will make it possible for us to reach an agreement.'

'How are you going to do it?'

'Well,' I said, 'it's over this question of waiting and bathing time. I think we've convinced Whitelaw that it would be perfectly reasonable to make an exception for us over that.'

He sat back, and took that pipe of his in his hand, and looked at me slowly, and then he said: 'Oh! Well, of course, Joe, you do realise you're pulling the Tory Government's irons out of the fire for them?'

'I'm not pulling anything out of any fire for the Tories,' I said. 'All I'm doing as a trade union leader is trying to avoid the need for an industrial dispute. And, if we can get this principle accepted, I'm quite sure my NEC will be in favour. I doubt it'll be unanimous, but there'll be a majority for recommending acceptance.' And I left him with that.

But, as I left, I had a funny feeling at the back of my mind, and I realised what it was—that remark about pulling the Tories' irons out of the fire had been a curious one. After all, it was we who were negotiating, not Harold Wilson. He was just the Leader of the Opposition, and I had gone along to see him, at his invitation, under the impression that he just wanted to be kept up to date. I couldn't have been more wrong.

That morning, we went once more to see the Coal Board. It was a long discussion, but at the end of it they agreed. Provided it was acceptable to the Pay Board, they were prepared to negotiate a payment for necessary time spent on waiting and washing before and after a shift. 'That's it,' I thought, 'it's all over. There'll be no problem with the Pay Board, knowing Whitelaw's reaction to the idea. So we've got a settlement.'

That afternoon, together with the Coal Board, we went to see the Pay Board. Sure enough, everything was going to plan. They said that, provided we could show that standard working hours in the industry, after allowing for meal breaks, were 'by custom and practice' more than forty hours a week, then they would consider allowing the overtime payments we wanted. At that point, it was as far as they could possibly go, and I felt that we were within only a few days of an agreement.

But, the moment I left that meeting, I knew it had been blown, and that all hope was gone, because I was given the news that that afternoon Harold Wilson had raised the idea in the House of Commons as if it were his very own. I went mad. It was bad enough to have the Tories playing politics with an industrial dispute, but to have our own Party doing the same thing to us was beyond belief. I think that was the most frustrating moment of my life.

The next time I saw Harold I told him: 'I'll never trust you again. That's the last time you'll ever get me on a confidential basis.' But by then it was too late, because the confidence had been betrayed.

Four years later, in the television programme I referred to earlier, Wilson said: 'He had mentioned this idea to me, and I naturally regarded it as confidential, until I heard on the radio that particular weekend a whole scheme put forward in a very rough speech—not a conciliatory speech—a very rough speech, I think by Mr McGahey—in Scotland. So I thought, 'Well, this is now open.' And at a meeting of the Trade Union Group, which included the miners, we were discussing what line we should take, and I tried to steer them in that direction. And of course I made it public.'

Well, that day, December 21, was a Friday. Mick had been with me the previous day with Whitelaw, and he was with me at the meeting with the Coal Board. And even the House of Commons doesn't meet on Christmas Eve. So I'm afraid that Harold's version fails to conform with the facts.

Of course, knowing Harold Wilson of old, and his love of the limelight, one could be charitable and say it was just him trying to grab the glory for himself as having found a solution to the dispute. But there was one little phrase which gives the lie to that theory, and that was the one about pulling the Tory irons from the fire. He knew what he was doing, all right. I had made it clear to him, privately, that if the Government and Pay Board agreed to this principle, and if it could be put into an acceptable form of words to all concerned, it was a big enough principle for us to recommend acceptance.

There was no way that he could have failed to realise the implications of what he was doing. Those implications were that, while the Government could perfectly easily have negotiated it privately and quietly with us, and told the Pay Board to accept it, and put it in such a way that they would not appear to have been defeated, once it had been raised as an idea coming from the Leader of the Opposition they could *never* accept it—nor would I expect them to.

What had been possible the night before was now quite impossible, and I will never forgive Harold Wilson for it. It was completely despicable, because he knew it would inevitably set the miners on another collision course with the Government. If Harold and company wanted an election, they should have forced it another way, by Parliamentary methods, rather than using the Union. It was wrong to use us just as much as it was wrong for the Tories to argue that we were acting politically, when the truth was that it was the politicians who were acting politically.

It was utterly ridiculous that we should have been placed in that position. But we were.

We still went through the motions, of course. Over the Christmas period, we had a number of meetings with the NCB and the Pay Board, in the shape of its Deputy Chairman. But now both Boards were starting to play silly buggers. First of all, the Coal Board came up with a set of figures by which they tried to show that the time we were talking about only amounted to five minutes.

I laughed them out of court. 'You've got to be out of your sweet minds,' I said. 'You can't say it only takes a man five minutes to wash and change and dress and all the rest of it. You can't get away with that!'

Then I turned to the man from the Pay Board and said: 'And I think *we're* out of our minds even being here. I don't intend to sit here like a bloody gaga—I came here with a determination to settle the damn dispute. It seems to me that you're putting things in the way of any settlement. All I say to you is that you've got to write words which will give us this principle of washing and bathing time. And you've got to phrase it in such a way that you can either say it's within Phase Three or Twenty-Three. I don't give a damn how you do it, or how you word it, as long as it's down—as long as it makes a settlement possible. How you do it I don't mind.'

Well, they thought about it, and then the Pay Board came back with a form of words which was a load of tripe, and I had to tell them: 'You're wasting your bloody time. It doesn't mean a damn thing. It's ridiculous.'

I wasn't the only person feeling frustrated. Even the Establishment-minded *Times,* in a leader on January 3 headed 'A Ruinous Dispute', said:'This dispute has taken on increasingly strong symbolic overtones as it has progressed. By putting the country on to a three-day week, the Government has signalled its resolve to dig in for a long confrontation.'

Further on, it continued: 'It is common ground between the Coal Board, the miners and the Government that the relative position of the industry's pay scales needs to be improved. This was the case even before the price of imported oil was doubled at the end of last year.

'Since these global energy developments, the importance of recreating a healthy and expanding domestic coal industry is still more evident. Since the industry, at present pay levels, is having difficulty in maintaining, let alone increasing, its work force, the clear conclusion is that pay and other conditions of employment need to be improved fairly rapidly. Since the recent dramatic change in the relative price of oil and coal, the industry as a whole could reasonably bear a higher wage bill, particularly if this was coupled with genuine productivity agreements.

'Since there is this much common ground between the parties, it is more and more aggravating to the general public that a solution cannot be found.'

It was aggravating to me, too. As far as I was concerned, Harold Wilson had effectively sabotaged our last chance of successful negotiations, and the Government, as *The Times* suggested, had dug in its heels. Even then, there was another chance they could have taken. On January 9 there was a meeting of the National Economic Development Council. Len Murray, who was at that meeting, had recently succeeded Vic Feather as General Secretary of the TUC. I found him a quiet, studious type, and a completely different animal to his predecessor. Vic was the extrovert, while Len is rather the introvert. He's not one for standing on platforms and shouting and screaming and all the rest of it. But he'll listen carefully to any comments you want to make. He's more in the mould of George Woodcock, who held the job before Vic Feather, and he showed his style by the offer he now made to Tony Barber, the Chancellor.

'If you pay the miners,' he said, 'we'll refuse to support any union which tries to use that settlement to further its own arguments.' It seems that Barber then rang Ted Heath, told him briefly what had been offered, and said he presumed there was no alternative but to turn the offer down. And Heath agreed.

That same day, our Executive went down to St James's Square to see Willie Whitelaw again. The meeting didn't start in a particularly good climate, because the day before Lord Carrington, who had just been made the first Minister of Energy, had made some public comments which seemed to us to close the door on negotiations. We made our protest about that, and at least Whitelaw said that he appreciated our concern. But he then proceeded to run through the arguments all over again, almost word for word what he'd told us back in December.

He did admit that mistakes had been made by governments of all parties, in putting too much reliance on oil and allowing the coal industry to run down. And he conceded that that was no fault of ours, since the Union had consistently warned of the dangers of such policies. And he said that, if we would settle under Phase Three, the Government would sit down immediately with us and the Board to discuss the industry's future, including problems of pay and manpower. But he was still claiming that Phase Three enabled us to be offered a settlement greater than could be offered to most other groups of workers.

This seemed to me to be plain daft. 'What I can't understand,' I said, 'is how can Phase Three be better for us than for the rest? Everything that's available under Phase Three is available to everybody. Are you suggesting that because a lot of other people previously enjoyed benefits which were denied to us, but which are now available to everyone under Phase Three, that this is the same thing as giving better terms to us? Because if so, that's bloody nonsense.' The meeting resulted, once again, in stalemate.

Now there was only one hope, and that was the offer which Len Murray had made to Tony Barber. In spite of the fact that Barber had turned it down, the TUC had left it on the table, and at a Special Conference of the TUC on January 16, the delegates gave it an overwhelming vote of support. So when, on January 21, Len Murray and some of the TUC leaders went to Downing Street for a last attempt at solving the problem, Ted Heath had no excuse for believing that the offer wasn't genuine - yet, that is apparently the impression he gave to the TUC, because it seems that at one point one of the TUC lads leaned across the table to him and said: 'Mr Heath, is there anything, *anything* we can do, to convince you that this is a genuine offer? Is there anything that you'd expect us to do beyond what we've offered to do already?' And Ted never replied.

But, from what he said in the Commons the following day, it became clear that he *did* believe the offer was sincere and genuine – what was worrying him was that there was no *guarantee* that other unions wouldn't press beyond Phase Three, riding on the backs of the miners.

Personally, I think he should have taken a chance on it. It certainly couldn't have made things any worse than they were. By the end of the first week in January it had been reported that 750,000 men had already been laid off work, and that number was increasing daily. The Government were lucky in that it was the mildest January since 1932, which helped their programme of fuel-saving, but even so there were already a number of Tory back-benchers pressing the Prime Minister to reach a settlement with us.

But, as for myself, I had had it. On the evening of Tuesday, January 22, following his remarks in the Commons, Heath had gone on television to tell the country that he intended to stand firm. 'The job of a Government is to accept its responsibility to govern and that is what we are doing,' he said, and the following morning the *Daily Express* carried the headline 'WE SHALL NOT BE MOVED—Heath takes a firm line'.

Well, you could call it firm, or you could call it stubborn, but if that was to be the attitude, after all the months of talking and arguing, then I was bloody well not going to be moved either. The same front page of that paper also carried a report by their Industrial Correspondent, Barrie Devney, a man I knew well and trusted.

He wrote: 'Mr Gormley, normally regarded as a moderate, made it angrily plain yesterday that he believes the time has come for a showdown. 'The fact is,' he said, 'that I have the feeling that the overtime ban is not having the effect we thought it would have in its early stages. The feeling is supported by the stock figures quoted last week by Lord Carrington. I feel we now have to be more positive if we are to succeed in our claim for wages for miners this year.

'My opinion is that the members are ripe to strengthen the action . . . so I shall be suggesting to the Executive that, if we hope for success, we should now have a ballot for a national strike. The action would be in the hope that we could convince the Government that it has made a big mistake in not accepting the TUC offer.'

On the following day, a Wednesday, Mick, Lawrence and i had a meeting at Euston Road, and agreed that that was what we would recommend to the Executive the following day. But, when that Executive met, it was by no means cut and dried. There were at that time six Communists on the Executive—Mick, who was on the Party's National Executive, Joe Whelan from Nottingham, Bill McLean from Scotland, Peter Tait from Yorkshire, Dai Francis from South Wales (the one who voted with me to end the previous strike) and Jack Collins from Kent, the one who had shaken the Wilberforce Inquiry when he told them about having to work naked underground.

Now, many people on the outside would automatically have assumed that they would all have been for a strike come what may. But, during the course of the three hours we spent discussing the situation, for example Joe Whelan and his Nottinghamshire colleague Len Clarke told us that their lads wanted further disruptive action, but stopping short of an all-out strike. Again, Dai Francis and Emlyn Williams reported that the members in South Wales wanted to go on a three-day week like the rest of industry. So it was by no means cut and dried.

And there was another factor. Just before the meeting started, I had received a long letter from Ted Heath, delivered by hand. He talked about the damage being done to people's jobs and earnings, the cuts in productivity, and the hardships in people's homes. We could end all that, he said. He appealed to us once again to accept the pay offer and his promised review of the industry's future.

'I hope,' he wrote, 'your executive will conclude that in the situation I have described acceptance of the offer and of the proposals which the Government has made would do justice not only to the aspirations of your members but also to the needs and circumstances of this country, of which we are all citizens.'

They had stonewalled every attempt we had made to get a settlement, and now, at the last minute, they were resorting to an appeal to patriotism. It was obviously designed for the public's ears, as much as for ours, and we were having none of it. If anything, it may have hardened the attitudes of some of our members. At the end of that meeting, we decided by 16 votes to 10 to hold a ballot of our members. The question on the ballot paper was to be a straightforward one—'Are you in favour of the National Executive being given the authority to call a national strike?' There was no need for it to be more complicated than that—by then, everyone in the country, let alone the miners, knew the issues involved inside out.

After the meeting, the Press were waiting. Two days earlier, I had predicted that if it came to a strike ballot, 70 percent of miners would vote in favour. The truth was that none of us was that certain, but with fuel stocks holding out, and spring around the corner, our final card had to be played now or never. So in answer to reporters' questions I said: 'There will be a massive campaign to instil in the members the necessity to vote, and vote the right way. The union would be in a difficult position if the members refused to vote for strike action in furtherance of the claim.

'The National Executive Committee will meet immediately we have the result of the ballot, and the strike could take place within a few days of that result.'

One of the reporters then pointed out that under the Industrial Relations Act there was supposed to be thirty days' notice given for a strike. My reply shows the bitter and angry mood I was in—'I think the picture is a bit too grim for us to be looking over our shoulders as to whether we are contravening the Act.' The following day, January 25, to prove the point, we sent the NCB notice that the Union might be on strike from midnight on February 9, 1974.

The ballot was to be held within a twenty-four-hour period on the following Thursday and Friday, January 31 and February 1. We had just one week to make sure the members knew precisely why we had reached the view we had. That weekend, John Fryer, Labour Correspondent of the *Sunday Times*, reported: 'This weekend miners' leaders launch a massive campaign to whip up support for a coal strike. The coming frenzy of rallies and leaflets reflects their concern about the outcome of a pithead ballot as much as enthusiasm for a final showdown with the Government. The odds on a vote in favour of a strike are little more than evens.'

'Little more than evens' wouldn't be enough. Under our Rules, we needed at least 55 percent in favour. Politically, morally, and psychologically, I knew we needed a lot more than that. On February 5, we knew we had it. 188,393 voted 'yes', as against 44,222 voting 'no'. 81 percent of the members who voted—and the vote itself was a huge turn-out—had backed us.

As I said before, we have always prided ourselves on being a very democratic union. And whereas you may *think* you've got the feeling of the membership right, there's nothing like an individual ballot to prove it. And that vote was more than even I had dared to hope.

The result of the ballot was announced at a meeting of our NEC on the same day, February 5, and in the light of it our decision could not be in doubt—unless a satisfactory offer was received in the next three days, the Union would be on strike as from midnight on February 9.

Two days after the NEC meeting, on Thursday the 7th, Ted Heath did what numerous commentators and politicians had, since the beginning of the year, been suggesting he might do—he called a General Election. Announcing it to the country on television, he said:'Only one thing can threaten our future. That is our continued tragic record of industrial strife. We can't afford the luxury of tearing ourselves apart any more. This time the strife has got to stop. Only you can stop it. It's time for you to speak with your vote. It's time for your voice to be heard, the voice of the moderate and reasonable people of Britain, the voice of the majority. It is time for you to say to the extremists, the militants, and to the plain and simple misguided: 'We've had enough. There's a lot to be done. For heaven's sake, let's get on with it.'

It was the start of a campaign whose major theme, for the Tories, was 'Who Governs Britain?'. To me, it was a spurious theme. They were simply continuing the argument, the truth of which they had now completely convinced themselves of, that our dispute was politically motivated and a direct attack on the Government. As I had said all along, it was *not* a political dispute but an industrial one, and if the Government had taken it upon themselves to interfere with normal negotiating machinery, forcing us to deal directly with them—well, that was their decision, not ours.

The calling of the Election, however, which was to take place on February 28, put the whole question of a strike into a different context, and for a whole number of reasons. So I convened a Special Meeting of our Executive for the following day, February 8.

It may have surprised some of the members, but I suggested straight away that we should suspend the strike. 'For a start,' I said,'the very fact this Election has been called means that we've won the battle. It doesn't matter a damn who wins the Election—whichever Party it is will be bound to reach a settlement with us.'

Secondly, I pointed out, the whole point of the strike was to get a better wages offer, and that could only now happen if the Government changed its tune. But, with Parliament dissolved, there was not *going* to be any effective Government for the next few weeks, so who would have the authority to make the cash available to meet our claim? 'It's true we've got a lot of the other unions behind us, but, like us, they'll be concentrating all their efforts on helping the Labour Party in the Election.'

I added: 'It's been reported that the Government has referred our claim to the Pay Board, for them to look at under the Relativities procedure. And, on the other side, Labour has called for an interim cash settlement for us. I don't believe we'll get anything more positive than that before the Election, and I can't see the point of striking in a period when the strike can't achieve anything.'

But I lost the argument. It was pointed out that, since neither the overtime ban nor the strike decision had been politically motivated, it would be wrong to call off the strike in the interests of one political Party—and I couldn't really disagree with that, after all I had said. Secondly, many members felt that, knowing the overwhelming result of the ballot, it would be very hard to call off or postpone the strike anyway, and impracticable to get it going again after the Election. Finally, it was argued, if we did postpone the strike it would weaken our bargaining position, because a lot of coal would be produced and put to stock before the Election was over. In the end, after a lot of discussion, these were the arguments which prevailed, and the strike went ahead the following day, February 9.

It was, as far as it could be, a low-key affair. We were determined not to present the media with any free propaganda for the Tories, and therefore put a strict limit of six men on any one picket line. This was especially important since we'd had reports that right-wing agitators were going to try to make trouble at the picket lines.

This inevitable linking of the strike with the political situation meant that public reaction was often more unpleasant than it had been in 1972. Then, many Tory supporters had openly sympathised with our case. Now, because of the impression which had been created that we were fighting their Party and had been trying to bring it down, some people were openly hostile. Nellie and I received a number of threatening letters, anonymous of course, some even telling her what car she was using and what would happen to her if she went out in it.

We were still living at Hurst Park, and our house was completely overlooked at the front by a block of flats, making it not only easy prey to Press or Television cameras, but also a simple target to anyone who wanted to get in and cause some mischief. So the Executive decided, for safety's sake, to move us to a flat in Lord's View, the big block overlooking the cricket ground, and in the end we stayed there for several months until moving to our present home. But the thing that worried me most of all was the effect it could have on our grandchildren —especially Frank's kids, since they had the name Gormley. Sure enough, Ian, his eldest boy, was baited into some bad scraps, and even had to put up with sarcasm from some of the teachers at his school.

On the other hand, some (presumably) Tory supporters came up with the most surprising offer of the whole affair, and it caused us to bring our next NEC meeting, due for the 14th, forward to the 12th in order to consider it.

The offer came from the London Mercantile Corporation. They said they could help to arrange for a group of industrialists to provide us with a single contribution of £2,470,000. This was to enable us to make payments, as and when we saw fit, to any of our members who resumed working, and represented an average single payment of £9.50p per man. In exchange, they wanted us to call off the strike by the 22nd at the latest, and to go back to normal working until the Pay Board had given its recommendations.

There was no doubt that the offer was genuine, and I think it must have been unique in the history of industrial disputes. To us, it was proof positive of how even industrialists were worried about the Government's rigid stand, and of how they realised the importance of a settlement. We felt, though, it was trying to lock the stable door after a whole string of horses—or chances of a settlement—had escaped, and that they should have been putting pressure on the Government long before. And even though they had obviously made the offer as a hard-headed business calculation, we decided we couldn't accept.

Yes, it would have given us the extra cash we wanted for a week or two, but in the end any agreement had to be with the Coal Board. It was rather like those stories which come up every so often, when someone goes to prison, on principle, rather than pay what he thinks is an unjustified fine. There are always many people prepared to pay the fine for him, but that doesn't solve the question of principle.

At that same meeting we considered a letter we had received from Willie Whitelaw, in which he told us officially that he had referred our case to the Pay Board, asking them to give it a full examination and to make their recommendations as quickly as possible. The Government, he said, undertook to back-date anything they recommended to March 1. We agreed to give evidence to the Pay Board, if invited, but on the understanding that we would not necessarily accept its findings.

The Inquiry was held from the 18th till the 22nd. The evidence we gave was very much along the lines of what we had told Wilberforce, with one vital difference. Paragraph 44 of their Relativities Report indicated that one criterion which would qualify a group for special consideration was a major change in the importance of their industry.

The upheavals in the energy picture, we said, represented just such a major change. After the War, when coal was badly needed, our wages, in relation to manufacturing industries, had been in the ratio of 130 to 100, and that had lasted until 1957, when our years of decline began. Now, it was agreed, Mining was just under 92 percent of Manufacturing, and what we wanted, we said, was to get back to the pre-1957 ratio, in order to attract the men to produce the coal.

As further proof, if proof were needed, of the Government's stubbornness, the Coal Board's evidence supported ours. And on February 21, the day before the Inquiry even ended, the Pay Board released information showing that, all along, we had been entitled to at least 8 percent more than we had been offered. We still hadn't got the cash, but it was a complete vindication of our position, and it was a body-blow for Ted Heath.

A week later, he lost the Election, the Tories getting 296 seats to Labour's 301. It wasn't a decisive vote, of course, since 14 seats had gone to the Liberals, and 23 to other Parties, and that weekend Ted Heath tried to hang on to power through deals with minority Parties. But he failed, and on the Monday, March 4, Harold Wilson returned to Downing Street. The following day, Michael Foot, the new Secretary of State for Employment, invited our National Officials to meet him at St James's Square at 2.00 in the afternoon.

There, he gave us the details of the Pay Board's report, and asked us to re-open negotiations immediately with the NCB. 'You can take it,' he said,'that any agreement you come to will be completely unfettered by any dictates of the previous Government. As for the Pay Board's report, it's up to you whether you want it to enter into the argument, but as far

as the Labour Government is concerned, it's not a governing document
in the situation.' But he did ask us to concentrate on settling the
immediate wages claim—any other matters we wanted to raise, like our
desire for a lump sum compensation for pneumoconiosis, could be dealt
with in the wide-ranging inquiry into the mining industry which he
wanted to begin as soon as we had reached a settlement.

Most important of all, to us, was the fact that, from what he had said,
Michael Foot was restoring to us, and to the NCB, the right of Free
Collective Bargaining, and we thanked him for it.

The following day, at the Industry's Joint National Negotiating
Committee, we had a long series of meetings, both formal and informal,
with the Coal Board. At the end of it all, they came up with a vastly
improved offer, including a commitment to an extra week's holiday the
following year, better holiday pay, a cost of living 'threshold' agreement,
and improved benefits on retirement and for men who were killed at
work.

But the main item, of course, was wages—a basic £32 a week for
surface workers, £36 underground, and £45 for men working at the face.
It was very close to what we had asked for in the first place, half a year of
unhappiness before.

Immediately these negotiations were finished, we remained at
Hobart House to hold a special meeting of the NEC, at which, after a
very long discussion, we agreed: 'That the NEC should strongly
recommend the members to accept the offer and to resume normal
working at the commencement of the first normal shift of the week in
which Monday, 11th March, 1974, occurred.' We also decided:'That
the matter be submitted to Areas for a proxy vote and the returns be
made to Head Office by not later than noon on Sunday, 10th March'.

That vote gave us unanimous backing, and the strike was over. A
month later, coal production had reached 93 percent of the output level
before the overtime ban started, a much faster recovery than had been
the case in 1972. This was partly because it had been a shorter stoppage,
but also because we were much more experienced the second time
around. Not only had we needed less men to make the strike effective,
but we knew all the snags and problems involved in allowing sufficient
men into the pits to provide proper maintenance and safety cover.

It was a strike which should never have happened. It has often been
said since that it was the miners who brought down Ted Heath. I can
only repeat what I have already said—as far as we were concerned, it
was *not* a political strike, but an industrial one. It was *not* the miners, but
Ted Heath who brought himself down. He didn't need to call an
election. He had a perfectly good working majority. But he had got
himself into a fixed position from which he felt he couldn't move, and I

believe that, as on the first occasion, it was due as much as anything else to his acceptance of bad advice from his Ministers.

At the end of it all, we had brought the miners back to the position in which, in the national interest, Ted Heath himself should have wanted to see them—at the top of the industrial wages league. We have remained there ever since.

Chapter Nine

The Wreckers

Shortly after the Election of 1974, we embarked on what the Government and the Coal Board had promised us as part of the settlement of the strike—a wide-ranging and long-term review of the Coal Industry. It was decidedly overdue, and something for which we had pressed for years.

It was called 'The Coal Industry Examination', a stuffy name and quite a strange one, sounding more like an entrance test for going down the pits. Eventually, it became generally known as the 'Plan for Coal'. *Everyone* concerned took part. It was chaired by Eric Varley, the newly-appointed Secretary of State for Industry, and included Joel Barnett, Albert Booth, and Alex Eadie from the Government, Derek Ezra (who—deservedly, I thought—became *Sir* Derek that June) and two of his top officials, and the National officials of NACODS, BACM, and ourselves.

The terms of reference were simple—'To consider and advise on the contribution which coal can best make to the country's energy requirements and the steps needed to secure that contribution.'

I won't go into all the long discussions which made up that Examination. It took a total of six months, with an Interim Report in June, but the most important thing was that, after nearly three years of bitterness, it was totally amicable. That was as it should be, though to people outside the Industry it may seem surprising. That's because they are fed a diet of supposed confrontation and antagonism between ourselves and the Board.

In reality, it's not like that at all. We sit together on the regular meeting of the Coal Industry National Consultative Council, on Welfare committees, on Pensions committees, on Health committees—in fact on every kind of committee you can think of. We are always consulted when it comes to the appointment of a new Chairman of the Board, and in practice the post of Industrial Relations Director is virtually ours to nominate, and Cliff Shephard, who held that position during the period of the two strikes, was actually an ex-NUM man. On occasions, the Board have even lent us their private plane when we have needed to get somewhere in a hurry.

So I would say that 90 percent of our dealings with the Board are conducted as by equal partners in trying to improve the Industry. But it's that other 10 percent, when we negotiate wage claims, which inevitably catches the public eye.

The final report of the Coal Industry Examination was published in the Autumn of 1974, and it was such a vital document that I propose to repeat in full the nine points under its heading 'General Conclusions'. They were:-

1. Events since the publication of our Interim Report reinforce our conviction that an efficient competitive coal industry has an assured long-term future.

2. The NCB's Plan for Coal has our full support as a general strategy involving as it does expansion and new developments wherever they are feasible, including the proposed exploitation of Selby and the expansion of opencast production.

3. To enable the required level of output to be reached as rapidly as possible and sustained, the industry will need both to overcome a number of technical and industrial constraints which at present impede existing collieries from achieving their true potential, and in addition to ensure that the whole of its projected new capacity is brought into full production efficiently and on time, subject to the normal planning procedures.

4. To facilitate the new mining developments, the Government intend to introduce legislation to give the NCB access to coal subject to 'retained copyhold' interests and to restore the power to make compulsory rights orders to promote the expansion of opencast coal production. This legislation will not impair the normal planning procedures for securing that full weight is given to environmental considerations.

5. We welcome the establishment of a financial framework for the industry which will give it the objective of long term competitiveness while covering its costs of production and contributing towards financing the the new investment programme, but at the same time recognising the special burdens of the past, the need to provide safeguards against short term fluctuations in the price of competing fuels, and the need to take appropriate action if other public policies prevent commercial pricing or impose exceptional burdens on the Board.

6. We welcome the new scheme for compensation for pneumoconiosis sufferers which has been worked out between the NCB and the Unions and the Government's intention to make a substantial contribution.

7. We are glad to note that progress has been made in working out improved pension arrangements in the industry and that the Government is prepared to assist in meeting the existing deficiency in the Mineworkers' Pension Scheme.

8. We again emphasise the importance of a sound and effective production incentive scheme and we trust that the current discussions between the NCB and the NUM will soon be successful and lead to a substantial increase in output.

9. We have studied proposals for research and development work into new uses of coal and recommend Government assistance for projects which offer good prospects for the long term future of the industry.

That document, which I refer to as 'my Bible', could, and should, have fashioned thinking in the Industry from its publication up to the end of the century. It was accepted by the Board, by ourselves and our colleagues in the other two unions, and by the Government. What's more, when it was presented to Parliament it was accepted unanimously there. So it should have been a blueprint, unaffected by the vagaries of political change. But it wasn't. Point number 5, which actually appeared in the document as paragraph 78, had a steamroller driven through it by the Tories' Coal Industry Act of 1980. And point 8, dealing with the need for a production incentive scheme, was to be the subject of bitter wrangling within our own Union for the next five years.

As with so many of the arguments I have tried to describe in previous chapters, the battle over a national incentive scheme was incredibly complex, probably the most complex of all. In order to understand properly the reasons why people took the positions they did, you would need to read a history of each of the individual Areas which make up our Union. Miners, as I have said before, are very conservative with a small 'c'. Each Area has its own traditions, different types of pit in which members work, different experiences of hardship during times of crisis.

So it would be vastly over-simplifying matters to say: 'Oh, of course he thought that way because he's a Communist', or, 'He voted that way because he's of the Right.' On other sorts of argument you could make such judgments, but not where the incentive scheme was concerned—it had its roots back in the days of the piece-work jungle that I lived and fought through, in fluctuating demands for the different types of coal produced by different Areas, in the vastly differing pit conditions and ease of working, and in the battle which had been fought in the Sixties over the National Power Loading Agreement.

The story of this new battle begins at our Annual Conference in 1972. It was held in the Dixieland Ballroom at Morecambe, and if the name 'Dixie' reminds people of the American Civil War, then that's not too inappropriate, because it was as near to civil war as I experienced in my term as President.

At that Conference, a resolution was put forward by the much-maligned COSA which read:'This Conference of the National Union of Mineworkers charges the National Executive Committee with the responsibility of ensuring that the wages of all the members are adjusted periodically to take account, not only of the cost of living and other factors affecting living standards, but also of ensuring that *members benefit from increased productivity and efficiency* my italics and that their real living standards are steadily improved.'

That resolution was carried, and as a result became Union policy—it was also, incidentally, one of the recommendations of Wilberforce that a productivity scheme for the Industry should be implemented by September 1972—with the onus on the NEC to do something about it, which we did. Over the next two years we negotiated with the Board on the subject, until we came to the position in September 1974 where we had a draft incentive agreement, which we discussed in the NEC. At the end of that discussion—stalemate. Dai Francis proposed that we reject the agreement, and he was defeated. Len Clarke proposed that we accept it, and he was defeated too. In other words, the NEC couldn't make up its mind.

So we decided to convene a Special Conference of the Union to receive a report on how matters stood, but without any recommendation from us, and with no decision to be taken by the Conference. Following that, the membership would be consulted by ballot.

That Conference duly took place, at the TUC headquarters, Congress House, on September 26, and was one of the most vitriolic meetings I can remember. It began with Arthur Scargill trying to raise procedural points, and points of order, referring to what had gone on at the NEC. I told him that, under our Rules, he couldn't raise them. He then said that he had taken legal advice—which made me bloody angry. As I said : 'You have to have all the Rules or not, and if this Union ever gets into the position when we have to go to law to decide how we are going to run our own damn Union, then we have no right to question the authority of a Government to introduce legal matters affecting the Union. If we want to get to legal issues all the time, don't come to these Conferences. Change the Rules. We have been running this Union over the years not as a legal ruling but by custom and practice.'

Anyway, when I wouldn't let Arthur have his way, he shouted, 'There's no point in stopping here,' and led the Yorkshire delegation out with him. That wasn't a good start.

The draft agreement we had arrived at was a national one, in the sense that the extra percentages earned for extra production would be the same throughout the country. But when it came to what 'extra' meant—in other words, what was the norm—he document held that this could only be decided on a face by face, pit by pit, and Area by Area basis. And that was what stuck in the craw of so many of the delegates. Time and again they stood up and said it would a return to the piece-work jungle which the Union had fought so long to demolish.

Jack Dunn from Kent, who had himself worked at the pitface for thirty years, perhaps summed up that point of view when he said:'I remember the arguments on piecework when one of our colleagues was getting a bit old and he could not swing his shovel as quick as some of the youngsters. You had the internecine warfare of the younger blokes wanting to get rid of the old chap because they felt their returns were being diminished. Men exploiting their bodies and ready to exploit their mates.'

Many had fears that the scheme would lead to miners throwing safety precautions to the wind in order to dig the extra coal to earn more of a bonus. Some felt that it would lead to men moving from pits where conditions were hard to those where it was easier, and so to pit closures.

Many delegates did support the agreement, on the grounds that at least it was opening the door to the principle, and that we could negotiate improvements later on. They also pointed out that no one would lose by it, and many would gain, though to that there was the counter-argument that the Coal Board would use those extra earnings as an excuse for offering us lesser increases in the basic wage.

The arguments were complicated by the fact that Harold Wilson, unable to govern properly with a minority in Parliament, had called another General Election for October 10, and our proposed date for a ballot of our members meant that the results would be known just before the Election. Many felt that if, as seemed likely, our members went against the productivity deal in its present form, that fact would be used and distorted by the Tory media to the detriment of Labour.

But the most vitriolic remarks of all were directed at the NEC in general, and the National Officials in particular, for not having come to a decision, and therefore not having brought a proposal to the Conference which delegates could either accept or reject. The fact that this was by no means the first purely 'reporting' conference we had held made no difference.

One delegate, Jack Collins from Kent, chose to attack the wage rise which we, the National Officials, had recently been voted, and went on: 'There was no question of a productivity deal, and if that is good enough for the leadership then it is good enough for the lads.'

To that, I replied from the chair: 'I don't take kindly to snide remarks about the motives of National Officials. We work in accordance with Resolutions carried at Annual Conferences. The decision for productivity was made at Annual Conference, and nobody therefore has the right to doubt the motives of those who have the honour to negotiate on behalf of the members of this Union. I think it is wrong to give any impression it is just the National Officials who have come here to try to push something through.

'We all have our feelings, and I have already spoken of my feelings on many platforms, but I shall not be seeking any platform for or against this agreement. I think it is for the members to decide and for us to explain what the agreement is all about. If they don't like it, all well and good.'

Even that didn't calm things. A few minutes later George Rees, from South Wales, launched into another bitter attack on the National Officials for 'failing to give a lead', which provoked me into saying: 'Let me just remind George and other people, never vilify your National Officials.'

It got nastier even than that. At one point, while Lawrence Daly was answering a question, one delegate tried to interrupt him, and the Report of the Conference records the following exchange:-

A Delegate: On a point of order . . .

Chairman: You cannot have a point of order on a thing like this. You come up to the rostrum when I call you.

Delegate: I will see you outside, Joe.

Chairman: We will have a pint in the first pub, and you will discover I am as big a boy as you are.

As I have said before, if people want to play it tough, well, I don't mind, though as it turned out we never did have that pint (and whatever was to follow!), because immediately after the Conference the NEC members stayed behind and we held a special meeting. At that, we decided to seek further negotiations with the Board, in the light of the many points which had been raised, and, as a consequence of that, to postpone the ballot.

By the time of the next meeting, October 3, the NEC had made up its mind. It agreed: 'That the proposed Productivity Scheme of the National Coal Board which was based on Faces, Pits, and Areas be rejected; and that the National Coal Board be informed that the Union would only accept a National Productivity Scheme which was based upon overall output per manshift, and which gave the same amount of bonus to everyone in the coalmining industry, irrespective of the job performed.'

But, to prove that we were also trying to act responsibly, we also agreed: 'That the National Executive Committee unanimously issue a call to all the members to co-operate fully with the National Coal Board to ensure that the industry achieves the production targets which had been jointly agreed as the objectives for this and for future years.'

So, it was back to the negotiating table. A whole series of meetings followed—during the course of which Labour were returned with an overall majority—until finally we came to a meeting with the Board on October 30. It was a long meeting, with the Board's representatives continually retiring to discuss the various amendments we wanted, until finally we came to the point where they agreed to have the productivity bonus shared out nationally.

And that, you might think, would be that. Not a bit of it. As the Minutes record: 'It was appreciated that the Board had conceded *all* [my italics] the amendments the Union had put forward, but after discussion it was agreed: 'That the revised draft agreement be submitted to the membership for decision through a ballot vote, and that the National Executive Committee recommend rejection of the proposed agreement.'

I think that was probably one of the daftest decisions the Executive of our Union has ever made. We had a policy. After hours and hours, and days of discussion and negotiation, we had got the Board to accept every point of that policy. And then we recommended rejection of it. If ever there was a bloody waste of time that was it. But the 'antis', the wreckers I should call them in this case, had had their way.

They had their way with the membership, too. A fortnight later, in the ballot, the NEC's recommendation was supported by 123,615 votes to 77,119. The National Incentive Scheme was dead.

Two and a half years later, in 1977, it came to life again. Once more there were long and arduous negotiations. And this time, the NEC voted to recommend its acceptance in a ballot. But the membership still didn't want it, and they turned it down by 110,634 votes to 87,901. That was its second death.

But there had always been certain Areas who were very anxious to have an incentive scheme, even if it were only local, and South Derbyshire was one of them. Towards the end of 1977, Ken Toon, the Area Secretary, approached the NEC for permission to negotiate such a scheme for their Area. This he had to do under Rule 36 of our constitution. And, on December 8, the NEC agreed, by a majority decision, that Areas be permitted to negotiate their own self-financing incentive schemes. In other words, we took a general decision, which we were entitled to do, rather than simply a decision about South Derby.

That didn't please the wreckers at all. The next thing we knew, in January 1978, the Union was taken to court by the Yorkshire, Kent, and South Wales Areas—all of them with leaders from the far Left—with a view to stopping the introduction of incentive schemes. I'm glad to say that the High Court threw them out on their ears, but, as I had said back in 1974, it was a very sad thing that miners should resort to taking each other to law.

Where South Derby led, others followed, and within eighteen months every Area had its own incentive scheme, which was exactly what people had been so worried about at that Special Conference in 1974.

Sooner or later, these local schemes were bound to lead to wider and wider discrepancies between the earnings of different Areas. In theory this ought not to be the case, because the norms are decided at pit level, according to the conditions at each coal face. This is a matter for negotiation between the local NUM representatives and the Colliery Manager. And the payment for achieving the norm—or percentages above and below it—is the same throughout Britain, so that theoretically everyone should be able to earn the same bonus.

But it hasn't worked out that way, and the curious thing is that the Areas with the lowest earnings are the same Areas which had the lowest earnings under the old piece-work system—the same Areas, incidentally, which supported the National Power Loading Agreement and opposed the Incentive Scheme. That suggests either that they're not interested in earning themselves more money, or that they just don't know how to negotiate properly for themselves. It is also true that, contrary to all the gloomy, and well-publicised, forecasts, the accident figures are actually *lower* in those Areas which are the highest producers.

Perhaps at this point I should pause, and recognise that to many, reading this, it may seem that the story of my life has become more the story of the Union. The truth is that that is exactly what, more and more over the years, it did become, especially during my time as President, which was almost more than a full-time job.

For example, when I became Area Secretary in Lancashire, and moved to Bolton, I had already served a number of years on the Bench as a County J.P. It gave me quite a few laughs that job—I remember one day when we had several cases of speeding, including some miners, all as a result of being caught by the radar trap in one little area. I said to the Clerk of the Court: 'Are these two police lads on piece work?' It certainly seemed they must have been!

On another occasion, I got caught myself. But it was in Manchester. I'd come back from London on the train with a colleague, who found he'd missed his last bus home to Ashton-under-Lyme. I had my car at the station, so I said I'd run him home. On the way back, going along this big wide dual-carriageway on the outskirts of Manchester, there wasn't another car in sight—until I pulled up at a traffic lights, that is, when a police car appeared.

Well, they told me I was speeding, and I said I hadn't seen any sign, and they said there was one back a while, so I just said, 'That's it, then.' Eventually my case came to court, and I pleaded guilty by letter, and on the very day it was heard, I was sitting in Bolton County Court, giving £5 fines to people who had been doing the same speed as I had done. And what did I get in Manchester? Eight quid! I thought, 'There's no justice but because there simply wasn't the time.

In the same way, in recent years, I've had little opportunity for anything like going to the theatre or the cinema. I enjoy the odd pint or so, and I don't suppose there's been much secret over the years that I like the horses and I like a good meal.

The horses began way back in those early days when I used to have the threepenny doubles and trebles with the local bookie, and got into Haydock Park free by the simple expedient of climbing over the wall with the other lads. In later years, my love of racing became known, and I'd get invited to people's boxes at big race meetings and so on, and in 1981 I was even invited to give away the trophy for the Tote Ebor Handicap at York. It got me a kiss from the owner's wife, and I had backed the winner and the second, so I was in good fettle that day!

I've had a few winners in my time, though mixed with my fair share of losers. I usually have a bet on a Saturday—nothing very much—and if there's anything to come Nellie picks it up on the Monday. Except for once. It was during my last year as President, and Nellie and I went for a drink on a Sunday at 'The Duke' in Walton, where we know a few people. One of them, a bloke called Bill, said: 'You're all right on Monday, aren't you, Nellie?'

'Why?' she asked.

'Well, didn't he back such a horse and such a horse yesterday?'

'I'm not sure,' she said, 'though he did say he'd had a good win.'

Maybe it's the Lancashire in me, but we don't give away too much about these things. Now I was on the spot, though, so I said: 'Aye, well, I have won—about five hundred quid.'

Nellie practically choked on her drink, and Bill in the land!' After three or four years I gave it up—not because of that, asked:'Well, are you giving it to Nellie to pick up on Monday?'

'I'm *not!*' I said, 'I'll not let Nellie pick *that* up! I think I'll have a morning rest that day, pick it up myself, and go in in the afternoon.'

As they say, a man can go so far . . .!

I'm by no means the only miner who likes the horses. A lot of them love the game. So I came up with the idea that the members of the miners' clubs could get together to buy shares in a horse, or horses, which would give them a bit of an interest, rather like the scheme the *Daily Mirror* runs. All harmless, and a bit of fun.

Then someone called Lady Olga Maitland, who wrote a gossip column on the *Sunday Express,* heard about it, and rang me up to find out what it was all about. I explained it to her, and she said: 'That's a good idea.' Well, so it was, but the way it appeared in her column made it seem as though somehow the Miners' Pension Fund was involved, together with a scheme to buy horses for *me!* That naturally scared everyone off it, and it came to a quick full stop.

I was furious. Normally I let what the papers say wash over me, but it was a bloody good idea which she'd killed stone dead, and I sued, and was awarded £3,500, which I put in the Coal Industry Benevolent Trust. A short while after that I was at some race meeting when I met Lord Matthews, owner of the *Express*. He invited Nellie and me up to his box, and we talked about the case, and he said: 'Yes, she's cost us a lot of money.'

'Well, fire her, then!' I said. And I meant it.

The only other occasion on which we went for a paper during my term of office was in September 1974. The TUC Congress was meeting at Brighton, and we had gone down on the previous Friday evening for a pre-Conference get-together of delegates. On the Monday, an article appeared in the *Evening News* describing how Joe Gormley and Mick McGahey were living it up, drinking champagne and eating caviar together at the Metropole Hotel. There was only one problem with the story—neither Mick nor I drink champagne, nor does either of us like caviar. And, on the night in question, we were at two separate places.

At the delegation meeting on the Monday, I took the article along and read it to the lads, who roared with laughter, because they knew we hadn't been together. But it made me a bit mad. As I said to them: 'This is the sort of stuff you have to face when you're in this job—condemnation of character.'

The Manager of the Metropole was just as concerned. He came up to me and said:'I don't know *where* they've got that from, Mr Gormley. We have no bill of this kind. No such bill.' Well, of course they hadn't. The reporter had just dreamed up the whole story. I wanted to make the paper pay for what, in my mind, was typical of the defamation of character that is always going on with trade union leaders. But our legal adviser said that we should be content with a retraction, and that's what we got, albeit a rather half-hearted one.

On other occasions, stories have been not so much inaccurate as deliberately snide. At the end of January 1974, during the run-up to the second strike, the NEC had a long-arranged visit by a delegation from the West German miners. Their President was a member of their Parliament, and was also President of the Mineworkers International Federation, and we took their party out to dinner at the White House restaurant, which naturally involved a large bill.

Well, one of the waiters showed a copy of the bill to a reporter, who made a big thing out of it, again along the lines of miners' leaders living it up while calling for a strike. But as I said at the time, and still say, where were we supposed to take them? To a fish and chip shop? Was that what a newspaper editor would have done with his guests? The whole thing was utterly childish, and the man who had shown the bill was sacked out of hand. I don't suppose *he* got much sympathy from the Press!

Not that I want to knock Fleet Street in general. I'm proud of the fact that I had a pretty good relationship with the industrial and political correspondents. I thought for many years that the Labour and Trade Union Movement tended to hide itself under a bushel. It didn't come into the open enough, and wasn't willing to put its point of view to the Press because of the old argument that the Press was Tory-controlled. But, of course, in a democracy even a Tory-controlled Press can't suppress everything. And I always argued that no publicity is bad publicity. On the other hand, if you do get publicity, it can't be all bad. Some of it will be good. The only thing I think the Press could do without is the gossip columns. I don't know whose egotism they satisfy, but they tend to give garbled tales, and innuendoes, which are neither good for the individuals they mention, nor for the Press itself, nor even for the country. They don't mean a damn thing.

On the serious side of reporting, it's no secret that a trade union leader, like a minister, will become more friendly with some reporters than with others, and that therefore they will tend to get any stories that are going. That often depends on the sort of trust that you can only get through personal friendship, and for many years, for instance, I have looked on Barrie Devney of the *Express* as a personal friend. I'm sure that the number of stories he's had, and not used, would get him sacked from the paper if they knew!

Of course, I recognise that there's a danger in this. Stories which ought to come out can get suppressed. And I've tried to be careful not to put too many things on a man's conscience, so that he has to keep quiet about them, and perhaps get scooped by someone who got the story from another source. But there are inevitably times when you have to say, 'This is what's what, but don't use it just yet, because there are still certain things to do and argue about.' It's a two-edged weapon, though, and you have to be careful how you use it, because we, and politicians, need the Press just as much as the Press needs us.

Barrie Devney it was, incidentally, who in an article about me in 1971 coined the phrase 'Battered Cherub' which I've taken as the title of this book. It's not for me to say whether the 'cherub' part is right, but 'battered' certainly! Barrie, too, knows what it's like to have wrong information fed to the papers. One evening late in 1973, during the negotiations before the strike, he was having a drink and a chat with Nellie and me, after which we decided to go out for a Chinese meal.

He was 'on call' for the *Express* that night, so after we had been at the restaurant for a while he went to the phone to check in with the news desk. When he got back to the table he was almost apoplectic. 'You won't believe this,' he said. 'They told me there wasn't much doing, but since I was in the area they said it might be worth popping down to this restaurant 'because Joe Gormley has been seen there, talking with a big fat man in glasses—obviously a Communist'. Big fat man, indeed!' Well, Barrie isn't exactly a waif, but I don't know whether he was more upset by the reference to his size or the crazy assumption as to his political leanings!

The only other Press story I would mention was when, at the Executive's suggestion, we moved, in August 1974, from Hurst Park to Sunbury-on-Thames, in order to enjoy a little more privacy. There we were to remain until I retired. Somehow they made a big deal out of the fact that it was a £30,000 house, and that the Union had bought it. Well, yes, so they did, and a bloody good investment it was too. It was effectively like a tied-cottage, and I paid rent and rates and all the rest of it like anyone else. So I never saw what was so strange about that. The best thing about it, for me, was that it's only a stone's throw from Kempton Park racecourse—funnily enough, the time we were in Bolton was the only time in my life I *didn't* live a short head away from a track.

It's a nice enough house, with a bit of a garden, in a quiet street where you'a think nothing ever happened. But we found out that, shortly before we arrived, a previous owner of a house nearby had been had up for embezzlement. Soon after we moved in, we were invited to a cocktail party up the road—not that we knew the people, but they were rather of the name-dropping sort. Anyway, Nellie and I decided it might be interesting, so we went, and Nellie was talking to the woman who lived next door to us and remarked what a pleasant place it was.

At that, the woman brought up the embezzlement business, and also how someone else locally had been taken away by the police.

'Oh,' said Nellie, in all innocence,'when we came here we thought we might be lowering the tone of the place!'

The woman looked straight at her and replied: 'Yes, and so did we, too.' As Nellie says, there's nothing like being truthful!

When we first moved into the house, there were a lot of bushes and trees, and after a while Nellie said to me:'I think they need trimming.' 'They *do* need trimming,' I said. Now, in the back garden there was this tall black-looking fir tree, which was always turning brown and shedding its needles into a bit of a paddling pool I have for when the grandchildren come to visit. I'd been telling Nellie we should have it down, and the reply was always, 'You're not, mate!' So I saw my chance.

There was a bloke I'd met in the pub who did a bit of tree surgery, and I told her I'd get him along. As it happened, the previous owner had taken the tops off a couple of other trees at the back, leaving four-foot stumps doing nothing. So Nellie said: 'When he comes, get him to take those down too.'

Well, along he came, and started with a big branch that was hanging over from the neighbour's garden in the front, and which he'd given me permission to cut off. Nellie stood watching us at the front door, and then we went round the side of the house to the back, while Nellie went through the house. On the way I said to him: 'Come on, mate, how long will it take you to get that big fir down?'

'About two seconds,' he said.

'Right then, get to it,' I told him, and by the time Nellie was through the house I had that bloody tree down. She played all holy hell, but there wasn't anything she could do about it. I don't like trees when they cause problems—though I've done some of my best work among the trees!

Mind you, I've never been one much for gardening. Nellie knew that. When we were at the bungalow in Bolton, I drove back home after a visit to London one day, and, as I stopped the car, I saw all these things I thought were weeds in the flower beds. I thought I'd surprise Nellie by giving her a hand, and I whipped them all out and into the rubbish bin. Then I walked in and told her: 'The garden's looking all right now. I've finished your weeding for you.'

'You what?!' she said. 'I've been all day at it, and I've only just finished setting those plants!' She swears to this day that I did it deliberately.

'Well, that's me finished,' I said. She didn't want me in the garden after that. But I wasn't too keen on digging anyway. I used to do it a bit as a young lad, but then, when I became a collier, I got to the point of view that, after a hard week of digging like hell for coal all day, there wasn't much sense in doing a load more digging at the weekend.

I can do without gardening, and I can do without shopping. That may be a bit of me that goes back to the early days, when it was very much looked on as women's work. The only time I went shopping was by mistake. The German Labour Attache was a friend of mine, and asked me to do him a favour.

'What is it?' I asked.

'One of our television stations is making a programme about me, and they want to know what I *do* in my spare time.'

'Well—what do you do in your spare time?'

He didn't answer. Instead he said:'I want you to come to Walton with me, and we'll do something there.'

'Okay, fair enough,' I said, and off we went to Walton, me thinking that we'd probably go into 'The Duke' for a pint. Then he said:'Well, what I generally do on a Saturday is go round Safeways.'

'You *what?!*'

'Well, that's when I usually do my shopping.'

I had no option. In I went with him, with Nellie following us, and we walked round with this bloody great trolley, and the TV crew following us. I thought, 'There's no sense in walking with this unless we fill it up,' so as we went round I grabbed everything I could get hold of and shoved it in. Nellie was going mad. As soon as I put something in, she would take it out. 'I've *done* my shopping,' she said. 'I don't want all this stuff.' In the meantime, the Attaché went merrily on, getting this great shopping list of his.

'Bloody hell, this is no good. I'm missing my drinking time here,' I said. 'I'll tell you what...'Then I got hold of this big bunch of grapes, and held it up high, and said to the crew: 'Now you take a picture of us and these grapes.' So they did, and I just said: 'That's it. We're finished now. We'll go for lunch now.' And that was all the shopping I ever did!

Not that it matters. As I said, the Union was my life, and sometimes made demands on me which could only be accepted by someone who felt that way about it. Towards the end of 1974, soon after we had moved to Sunbury, I became ill, and as a result we nearly had a constitutional crisis in the Union.

On December 10, the Union's side of the Joint National Negotiating Committee held a meeting, chaired in my absence by the Vice-President, Mick McGahey. Thirteen members were present, and in the absence of myself, Lawrence Daly, and Len Clarke, the 'antis' as I call them had a majority of 7 to 6.

Now, at our Annual Conference that July, we had passed a composite resolution which read as follows:- 'This Conference of the National Union of Mineworkers, recognising the importance and necessity of attracting recruits to the Mining Industry, instructs the National Executive Committee to seek substantial increases in wages and improvements in conditions, which reflect the new relative importance of the mineworkers in the country's economy. Long-term agreements should be introduced to protect wage levels, ensure adequate pensions, continue flexible cost of living payments, increase holidays and holiday payments.'

The key point is that it asked for 'substantial' increases, rather than anything specific.

In the meantime, the Government had come out with the idea of Harold Wilson's 'Social Contract'. Originally he had called it the 'Social Compact', a play on Rousseau's *Du Contrat Social*, which held that power resided in the people, and that government could only be by general consent. But, as was often the case, Harold was being a bit too clever for his own boots, and people quickly called it the 'Social Contract' anyway!

I didn't like it. To me, it was just pay restraint under another guise, but the TUC were going along with it, and we went along with it in order to give the Labour Party as much of a chance as possible.

Midway through that meeting on December 10, they adjourned, in order to keep a meeting I had arranged with the TUC. At that meeting, the TUC said that, although they didn't wish to interfere with our wage negotiations, they hoped we would bear in mind the Movement's need to preserve employment prospects, to help the low-paid, and to achieve the long-term aims of the Social Contract.

So what did our Committee, when they resumed, decide? They decided by seven votes to six, on Mick McGahey's casting vote, first that, instead of running from March 1, there should be a demand for an interim wages settlement as from November 1. This, they decided, should be for £2.50p, plus £4.40 agreed cost-of-living threshold payment, *plus* another £2.50p on March 1—a total increase of £29.40p. Round about 65 percent! Well, I suppose 'substantial' could mean anything, but that was certainly a free translation!

Two days later, on December 12, the NEC met, again in the absence of Lawrence and myself, both of us being still ill. By all accounts it was a bitter meeting. Mick McGahey, who was in the chair, was challenged for his conduct of the sub-committee two days before, on the grounds that he had gone far beyond what our conference resolution said in terms of wages, while at the same time ignoring some of the other elements in that resolution. After a lot of argument, Mick ruled that the motion challenging his conduct could not be put.

Someone then moved that the sub-committee's recommendation be accepted, but Mick would not allow those six members, who had originally been against it in the sub-committee, to vote against it in the NEC, and he declared the motion carried. At that, twelve members of the NEC, including the six, walked out of the meeting in protest, demanding a ruling from the President.

Back home, ill in bed with bronchitis, I had been told, in a frantic telephone call from Tommy Bartle of the Durham Area, of the Negotiating Committee's decision, and in particular how Mick had used his casting vote. I told Tommy that Mick might try to do this to the six NEC members who had been in the minority in the sub-committee, and said that if it happened they should do this walk-out. So I wasn't too surprised when Tommy called again to tell me it had gone as I suspected it would. Straight away I called Mick at the meeting and told him that I was coming in, and that I wanted all the NEC members to stay in the building until I arrived. So they adjourned the meeting, resuming when I finally got there in mid-afternoon.

Taking the chair, I said: 'It seems I can't even be bloody ill for a couple of days without something going on that oughtn't. But I've been told what's happened, and that's why I've come in, because as Rule 15 says it's my job to see that the business of this Union is conducted in a proper manner and in accordance with the Rules.

'Well, it hasn't been.' Then I gave my ruling. 'Any member of this NEC is entitled to vote here in accordance with his conscience. It's got bugger all to do with whether he was on a sub-committee whose recommendation is being discussed.'

My ruling was promptly challenged, but was upheld by the vote, and we then went on to reject the sub-committee's recommendation and to authorise the National Officials to have informal talks with the Board along the lines of our Conference Resolution—which is what should have happened in the first place. Our constitution had been upheld, but it shouldn't have needed me to get up from my sick bed to do it.

After the meeting, the Press lads asked me what I had been reading in bed, and they fell about laughing when I told them: 'The Day of the Jackal.'

In fact, Mick was theoretically correct. That was how we used to operate when I was first on the NEC. Once a sub-committee had made a decision, all its members were supposed to support that decision in the NEC. But, in my time as President, the 'antis' had consistently voted in the NEC against sub-committee decisions where they had been in the minority, and in the cause of peace and harmony I had let them get away with it. Had I not done so, we wouldn't have had nearly so many narrowly-split votes over the years. The split would more often have been something like 19-5.

But they couldn't have it both ways, and that was why I gave the ruling I did. And I should add that even today the 'antis' will campaign in their Areas against NEC decisions they don't like—they forget about NEC loyalty.

That was typical of the sort of tightrope I had to walk throughout my term of office. There were never more than two or three votes between what I call the 'antis', and what the Press calls the 'moderates', but which I prefer to call the 'progressives'. The 'antis' would always vote against anything, even though they might think that what was being offered was a very good deal. In fact, they often voted against things knowing, and even hoping, that they would be defeated, just so that they could appear on the records to have been 'militant'.

It was well summed up by an apocryphal story that was told about me at an NUM Conference. The story went that I had been ill, that someone on the NEC had suggested sending me a get-well telegram, and that the vote had been carried by 13 votes to 12!

In fact, it wasn't that apocryphal. In March of 1975, the students of University College London, which is just across Euston Road from our headquarters, asked me if I would agree to be 'kidnapped' in support of their Rag. The charities they were helping were all very worthwhile, so I agreed, and they put me in the back of this van, with my legs hanging out! Then they asked the Union to buy me back at a penny a head for every miner, which would have amounted to £2,500. Arthur Scargill rang them up and offered ten times that amount if they would keep me!

But they didn't, and that month we achieved, through negotiation, the biggest percentage increase in the history of the NUM. The basic wage of the faceworkers rose from £45 a week to £61, the lowest underground workers from £36 to £47, and the surface workers from £32 to £41. Now that was achieved, not through any strike or threat, but through what is called 'free collective bargaining'.

I put it like that because, although I'm obviously in favour of it, the word 'free' in that context has always amused me. Negotiations never *have* been free. They never will be. They are always subject to the situation at the time, whereas some people get the idea that 'free' means you can go in and automatically get a massive wage increase. You can't. I've never found any employers willing to say, 'Here's a pocketful of money, you share it out.' You have to fight and prove your entitlement to every last penny. You *must* have a good case to put to employers, or to conciliation if it comes to that. We only got what we did out of Wilberforce because we had a good case, not out of any sentimentality. So I want to stress here that the idea that free collective bargaining inevitably leads to a great wage explosion is a complete fallacy.

What *did* lead to such an explosion was the Social Contract. I have to say that I suspected it from the start, and said so. It was simply an incomes policy under another name. Harold Wilson knew perfectly well what he was doing, because it had been tried before. He and Barbara Castle had tried it with 'In Place of Strife', and Ted Heath had tried it with his percentage norms and what have you, and now here it was again. It was a con-trick, a political conjuror's illusion that somehow all would be well because there was this marvellous piece of mutual trust between the Government and the TUC.

Looking back, I don't see why any of us went along with it, though I suppose at the start it was because, having got Labour back in power, we wanted to give them all the support we could. But at least the NUM was the only union to ballot its members consistently to see whether they agreed.

Well, in 1975, following our wages agreement, there came the explosion I mentioned, though for some reason I can't fathom no one seemed able to see that it was such. The terms of the Social Contract for that year were that there was to be a £6 wage increase across the board, for everybody. Six pounds! I'll guarantee that was the biggest inflationary factor in the last half-century.

I don't think there were half a dozen unions in the country who could have negotiated six quid for their members. With the exception of a few unions, who wouldn't have constituted even a quarter of the TUC, it was far in excess of any agreements that had ever been reached. For most, it was a figure they wouldn't even have dreamed of. For most, it was above 10 percent, and for many it was up to 20 percent.

I don't want to be misunderstood on this. It was a marvellous thing for a lot of unions and their members, and I supported it. But it was a far bigger inflationary factor than anything which would have come from so-called free collective bargaining.

Our NEC ended up supporting it, and in turn our members supported the NEC in a ballot, with 116,076 in favour and 75,743 against. Maybe it seems surprising that so many voted against, but perhaps their instinctive feeling told the truth of the matter, which was that this sort of deal would erode all the differentials which the miners had won in their fight to the top of the wages league—if, that is, this was the sort of deal we were going to be asked to continue to support. At the time, I couldn't believe that we would.

That ballot got us out of what could have been one of the biggest fiascos in our history. It took place two or three weeks after our Annual Conference, which that July was at Scarborough. Arthur Scargill and his Yorkshiremen had a resolution down which demanded £100 a week for faceworkers, £85 for the underground men, and £80 for the surface workers. It was a resolution which I described publicly as 'plain bloody daft . . . bloody silly'.

I did everything I could in the NEC to persuade Arthur to withdraw it, but he wouldn't. The only thing we could manage was to get the resolution composited with a couple of others, which watered it down slightly. Whereas the Yorkshire resolution had said that, failing an unsatisfactory response, we should ballot the members for industrial action, the Composite Resolution, while still 'seeking' (rather than Yorkshire's 'demanding') £100 a week for faceworkers, said that in the event of an unsatisfactory offer we should consult the members 'in accordance with Rule'.

But it was still a ridiculous claim, and in my Presidential address I made what was probably the most impassioned plea I ever made in my life for it to be rejected. I told the delegates: 'There is not a great negotiating merit in picking figures out of the air, and after repeating them a few times to make out that they are sacred . . . we keep constantly hearing resolutions being carried in Areas of the Union demanding free collective bargaining, and at the same time supporting a resolution which lays down certain wage levels, not as a target, not as something to be achieved eventually by negotiations, but as specific demands, failing which we start talking about strike action.

'The two things don't go together,' I told them, 'because free bargaining is not possible where either side ties the hands of the negotiators. I appeal to Conference not to tie the hands and feet of your NEC. But the Resolution itself . . . is asking this Union to pledge itself to insist on an increase in wages for all its members—and I stress the word 'all'—which is higher than the amount of the National minimum wage being demanded at the moment by the TUC. This, in the economic position facing us, is neither logical or even militant. It is madness.

'If the resolution is carried and our claim is not accepted, do we believe we would get much support from the rest of the Movement, when we are asking for all our members an increase in wages higher than the wage being earned by the big majority of workers in many other fields?

'We have proved in the last three to four years that this Union has great industrial power, and maybe some of us have become a little drunk with this power and are constantly wanting to be flexing our muscles. I believe that when you get that way, it's necessary to stop and reflect as to whether we should use that strength to further our own ends, or whether we should use it wisely to create a better position for all workers. It is my candid opinion that it would help to destroy us if we were seen to be driving a big wedge, not only into the TUC, but also between the TUC and the Labour Movement.'

I went on to warn them that, if they passed the resolution, the Labour Government 'much against its will, would be forced to introduce statutory legislation to deal with wages'.

And on the subject of militancy I said: 'If such ideas as contained in these resolutions are stemming from feelings of militancy, I must remark that it is not militant to be seen to be trying to split the Movement; it is not militant to create feelings of insecurity in the Industry, to create once again a feeling of uncertainty amongst our members. But, worst of all, I do not believe that it can be termed 'militancy' when we are trying to do something which may endanger the life of the Labour Government.

'Because, although we may disagree with the way in which the Chancellor is trying to deal with the emergency which exists, or even with the approach of the TUC on the issue, we cannot disagree with the fact that there is a serious economic emergency existing. This is affecting everyone in the country, not only the work people, but more so the sick and the injured and the retired people. The value of their money is falling as rapidly as that of the miners, and their purchasing power is becoming weaker and weaker.

'Whilst we may spend our time arguing as to who is responsible for this position, the whole situation is deteriorating from hour to hour, and if we, as a Union, can be seen to be giving a lead to other Trade Unions

in Britain by saying that we are determined to help as far as is humanly possible to solve the immediate problem, we can set an example to those vocal critics of the Trade Union Movement, who by their own actions may have caused the situation to deteriorate. I refer to the financial manipulators and other people like them, who have been selling us short in the world markets, and who need to be dealt with in the long run. There is no time for recriminations now, because whilst we are doing that we are not helping to solve the problem.'

I then said that I appreciated that the delegates were all mandated, but appealed for the resolution to be withdrawn. 'Try to trust your negotiators,' I said, 'to get the best possible deal in the circumstances which face us at any one time. There's no point in shackling us.'

But in spite of that appeal, and in spite of an appeal from Harold Wilson who also spoke, the resolution was carried. As I had forecast back at the time of the first strike, it was the first of a whole line of demands-backed-by-threat which have come to dominate the proceedings of our Union, and which run directly contrary to all I have learned in a lifetime dedicated to negotiation.

That year, however, the threat was averted. The Government and the TUC came out with their plan for the £6 across-the-board increase, and on July 17 at our NEC meeting, following more bitter argument, it was decided by 14 votes to 10 to ballot our members on whether to support that plan. Once they had voted as they did, the question of seeking that £100 a week no longer applied. But it had been touch and go.

Early in the following year, 1976, Harold Wilson resigned as Prime Minister. As to why he did that, I'm no wiser than anyone else. As I said at the time, it was completely unexpected to me, and a shock in that sense, though I can't say I was all that sorry. Harold was a wily man. He was all things to all men, but he was never a warm man, never able to draw people to him in the way I believe is essential for a Labour leader. It's true that he was able to keep warring factions within the Party appeased, but I'm not sure that it solved many problems for us, or that it gained us any more voters. I was never drawn to Harold, but then, since I can never forgive him for what happened in 1974, I make no apology for the fact that my opinion is biased.

Jim Callaghan, who succeeded him, was quite another thing. I looked on him as an old friend and colleague, and we'd certainly fought a number of battles together. I'm not sure that Jim ever got his hands dirty, except maybe on his farm, but at least he had a solid trade union background, and was a much warmer person, in private as in public rather like everyone's favourite uncle.

So it may have been something to do with this personal loyalty which made me, for the second year, support the Social Contract which Jim had inherited, and which he decided to carry on—even though it may have been against my better judgement. Jim took over on April 5, and soon afterwards it was announced that that year's 'norm' within the Contract would be 4.5 percent. I didn't like it at all. We seemed to be going down the well-trodden path which had always led to disaster before. But as I told the Press: 'We can't be seen leading the Union towards the demise of the Government.'

Again, it was going to mean a hard fight. Our faceworkers, for example, had had a rise of £16 in 1975, £6 in 1976, and now it would mean a rise of only just over £3 for 1977. And I knew that once again there were resolutions down for our 1976 Conference in the Isle of Man demanding that 'magic' figure of £100. I knew there was only one way to forestall those demands, and that was to have a ballot *before* the Conference.

On May 13 we had an NEC meeting, which was very close-run. Arthur Scargill proposed that we should call a National Delegate Meeting to discuss the new terms of the Contract, knowing that at such a meeting he and his supporters were likely to command a majority. But his motion was defeated by 14 votes to 10. Len Clarke, President of the Nottingham miners, then proposed that the NEC support the Government's policy, and that squeaked through by 13 votes to 11, the difference in the voting pattern being due to the fact that one NEC member didn't want us to take a position either way.

Voting on the NEC was one thing. Getting our members to vote the right way in the ballot we had called was quite another, especially with Arthur in Yorkshire, and Mick in Scotland, mounting a massive propaganda battle against the policy. I should say at this point that there is nothing in our Rules which says that we *have* to have a ballot on every wage agreement. But, as I have pointed out earlier, the union runs itself by custom and practice, and it's clearly more democratic to hold a ballot when the NEC is so narrowly split, and holds such strongly differing views, on such an important issue.

That ballot was held in the last week of May, and it wouldn't be putting it too strongly to say that a good deal of the world was waiting on the result. There had been a terrific run on the pound sterling, and many felt, as usual, that where we led, other unions would follow. Once again, it was to be the miners who decided whether the Government's counter-inflation policy would hold together.

It wasn't a situation I relished. I had always taken the view that it was up to each union to negotiate for itself. I never liked the idea of others riding in with large wage claims on the backs of the miners, nor, equally, did I like the idea of the rest holding back, if they had a good case, simply because *we* held back. Yes, as I had said the year before, it was good to be setting an example. But the example was rapidly becoming looked upon as the rule, to such an extent that when, during the ballot, someone at a pit in Gwent said he thought the vote had gone against acceptance, the pound promptly lost another 1.5 cents.

By the time the voting was done, I had no idea which way it had gone, though I feared we might have lost. At the same time, as I said in a radio interview at the beginning of June, the run on the pound had thrown into question the whole idea that Britain's economic situation could be solved by holding back wages. 'The miners,' I said, 'along with other workers, quite rightly say "we are not to be blamed for this". We cannot accept wage restraint in the hope of creating a stronger pound.'

And especially not when all that seemed to be happening was that the pound was getting weaker. On the morning of June 7, it was standing at £1.7240 on the New York Market. Early that afternoon, after a pub lunch of sandwiches and a beer, I went back to our headquarters to hear Frank Britton, Controller of the Electoral Reform Society, give us the result. The Press of the world seemed to be listening as Frank made his announcement—103,506 supporting the NEC and accepting the Contract, 90,387 against, at 6.8 percent the tiniest of majorities. Inwardly, I heaved one great big sigh of relief. Outwardly, all I said was: 'There it is then, lads. You've had the figures. That's that.' Sometimes it doesn't do to show your feelings too much. But when some reporter asked me what I thought the vote would do for the pound, I said: 'If you've invested in dollars you'd be catching a draught by sitting here. The pound will be up three or four cents.'

At mid-trading in New York, the pound rocketed up to £1.7580.

Some people might derive a good deal of self-glorification from a situation like that. I honestly didn't. I just thought it bloody crazy that people's lives, and jobs, and savings, should be subjected to that sort of whim.

The following month, in the Isle of Man, the agenda for our Annual Conference contained six motions dealing with wages. Four of them, including naturally one from Yorkshire, brought up that £100 figure again. But at the preceding NEC meeting I ruled the whole lot out of order, on the grounds that the ballot of the membership, which quite properly is the ultimate voice in our Union, had already determined our wages policy for the next year. We couldn't override that vote, and therefore the resolutions were invalidated. They didn't like it, of course, and when we came to the Conference my ruling was challenged by—no prizes for guessing—the Yorkshire delegation. But the delegates supported me, on a card vote, by 145,000 votes to 128,000. That was a nice fifty-ninth birthday present. I had got away with it!

Shortly after that Conference, I was given something quite different to think about. Derek Ezra's contract as Chairman of the Coal Board was about to run out, and Tony Benn, the Energy Minister, offered it to me. My immediate instinct was to refuse, but it was too important an offer to take lightly, and as usual I discussed it with Nellie. Anything I ever achieved in life, or any move I made, was always after discussion with her, and then with her backing. It wasn't just the usual husband-and-wife thing—Nellie had been in politics even before me. She started at sixteen, and so her advice was always worthwhile, and then, when I'd made a decision, she would always fight alongside me to get what I wanted.

On this occasion, the first question she asked was: 'What do you gain if you go as Chairman?' I thought about it for a minute and then said: 'Well, nothing really.'

'So, why change?' she said. 'You've got the respect of your men. You can't go any higher. I think we're better off as we are.'

And that, of course, was the decision I took. I went to see Tony and told him: 'I've thought about it, and I've come to the conclusion that I can't see any need to change the Chairmanship at the moment. Derek is doing a damn good job—let him get on with it.'

Why they wanted the change, I was never certain, though I heard whispers that the move started with a few members of the Board, and also from some of the civil servants, who had ideas of their own. But I wasn't going to have civil servants pulling the damn furrow in, and determining who was to be the next Chairman, and I didn't see anyone in our own organisation who had ambitions that way.

So I told Tony: 'The delaying tactics aren't helping the situation. A man can't be left waiting, wondering whether you're going to ask him to continue or not. You'll find yourself in a hell of a position. To remove any doubt, you ought to announce the reappointment as soon as possible.' I'm glad to say he took my advice, and the announcement was made the same week. I've had enough fights with Derek in my time, but in my view there wasn't a fellow in the country who fought harder for the coal industry than he. His heart was totally in it, and unlike some Chairmen of Boards there was never any suspicion of personal ambition about him, no feeling that he was using the job as a step towards other things.

He takes his job very seriously, and in all our arguments I've never seen him lose his temper—in fact, I've told him many times that it would have been better if he had stood up and shaken his hands around a bit and shown emotion. But he's not that kind of man. Above all, he's a man you would call 'dedicated'.

And he *did* understand what negotiation was all about. In 1977, with the Social Contract going to tatters, we held our Annual Conference at Tynemouth—we certainly got about!—and once again Yorkshire,

Scotland, and South Wales, always the so-called militants, had resolutions, with the usual threats attached, demanding massive wage increases. By now they'd dropped the £100. Instead, it was £110! Well, it got rejected, and we negotiated, and in March 1978 we achieved an increase of more than £8 for faceworkers, and commensurate increases for the rest.

That July, in Torquay this time, Yorkshire went all up-market on us. Their resolution contained its standard threat at the end, but this time they wanted us to 'secure a salary of £6,500 per year for face workers'. That was roughly equivalent to £130 a week, and the resolution was rejected. Not that it was the highest bid. Another resolution called for £135. I can't think why they stopped at that! Anyway, we negotiated quietly away again, and this time achieved an increase of £6.50p at the face, bringing the basic wage to £84.95p as from March 1979. This was overwhelmingly accepted by the members in a ballot vote, by 131,316 votes to 63,431.

In 1977, we hadn't thought it necessary to ballot the membership on the wage agreement for 1978, but in 1979 we made up for it by having two, the one I have just mentioned, and another at the end of the year which resulted from yet another fiasco.

In May, of course, we had had the General Election, and the Tories under Margaret Thatcher won a big victory. It came as no surprise to me. I had been predicting for a couple of years that Labour were bound to lose, for the simple reason that they were souring their supporters in the same way that they had done in the late Sixties.

Two months after the Election, at our Annual Conference (in Jersey, this time—*almost* abroad!) there were yet more tough resolutions on wages. They were composited into a resolution which demanded a basic £140 for face workers, and £80 for surface workers, with appropriate differentials for other grades. As was becoming normal, it added that if the Coal Board rejected these demands, the membership should be consulted 'on organising various forms of industrial action'.

Well, that motion was carried unanimously. Why? Partly perhaps because of a backlash against the previous years of holding back under Labour, and partly through utter resentment at Sir Geoffrey Howe's first, blatantly Tory Budget.

So we duly went to the Board, and negotiated, with those of us who were realists knowing perfectly well that £140 was out of the question. It would have represented an increase of around 65 percent! But after months of talking, we got the Board to make us an offer of 20 percent. To me, that was a great achievement, and it should have made a lot of the 'antis' happy, too, because at last it took the faceworkers above the magic £100—in fact to £101.95p.

We held a Special Meeting of the NEC to consider the offer, which I urged them to accept. Well, for once we got unanimity on the NEC, but not the way I wanted. The moderates had switched their position and joined the 'antis'—and *they* must have been a bit shaken by it, too—in voting to recommend non-acceptance to our members. Now, it's true that the Conference Resolution had not included the usual moderate 'get-out' by using the phrase 'failing a satisfactory response'. It had simply made a demand for a specific sum, without any caveats. So, taken literally, you could say that the moderates were only obeying that Conference decision.

But the truth was that it went deeper than that. They were fed up with years and years of the 'antis' voting against everything. They had had enough of all the years of mud-slinging they had had to endure, and the accusations of being too soft. So now they just said 'Bugger it! We're sick and tired of these people riding on our backs. We'll join them, for once, and recommend non-acceptance, and see what happens.'

I, the President, was the odd man out. I could hardly believe it was happening. I rounded on the lot of them and said: 'You're all bloody mad. Twenty percent and you're wanting to reject it! You really must be mad. When it comes to the ballot, the members will skin you.'

And so they did, going against the Executive, and accepting the offer, by a majority of 113,160 to 107,656. The day of the £100 a week miner had arrived, but I'd have been happier if it could have been arrived at a bit more gracefully. What's more, a turn-about like that can be demoralising for the Union. The Executive should try to lead, but seek to do it by reading its members' feelings correctly. It can't afford to have that sort of rebuff too often, because then it becomes a delegation of leadership to the members, and that's not what the NEC is elected to do.

The following year, 1980, the NEC had learned its lesson. It recommended acceptance of a 9.8 percent offer, as from January 1981, plus increases in bonus payments, and the members agreed by a substantial majority. In the ten years since I had taken office, the basic wages of faceworkers had risen from £27 to £111.95p, an increase of more than 300 percent, the lowest underground workers from £19 to £90.20p (just under 375 percent), and the lowest surface workers from £18 to £80.85p (almost 350 percent).

Wages and incentives, which I've dealt with in some detail, were by no means, of course, the only achievements for which we had to struggle. There is a long list of them, from pensions to safety in the pits, from concessionary coal to the ever-present problems of health, in particular the dreadful work-related diseases like pneumoconiosis. And one battle I should mention specially is the long-running, and often acrimonious, fight for early retirement for miners. With my own father, as I have described, having died in the pits, simply because he couldn't afford to retire, it was a battle I felt very personally.

At the start of 1977, a ballot of the members endorsed an agreement we had reached with the Board after literally years of negotiation. It was a complicated settlement, but its main provisions were that a miner, provided he had served twenty years underground, could retire at sixty-two in 1977, sixty-one in 1978, and finally our goal of sixty in 1979. He would, if he volunteered to do so, receive a lump sum payment of £500, and weekly payments, until the normal retiring age of sixty-five, representing an average 95 percent of his take-home pay in the year before he retired. In essence, it was a recognition of the fact that mining is the toughest industry there is.

Now, you might have been forgiven for believing that with all those things achieved, and with the Board and the Union united in their desire to make the 1974 Plan for Coal work, the Industry should have been well set for a period of retrenchment, and consolidation, and orderly progress. Well, it *should* have been, but no sooner had the Tories got into power than they started to stir up the hornets' nest all over again.

The stick with which they prodded that nest was the Coal Industry Act of 1980. In line with the monetarist line they had adopted, that Act cut right across the Plan for Coal, which had been accepted unanimously in Parliament. Now they were saying that the Industry had to be self-financing within three or four years, by 1983-84.

I knew that was impossible to achieve, unless they cut off huge chunks of the industry, to which we would never agree. And I said as much to David Howell, the Energy Minister. 'This is bloody stupid,' I told him, 'you're tying us hand and foot. We can't meet the conditions in this Act, and there'll be trouble.'

So he then started talking about all the financial assistance they were giving the industry, and how they intended to make it pay its own way. 'But you can't do it,' I said, 'because as soon as someone tries to fulfil the requirements of your Bill, you'll realise that it can only be done with a hell of a lot of problems.'

They didn't listen, of course, and went ahead and passed it in Parliament, although Labour did vote against it. Personally, I think Derek Ezra should have taken a tougher stand. He should have said, 'I'm not going to be Chairman of the Board under these conditions. It's physically impossible to achieve what you want.' But apparently he hadn't the courage to do that, although he must have known as well as I the trouble it would cause.

That trouble erupted at the start of 1981, though there had been rumblings of it for a few months previously. I had been getting an increasing flow of whispers from the Areas as to what the Board's Area directors were saying. They have various ways of getting their messages across, or simply flying kites. They, and the Union's Area officials, often pretend to be at daggers drawn, but in fact they frequently meet for a little tête-à-tête, perhaps over a drink or a meal, where various suggestions are put out and tried on for size.

Individual Areas, of course, wouldn't get the full picture of what was happening elsewhere, but it was all filtering back to me, as the President, and finally I became incensed, because it was clear that things were happening behind the scenes which shouldn't happen.In other words, as I had predicted, the Coal Board, as a statutory body, were preparing an attempt to make the provisions of the 1980 Act work, and in so doing were putting a match to a powder keg. So I demanded that we have a meeting of the full Executive, and the full Board, to discuss the whole situation.

Derek asked me: 'What about the other two unions, NACODS and BACM?'

'It doesn't matter to me if you want to arrange for their executives to be present,' I said. 'I don't mind, as long as we're all talking about the same problems, because we're all part of the tripartite agreement.'

The meeting was set for February 10, a Tuesday, and I went to it with a good deal of foreboding. It seemed clear to me that, for the third time in my Presidency, the Union was being forced into the position of all-out confrontation with a Tory Government and its policy.

Chapter Ten

Miners v Tories

There's a phrase I've used more than once in this book, which I make no excuse for using again. The whole thing was bloody stupid, and it should never have had to happen the way it did.

The reasons were a long chain of cause and effect and interrelated circumstances which combined to bring the Industry to the brink of another abyss. For a start, there was the 1980 Coal Industry Act. After the universal acceptance of the 1974 Plan for Coal, Maggie Thatcher and her cronies should have had the commonsense to see that mining should be left out of the tough monetary policies. Unfortunately, commonsense is a fairly rare commodity among politicians.

Then there was David Howell, the new boy at the Department of Energy. He was a pleasant enough fellow, and he certainly kept on *saying* he supported the Plan for Coal, but when it came to the crunch he didn't have the courage, or the seniority, or the plain nous to tell the Cabinet that it was impossible to place the financial restrictions on the industry which they wanted. This was in spite of the fact that I had on several occasions reminded him of what was contained in that key paragraph 78 of the Plan for Coal, namely—and I will repeat part of it—'the need to provide safeguards against short-term fluctuations in the price of competing fuels, and the need to take appropriate action if other public policies prevent commercial pricing or impose exceptional burdens on the Board'. It couldn't be plainer, really, could it?

At the same time, Howell, perhaps still a bit wet behind the ears, perhaps with a memory which did not extend back to 1972 or 1974, couldn't understand the temperament of the miners. He's not the first to fail in that respect, and some have had to learn it at their cost. If that lesson hasn't now be learned by everyone, it's time it was, because they can play around with lots of things, but not with the emotions of miners when it comes to an issue like jobs.

Then there was the attitude of the members of the Coal Board. The majority of them are mining engineers. I've accused them many times of being so conservative in their outlook that I get frightened for them. As full-time paid members, they're always looking to preserve their jobs, which is fair enough, except that the way they do it is by thinking of themselves more in terms of businessmen than as part of a great industry. They look at what they consider an 'uneconomic' pit, and they decide that it's an encumbrance to them, because the world at large doesn't consider it good business to keep something going if it's 'uneconomic'.

But it's a question of what you mean by 'uneconomic'. In a time of massive unemployment, is it better for the country to close a pit, with the probability that there won't be any other jobs going in the area, and therefore the necessity to pay out dole money, rather than keeping the men in work and at least getting *some* coal out of it, which sooner or later will be of use to the nation? I know my answer.

That huge unemployment, of course, was partly due to yet another factor, namely the slump which was hitting Britain in particular and falling, while at the same time we were increasing productivity, which was our part of the original bargain. The result was that the Board was being forced to put eight million tons of coal a year into stock.

'Forced', did I say? An odd word, that, in light of the fact that at the same time we were *importing* eight million tons of coal! Now, it's true that a little bit of coal will always need to be imported. People may think that coal is coal is coal. But it isn't. There are many different types, with different characteristics, and there is in particular a certain kind of coking coal, used in the steel industry for what they call 'baking powder', which we just don't have in these islands. But, apart from that, the main reason for the imports, especially by the CEGB, our biggest customer, was on the grounds of cheapness.

It was an irony that, in the days to come, this was an argument used against us. Typical of some public thinking was a letter in *The Times* which declared:'In the last decade the National Union of Mineworkers used its industrial muscle to push wages to a level where coal ceased to be priced competitively. As a result we were sucking in exports from Europe and elsewhere.'

I'm afraid the lad who wrote that was typical of many in his sheer ignorance. The truth was—and here was the irony—we were actually producing the *cheapest* coal in Europe. The difference was that all the other Governments concerned were subsidising their coal industries to a *far* greater extent than ours. In 1979, for example, France subsidised its coal to the tune of £28 a ton, West Germany £15. Britain—a mere £1.50p. It's true that American coal was cheaper, but that was easily explained. Most of their coal came from big opencast sites—often as much as ten square miles of coal. All they had to do was remove twenty feet of topsoil, and then they'd get to fifty feet of solid coal, which they would just take off with a drag line. There's a bit of difference between that and having to go three thousand feet down a shaft, and then a couple of miles underground, the last few hundred yards probably crawling, to get to the stuff.

The Coal Board *had* tried to stop the rot. The previous year, 1980, there was talk of the Steel Board placing a big order from America for their cheaper coal, and that had been forestalled by the Board subsidising our coal to the tune of £40 million. That's the Coal Board, not the Government, and yet here were the Government saying that the Industry had to be paying its own way within three years or so. It was ludicrous.

And finally—and this was the last factor in the equation—the Board themselves, I believe, saw that it *was* ludicrous, and that they were being asked to achieve the impossible. But, it is my firm belief, because of this innate desire the Board members have, to be seen as good businessmen, they weren't prepared to come out and say it themselves. That's why they embarked on this policy of pushing all these rumours of pit closures out into the Areas, knowing that they would soon filter back to the National Officials. I'll say it straight – they wanted us to do their dirty work for them. I told them to their faces that that was what I believed was happening, and of course they denied it, but from all that happened subsequently, that denial was shown to be false.

The meeting we had with the Board on February 10 turned out to be one of the rowdiest ever. It started off quietly enough. For the first forty minutes or so they gave us a résumé of what was happening in the Industry. We'd increased overall production. We'd increased productivity per manshift. We were getting better machine performance, better absentee figures, better safety figures. In fact, a huge success story the whole way through.

At the end of it I said: 'Well, what the hell are we meeting for? What's all the crisis about? What are all these rumours we keep getting?'

They replied that, because of the financial situation, they would like to take some action over certain pits. But we had already *been* discussing pit-closures in the normal procedures. In fact, since 1974, we had agreed the closure of about forty pits, either because they were worked out, or because the geological position was impossible. Only that week, for example, we had agreed the closure of the Lady Victoria pit in Scotland, because there was no practicable way of getting any more coal out of it. Another, in Durham, had been agreed because the water conditions had become impossible. So it was happening all the time.

'But if you're talking about a return to the Sixties,' I said, 'with pits being closed just for the sake of it, then I've got to tell you here and now that we won't allow it. We're not going to sterilise areas of valuable coal, which Britain is going to need, just because of short-term problems.'

Then all hell broke loose. Every one of our lads seemed to be talking, or shouting, at once, the general cry being, 'Tell us how many pits you're talking about.' It got so hectic that I had to change sides at the table, and sit next to Derek Ezra in order to get some control of the meeting. Derek, it appeared, didn't want to answer the question. But we pressed him and pressed him, and finally I said:'You might as well tell them, Derek. You must *know* the numbers.' That, at last, persuaded him to reply: 'Well, between twenty and fifty pits over the next five years.'

It was probably the most stupid statement he ever made. The fact was that he was only talking about a two-year closure programme of about twenty-three pits, eighteen of which had already been discussed, and a few already agreed. And, over a five-year period, it probably *would* have been about fifty pits in the normal course of events. But, by putting it blatantly as a target figure like that, he gave the 'militants' the perfect platform they needed. 'Fifty pits' became the issue, along with the projected loss of 30,000 jobs. It wasn't just the 'militants' either. The whole Executive, myself included, was angry and bitter.

As I told the Press after that meeting: 'We'll be going to the Cabinet to ask them to help, and if they won't we'll ballot the lads and ask if they'll support us in national strike action. It's economic madness to be importing coal and at the same time putting eight million tons of British coal to stock. I'm not going to allow the industry to be raped in this way.'

Said one NEC member: 'Mrs Thatcher has been out to get the miners since 1972 and 1974. If she throws down the gauntlet, I can assure her of one thing: we will pick it up.' Even before that meeting, Arthur Scargill had organised a ballot of Yorkshire members to ask if they supported the principle of industrial action to fight closures, and he had had an 86 percent vote saying 'Yes'. And with the threatened closure of a pit called Orgreave, near Sheffield, as the platform he needed, plans had already been made for a strike up there.

On Thursday, two days later, there was total unanimity on the NEC for once. We all knew perfectly well that sooner or later the pits which were under discussion would have to close, but it was supposed to be part of an orderly process, keeping pace with the opening of new pits like Selby, and the development of new seams in older-established pits. What the Board was seeking to do was accelerate those closures, not only to save money where they were 'uneconomic', but also to reduce our overall output.

We weren't having it. By 25 votes to none we agreed that the NEC was 'unanimous in its total opposition to the National Coal Board's plans to reduce the capacity of the industry with its resultant effects on manpower, and warns of the danger of industrial action starting in various Areas. If any attempt is made to put these plans into effect, either in individual Areas or collectively, the National Executive Committee will recommend, through a Ballot Vote, that the members take national strike action'. We also decided to seek an urgent meeting with the Government, but when my office phoned David Howell to arrange it, the reply was 'Yes, we can have a meeting, perhaps in a fortnight's time.'

'In no way are we having a meeting in a fortnight's time,' I said. 'We are having a meeting at the very earliest possible opportunity.' What he was thinking about I cannot imagine. Even at that point, apparently, he didn't realise that he had a major crisis on his hands.

It was suggested in many parts of the Press that this was to be a 'listening' meeting, with us talking and Howell doing the listening, but I let it be known very clearly that as far as I was concerned that was *not* what it was going to be. I wanted to know what the Government's position was, and I wanted some decisions taken.

I knew miners, and I *knew* the difference between the times of playing silly buggers and the times of being deadly serious. There was no doubt which this was. The members were boiling over, and that weekend the lads in South Wales began an unofficial strike in opposition to the closure of Coegnant pit in Glamorgan. In Kent, they began an overtime ban in protest against the threat to close one of their pits.

What I *couldn't* know was just how stubborn Mrs Thatcher was prepared to be. After all, only a few days previously, when trouble was obviously brewing, she had said: 'We have fixed the amount available for the industry. It is for the management of the National Coal Board to make the arrangement and we shall stand by that arrangement.' What's more, Michael Foot had asked her in the Commons: 'Is the Right Honourable Lady seriously saying that in this critical situation she will refuse to call together the tripartite meetings which we had on the Coal Industry, and which saved the Coal Industry following the experiences of 1974? Will she not decide to do it now, instead of being forced to do it later?' To that, she had given a typical Thatcher reply: 'No, Sir, and I am not forced to do many things.'

But, then, she hadn't faced the miners before. On Tuesday the 17th, Lawrence and I went down to the House of Commons to discuss the situation with Michael Foot and Len Murray. During that meeting, I phoned Derek Ezra to tell him that the uproar in the coalfields was rapidly getting out of control, with strikes being threatened by even the traditionally moderate Areas.

'We've got our NEC meeting on Thursday,' I told him, 'and Michael has suggested that we ought to try to hold tripartite talks with the Government tomorrow, to see if they can give us enough to calm things down a bit.'

Derek said he agreed with me and would see what he could do. As it happened, David Howell was at that moment at Downing Street, discussing the situation with the Prime Minister. I don't know what

Derek told him, but presumably he passed on my warning, and presumably Mrs Thatcher and Howell were at last prepared to heed it, because the first round of the talks were set for the following evening, February 18.

The Coal Board started that meeting by telling Howell that the financial position they had been put in by the 1980 Act was forcing them to bring the pit closures forward. They also said they needed help on the control of imports. Then I spoke on behalf of all the three mining unions —the other two had asked me to speak for them—and backed up what the Board had said, though perhaps putting it a bit more strongly! I emphasised that the first essential was to maximise production in our own industry, and that imports should only be used as a top-up operation if we couldn't ourselves produce the coal to meet the British demand—and, of course, for the specialised coals which we couldn't produce ourselves.

Now, that meeting was only supposed, according to officials of the Energy Department, to be a 'preliminary' meeting. Few people believed that anything could happen very fast, and many didn't believe they'd happen at all. After all, *The Times* had carried a large leader-page article the previous morning headed 'Miners v Tories: the supreme test that faces Mrs Thatcher'. With most of the country seeing it in those terms, and with her reputation for stubbornness, confirmed by what she had said in Parliament, it seemed unlikely in the extreme that she would bow the knee to us. But she did. Or, rather, Howell did on her behalf.

He said the Government was prepared to discuss the financial constraints on the industry. He was prepared to look at the question of imports, with a view to bringing them down to an 'irreducible level' (ie taking into account the need to import specialist coals), and by the same token he was therefore also prepared to look at the cost of keeping the threatened pits open. He told us he would look at these things with an open mind, with a view to coming to some different financial arrangements with the Coal Board, and with a view to removing the financial straitjacket which the 1980 Act had imposed.

It was as near to a total climb-down as we could have hoped. But I couldn't afford to let them off the hook too easily. 'There are many, many other things which have to be talked about,' I said, 'but I think what I've heard this evening will be sufficient for my Executive to cool things down. In the circumstances, though, we must obviously demand that the Coal Board withdraw that pit closure list.'

Derek Ezra immediately said: 'On the understanding of what the Minister has said, I'm prepared to withdraw the whole of that list. We will withdraw everything that was said on February 10, and we'll just go into the normal procedures.'

The following day, our NEC met and approved, by 15 votes to 8, the following resolution:—

(a) Accept the report of the meeting with the Minister of Energy as a victory for NUM policy and commonsense.

(b) Instruct the National Officials to meet the National Coal Board and other Unions to formulate the biggest financial package to put to the Government at the next meeting.

(c) In the meantime, we instruct our members who are now on strike to return to work immediately.

(d) In the event of an unsatisfactory outcome of our negotiations, we implement the resolution carried unanimously at the National Executive Committee on the 12th of February, 1981.

The plea to return to work took a bit of time to take effect. Men remained on strike in parts of South Wales, Yorkshire, Kent, Durham, and Scotland, but by the weekend those unofficial strikes had collapsed, although in many cases it was, understandably, only on the basis of 'wait and see' what concrete agreements we could reach.

I knew that was going to take a lot more hard bargaining, which wasn't going to be made any easier by the derision which Mrs Thatcher had had to suffer in Parliament for her reversal of policy, and by the rough ride which David Howell had been given by Tory back-benchers. As that Sunday's *Observer* quoted someone as saying: 'They didn't even wait to see the whites of the miners' eyes before climbing down.'

Well, if it was necessary to make sure they did see the whites of our eyes, I didn't mind. Following the first meeting with Howell, we met the Board, and I told them: 'This is a wonderful opportunity for you to put maximum pressure on the Government, and bring out the biggest financial list you can.

'For example, you've said that by further subsidies from the Board's own pocket you're hoping to reduce imports by two million tons, and then there's another three million you could whittle down with Government help. Well, don't just ask for that – ask for the whole five million.

'And while we're talking about closures, let's talk about a lot of other things – for example interest charges.'

Following the Plan for Coal in 1974, the Industry had had to spend fortunes—between £700 and £800 million a year of borrowed money—in rectifying the mistakes of the Sixties. That money was spent on the search for new coal, opening new pits, new machinery, the modernising of old pits, and so on. Mining *is* a costly industry, in more senses than one. In purely financial terms, we were having to pay £245 million a year in *interest charges* alone, to cover that borrowing – a figure which by the end of 1981 had risen to £400 million. It was a hell of a burden, and I believed the Government should help us with it.

'And until we do get imports down, and as long as we *have* to stock coal,' I said,'for God's sake let's get help with stocking costs as well.' That's an expensive business in itself. First you have to find, and either buy or rent, the land to put it on. Then it takes machines and men to put the coal down on the ground, and, later, machines and men to pick it up again. The Coal Board reckoned it cost them £5.60p a ton to stock coal, and with seven million tons currently on the ground, that was another financial burden we could do without.

We pushed the Board into drawing up a whole shopping list, which also included things like increases in the social grants for the miners' pension scheme, the redundant miners' payment scheme, the need for investment in research and development, regional grants, and financial assistance for converting industrial generating plants from oil to coal.

That meeting was on Monday, February 23, and two days later we went back with the Board for a second meeting with David Howell. The Board had told us they needed a little more time to work things out, but I didn't believe it, and I insisted that they put the list to the Minister.

So what did they do? They got up and said that they wanted help with the extra three million tons of imports that they wanted to eliminate, and that that, together with keeping the pits open longer than they had planned, would cost between £100 and £200 million. Just that. I was appalled that they should be aiming so low. They didn't realise that they were negotiating in a different direction from when they negotiated with us over wages. They thought they were still negotiating upwards, instead of downwards.

I was under no such illusion. 'Well, what the hell does *that* cover, Derek?' I asked. 'Does it cover the other two million tons of coal you've dealt with already, or rather, which you're proposing to deal with in this financial year? Does it include the cost of the interest charges, and the stocking charges, and the coking coal subsidies? Does it cover *any* of these?'

Derek looked at the Minister, and looked at me, and then said simply: 'No.'

'Well, why the hell doesn't it? I'll tell you what, I'm bloody glad you're not negotiating for *my* wages, Derek. I'd be living with clean teeth! This is negotiating gone mad. We agreed to a shopping list, and if you won't give it, I will.'

And I did. I trotted the whole thing out to the Minister. Well, straight away he told us that they'd already made a decision to put £50 million to one side to help with the conversions from oil to solid fuel, which was a start in the right direction. Then he said that they'd laid an Order on the floor of the House of Commons that day, with a view to increasing benefits under the redundant mineworkers' payments scheme.

That was a good move, too, except that I had to warn them: 'But we're not going to allow that to be used as an excuse for selling jobs. We're in the game to maximise jobs, and to maximise the industry, and maximise production in the future interests of Britain. Because we don't believe that the cheap coal which is currently available from abroad is going to be there for very long. Once it becomes commercially possible to produce gas and oil from coal, no one is going to want to export coal. So, if our consumers base all their needs on imported energy, we're going to find ourselves back in exactly the same position as in the Sixties. The same trap. The reliance on a flow of cheap oil which suddenly dried up.'

And so the argument went on. The Board agreed with us, but they weren't willing to do the negotiating. We were doing their job for them. I knew that it was far better, from a negotiating point of view, to be a bit on the high side, so that the Minister could feel he was whittling it down a bit, rather than be on the low side and expect him to keep on upping the ante.

The Board didn't seem to realise that, and in fact I told them privately:'I don't trust your negotiating abilities. And we're going to keep the pressure on you, to make sure you put forward the biggest possible scheme.'

Meanwhile, there was one matter which occurred during the dispute which perhaps I should clear up once and for all. During the third week of February, the *Daily Express* ran a story that I had had a secret meeting with Jim Prior, then the Secretary of State for Employment. The implication was that, as a result of this meeting, the Department of Energy had been outflanked and given no room for manoeuvre.

Jim Prior, whom I knew and liked, and who had a much more reasonable attitude towards the unions than some of his colleagues, issued a denial of the story and called it 'scandalous'. He was quite right in that denial. It *was* true, however, that about three weeks previously I did have a private meeting with him at his flat, lasting about fifteen minutes.

The real purpose of that meeting was nothing to do with the current problems. It was simply that he was testing the reactions of various union leaders to the proposed Trade Union Bill. But during that meeting he did refer to the rumblings of discontent which were going on, and he asked me:'What do you think we can do about this problem, Joe?'

I simply told him the facts. 'We need import controls,' I said, 'and help for our exports of coal, and help with our stocking costs. We need a lot of things which weren't contained in last year's Coal Industry Act, and the fact is, we can't be involved in financial straitjackets like that.'

His reaction was sympathetic, as I would have anticipated from a reasonable man, but he said very little. I wouldn't have expected him to say much anyway. But I was always meeting Ministers, from both Parties, and, if they asked me a question, it was only polite to answer. But there was certainly no collusion of the type which the Press suggested, and which was apparently being widely rumoured in the Cabinet.

As for our demands, after weeks and weeks of argument we finally got nearly everything we wanted, including, most important of all, the financial help to cut imports to a minimum and to keep the threatened pits open. Before the year was out, it's true, some of them had been closed. But it was done in the normal way, after consultation with us at pit level. Each and every pit was discussed on its own merits, and closure was only after our complete agreement. After all, even the most militant of miners knows that you can't dig coal with water up to your waist, or if there simply isn't any coal to dig.

Whether Maggie Thatcher knew what her climb-down would cost, I have no idea. Estimates for the first year were between £300 and £500 million. But I wasn't crowing. I didn't regard it as a victory for the miners, as such, but for the Industry, and for Britain, and for commonsense.

After that first meeting with Howell, the *Observer* quoted a Coal Board official as having admired what I did at the meeting, and saying: 'Joe could bargain the buttons off their trousers.' Well, I'm not sure I wanted *that!* But I wouldn't ask for a much better summary of anything I've been able to achieve.

Negotiating has been my life.

Chapter Eleven

The Philosophy of a Democratic Socialist

I've been called a lot of things in my time, and not all of them flattering. I've been called a militant, and an extremist, and a trouble-maker, and even sometimes a moderate. But I don't worry. Whether people call me a right-winger or a left-winger, or even a centre-winger, I don't give two hoots. I stood where I stood, and if people didn't understand, well, that's their problem, not mine.

But now, perhaps, is the time to spell out once and for all the philosophy in which I believe, and by which I have tried to guide my actions, both in politics and in trade unionism.

I am a Socialist. I was born a Socialist, and I shall die a Socialist. That is unalterable. But, in my attitude towards achieving Socialism, I believe in negotiation, and I believe in compromise. I make no excuse for it. There are those who want to change everything overnight. They try to jump from the ground over the top of the wall. Nine times out of ten, they fall back and hurt themselves. I believe in putting a ladder to the wall, and climbing it step by step.

I remember once, many years ago, when Will Paynter was General Secretary of the Union, we were coming up to Conference time, and we had two resolutions down on the agenda which were totally contradictory to each other. I can't even remember whether they were on the question of wages. It doesn't matter. The point is that I was Chairman of the committee which dealt with Conference arrangements, and I asked Will, who wanted them composited:'How the hell do you get a composite out of two resolutions, one of which says 'yes' and the other says 'no'?'

He replied:'Oh, Joe, we'll leave it to you.'

So we came up with a composite resolution which said 'maybe'. And it was carried unanimously!

Of course, it isn't often quite as down-the-middle as that, or no progress would be made at all. I'm simply trying to indicate that I believe progress should be made gradually, rather than by revolution, because the essence of change is that it should be achieved with the support of the majority of the people; and I'm not sure that there would be many in Britain who would favour a revolution. You have to carry people with you and, most of all, the people on whose votes you rely to win power.

As I have written more than once, my years as President were always tempered by the fact that there was an 'anti' block on the NEC who would nearly always vote against anything, and who certainly wouldn't agree with my ideas on how things should be achieved. Many of them, like Mick McGahey, were avowedly Communists. And I respect that. I prefer a man who states his convictions and applies to belong to a Party which meets those convictions. Others, like Arthur Scargill, were members of the Labour Party, though from some of the things that Arthur said from time to time I would have thought he would be an embarrassment to the International Marxists!

But I should make it clear, once and for all, that I am not anti-Communist as such. I'm against the way in which the Communist Party in Britain applies its ideas, always seeking confrontation. That gets nowhere, and even the most left-wing of union leaders finds, when he reaches the top of the tree, that it's just too exhausting and non-productive to have battles going on *all* the time. I also resented the fact that, as I knew perfectly well, our affairs were being discussed within the Communist Party, with a view to deciding the line which their members on our Executive should take. And that meant jumping on to the bandwagon of any dispute, whether it was right, wrong, or indifferent, without thinking it through properly.

At the same time, I have to say that I found both Mick and Arthur, and some of those who thought like them, to be fair colleagues when it came to discussing purely industrial matters. As the leaders of Scotland and Yorkshire, they did their jobs in their Areas successfully in their own way. Few problems came to National level, and when they did they were usually settled amicably. Mick, in particular, is one of the most reasonable men for the Board to get along with when he's ploughing his own furrow in Scotland, looking after the interests of the lads up there. But that reasonableness finishes the moment he gets over the border. Socially he's fine—in fact, a very kind man—but it's when he gets on the NEC as the Vice-President that the political animal comes out. Then, as he himself will admit, he'll vote against anything.

As for Communism internationally, it may surprise many people to know that, having visited many Communist countries, I believe that for a lot of them it may be a good thing. It seems to me that the systems are being made to work, even though the general opinion in those countries might be against me. People forget that many of those regimes started in countries which were way behind the rest of the world. Many of them hadn't even had an Industrial Revolution. So they have had to pull themselves up from nowhere.

Their single greatest weakness is the lack of freedom of speech and opinion. That is *not* something I would ever tolerate. I don't believe that even my opponents would deny that I have always been ready to listen to any argument, and at the same time expect people to listen to mine. But there is no intrinsic reason why that shouldn't be possible in a one-Party state, nor have I ever seen anything essentially *wrong* in a one-Party state. As I pointed out in an earlier chapter, there was a great deal more democracy, and progress achieved, on Ashton Council when it was one-Party than when it acquired an Opposition.

In fact, I believe that democratic socialism, which is what I want to see achieved, means accepting disciplines, not only self-discipline, but also collective discipline. And those disciplines are not always apparent when you have too much of a democratic society. Again, Communist colleagues may find it strange to read this, but perhaps I am a bit in advance of their position in this respect.

For example, when I visited India, I found that one of the problems there was that nobody could be given the sack. That's very inefficient. It was 1975, at the Miners' International Federation Congress in Delhi, and during a conversation with the Indian President and the Prime Minister, Mrs Gandhi, I asked them: 'Do you think it's possible to solve the problems of India and still remain a true democracy?'

They said 'Yes', but I told them I thought the answer was 'No'. And from what I saw a few days later, I thought my argument was proved. From Delhi, we went to Calcutta, where the utter desolation and poverty was impossible to describe. From there, we went to visit some of the mining regions in the North Eastern States, near the Nepal border. As we drove along those dusty roads, through straggly little villages, we could see the miners walking along with their picks and shovels on their shoulders, but not too often with shoes on their feet.

There were the women, too, carrying coal in baskets on their heads, and I was appalled to hear how many tons they were expected to carry from one place to another each day. I couldn't help thinking that perhaps it needed a bit of a dictator to put things right.

Then, suddenly, we came to a village where everything was quite different. It was still a mining village, but everything looked orderly, the streets were paved and tidy, even the gardens were green. We came to the pithead, and that, too, was neat and well-kept, with the workers wearing proper safety shoes, helmets, and so on. Lo and behold, when I was introduced to the colliery manager, he turned out to be a Polish mining engineer. With a little discipline, he had made things run smoothly. He had proved that by being a bit authoritarian it was possible to change the whole pattern.

Even as a democratic socialist, I have feeling that sometimes you can choke on democracy.

I don't believe it's democracy to allow people to please themselves what the hell they do. That's anarchy. The laws of the land are there and have to be obeyed. That's discipline. I couldn't ask miners to go into the pits and ignore the laws, on safety and everything else, which govern the production of coal. They have to follow the rules and regulations, and if they want to change them, well, there are procedures for doing it, just as there are for the laws of the land.

So I'm not talking about outright dictatorship, but a bit more discipline and a bit more authority. In India, for example, as I saw, caste is taken as being more important than people's lives. And there comes a time when you have to ask yourself, 'Which is more important—people being able to enjoy an orderly and well-provided life, or the fanaticism of long-forgotten rites and gods which dictates how things should be?' As a realist, I say that it's more important that people should have decent lives, and that it is ridiculous that they should be starving as a result of old religious laws.

But then, I *would* think that. I start off from the basic premise that everyone is equal. Nobody's more equal. I remember when I first met Prince Charles, he asked me what I liked to be called, and I said 'Joe'. 'In that case, I like to be called 'Charlie',' he said, and that's how it has remained. It was the same position on which I insisted with some of my black colleagues in the Union, which does have a few black miners. They would come to meetings and want special treatment because they were black.

'You're not *having* special treatment because you're black,' I would tell them. 'You're no more equal than I am. You're no less equal, but you're no more equal. So, if you want equality, it's equality you shall have.'

From that belief in equality, it seems natural to me to accept totally the principle: 'From each according to his ability, to each according to his need.' I have fought all my life for the time when my members, and people as a whole, are not worse off when they retire, or when they are sick, or when they are disabled, or when they are, through no fault of their own, unemployed. That is what democratic socialism, to me, should be about.

But I want everyone to be pulled *up* to a decent standard, not have a levelling down. As I said once at an Area Conference:'What is wrong with the leader of a union wanting a nice house for each of his members to live in? What is wrong with wanting a good standard of living for his wife and family, a good education for the children, a Jaguar at the front door to take him to work, and a Mini at the side to take his wife shopping?'

It got a great round of applause, although we're still a long way from achieving it. But I don't believe those aims make a person any less of a socialist. In fact, I think that where many of the Communist regimes have gone wrong is that they have built up a new elite who enjoy all the old privileges which were afforded to the Lords and Ladies under the previous systems.

Mind you, there are those on the so-called Left wing in Britain who haven't held back in feathering their own nests very comfortably. It led me once to a furious row when I was on a visit to Rumania, as a member of a delegation from the National Executive of the Labour Party. Frank Lane, of the NUR, was with us, and Peggy Herbison. The leader of the delegation, since someone else had dropped out, was Jennie Lee.

On the way over in the plane, I was reading *The Times*, and I happened to notice in it an advertisement offering a property for sale outside London. It was the estate which Jennie, and her late husband Aneurin Bevan, had enjoyed. I was interested, because Aneurin had always been something of a hero of mine. The reserve price on that estate was £125,000.

Well, we got to Bucharest, and in due course we were taken to meet Mr Ceausescu, the Rumanian leader. Jennie performed the introductions, and when she came to me she said: 'Now I'd like you to meet Mr Gormley, who is an ultra-right-wing socialist.' That made me flaming mad, and the British ambassador, who could see how angry I was, grabbed my hand and pulled me back a bit.

So we sat down and talked for two or three hours, and towards the end of the discussion I found that Ceausescu and I were arguing in an exactly similar way as to how we would solve the economic problems facing Europe. I suddenly broke into the argument and said: 'This is fascinating. Here am I, introduced to you, Mr Ceausescu, as an ultra-right-wing socialist. And there are you, the head of a socialist state, the leader of a Communist Party. Yet you and I are agreeing on everything we should do to solve these problems. It makes me wonder who's looking at who, and whether you're left or right in the eye of the beholder.'

He just smiled, and at least Jennie Lee had the decency to blush. But when we got back to the hotel, I gave her a warning.

'Jennie,' I said, 'never be so stupid as to do that again. And what's more, let me give you one little word of advice. Joe Gormley, for all his sins as a socialist, will never be able to put any money together. Yet you and Aneurin, he as a miner at a time of low wages, and you as the daughter of a miner, were able to amass a fortune sufficient to let you put an estate on the market with a reserve price of £125,000. So don't talk to *me* about anti-materialism, girl. And don't ever do that to me again.'

She said nothing, and went upstairs to her room. But then, what *could* she say?

What I cannot stand is hypocrisy like that, whether it comes from individuals or from nations, and certainly there's a massive amount of it in international politics. For example, I used to get exasperated by Jimmy Carter and all his grandiose statements about how America was leading the world in the fight for civil rights and freedom of speech. It was a load of twaddle. It came from the leader of a country where everyone starts ranting and raving the moment a man says he's a Communist or a Socialist. That's an attitude which exists even among working class people in America, even among miners.

There's no freedom if it doesn't include freedom of political thinking, freedom of religious thinking, the freedom to vote, freedom from racial inequality.

But there's hypocrisy on the other side of the world, too. Leonid Brezhnev gets up and talks about peace in the world, and gets well-supported by the British Communist Party, arguing that we should cut our defence expenditure to nil, yet saying nothing about the huge build-up of arms in the Eastern Bloc. I've said this to members of Politburos in many countries of Eastern Europe—if we talk about peace, then for God's sake *make* peace, rather than spend fortunes making goods whose sole purpose is destruction.

They pretend that they believe in the notion of co-existence, but that's hypocrisy, too. If I believed what they believe, namely that the world will one day all be ruled by Communism, I would say so. I would say, 'Within a peaceful framework we will be working gradually towards persuading people to our way of thinking.' But they don't do that. They simply produce more and more arms as a means of frightening people into believing the inevitability of Communism.

This is one reason why, during my term of office, I tried to get the NUM increasingly involved in international affairs, even to the extent of forming an international department at our headquarters. Because mining is unique among industries. Other groups of workers may share certain things in common, but miners alone share that particular degree of discomfort and danger. When a miner talks to another miner, from another country, his first thought is that it is to a miner he is talking, not to a foreigner.

That communality of interest is a marvellous stepping-stone to breaking down barriers of politics, or even barriers of barbed wire—many mines cross borders! It's not at all uncommon for a Western European mine to have Communist soil at the other end of the workings. When you're spending all your working life fighting the same dangers, and the same geological conditions, as your neighbour, it's difficult to get too aggravated about some of the other facets of life.

That's why, in the many years I was Vice-President of the Miners International Federation, I gave a great deal of time to the job. It's a bridge-builder. That, too, is why the NUM has gone to great lengths to help miners in parts of the world where they have suffered under harsh regimes, even to the extent, in 1977, of sending a delegation to Chile under the guise of tourists. We knew that, as a miners' delegation, they wouldn't be allowed in, so we made elaborate arrangements to hide the fact that they were who they were. Once they got there, we had contacts who were able to get them to talk to the Chilean miners, and find out what was happening to them, following the coup which deposed Allende. Since then, we have been able to help them quite a lot, both materially and financially.

We do everything we can to help our less fortunate colleagues, and that's why I was livid when Bernard Levin, in *The Times*, had the temerity to attack the Union and myself for not doing enough to help a Russian miner, Vladimir Klebanov, who had been sent to one of their psychiatric hospitals. I had, in fact, as I wrote in *The Times* in an article of reply, raised the case not only of Klebanov, but also of a dozen other Russian miners, with the Soviet Miners' Union—we had probably been fighting these battles long before Levin had even heard of them. I had raised the case first by letter, then later face to face with Mr Effremenko, then the leader of the Soviet Miners. And when *that,* too, failed to get a satisfactory response, we raised the matter with the International Labour Organisation in Geneva.

This had all happened in 1977 and 1978, three years before Levin's article, and had he had the courtesy, or even the good sense of journalism, to telephone us and ask, we could have told him. But he didn't, and so once again an unnecessary slur was cast on the Union. It was typical of the sort of thoughtless and irresponsible journalism which gives the profession a bad name.

Not only do we send delegations all over the world, but I made sure that our Annual Conferences were always addressed by representatives of foreign miners, and that includes all sorts of mining, tin, diamonds, copper and whatever. They came from every corner, from Norway to Australia, from China to Bolivia. But, as I told my last Annual Conference, in July 1981: 'I have one regret. As I am coming to the back end of my useful life as President, it is the fact that we have not been able to get the whole of the mining fraternity assembled round one Conference chamber in order that they could agree a common strategy on peace and détente, which we could then put to the wider Trade Union Movement, and then put the pressure on the politicians and say, 'This madness has gone on long enough. Let's call a halt to it.'

Well, I was being a bit pessimistic, because at the end of November 1981 I finally brought that dream of mine to reality, when we held an International Miners' Conference on Peace and Détente up in Newcastle.

They say there's no point in taking coals to Newcastle, because that was where all the coal used to be exported from. I just hope we managed to export a bit of peace as well.

We could do with some of that within the Labour Movement, too, without charades like the Special Conference of 1980. It was supposed to discuss new methods of electing the Party leader, but it didn't discuss aything too much, because it was a load of shouting. It was typical of what had been starting to happen over a few years, with people coming into the Party who were simply not willing to listen to anybody else's point of view.

But I knew it was going to be a farce. Our members had mandated us to vote for the status quo, but I said to the Executive: 'It's a bit stupid to go into a conference knowing that that is not a resolution which is going to be debated anyway. And, if that's not on the agenda, you'll nullify your own damn vote. And it's too important for the NUM not to register its vote.' So we looked at each different formula, and decided to support the one which gave 50 percent of the votes to the Parliamentary Party, and 25 percent each to the unions and the constituency Parties. Failing that, we would vote for whichever gave the Parliamentary Party the highest percentage.

But, just before the Conference started, I looked at one resolution which, if carried, would have stopped all the arguments. It said, in effect, that the whole matter should not be debated. I got my Executive to agree to support that resolution, and then went and talked to a group of other union leaders, including David Basnett of the MGWU, and Terry Duffy of the AUEW. 'Listen,' I said,'we can get out of a bloody problem here. If we all demand that that resolution's taken, and voted on, and if we support it, we can do away with all the acrimonious debate.'

But they just said:'Oh, well, it's a bit late now, Joe.'

'How is it too bloody late?' I said. 'Just yesterday I got my Executive Committee to agree that we'll vote for this resolution before anything else. And you can do the same.'

But of course, they couldn't, because they weren't in proper control of their delegations anyway. So their refusal to move meant that we had to go through the farce of the Conference, and then a further farce when it came to the voting. Because we could *still* have got the 50 percent for the Parliamentary Party if it hadn't been for the stubbornness of the AUEW.

They had been mandated to support a resolution giving 51 percent to the MPs, but when that failed to carry we got to the vote on giving them the 50 percent. And they were proposing to abstain, just because it wasn't exactly what they had been mandated to do. I went to the rostrum and said:'For God's sake, use your bloody vote. What's the good of coming to Conference and then nullifying your vote by not voting?'

But I was told by delegates from the AUEW: 'Our vote must only be to give the absolute majority to the Parliamentary Party' . . . even though that had already been defeated.

'Get the hell,' I said,'what sort of bleeding decision is *that?*' If they had voted according to commonsense, the 50 percent would have been carried. I just hope their rank and file members were proud of them.

As for me, I left that Conference before the final vote was even taken, because I was so disgusted by the way the whole thing had been conducted. Our delegation cast its votes, of course, but after twenty-five years of going to Labour Party Conferences, I was totally saddened that we had reached a point where people were no longer prepared to listen to each other.

I was saddened, too, by the fact that following that Conference a number of prominent members of the Party saw fit to break away and form the SDP. I thought then, and still do, that when it comes to a General Election, the Tories and Labour will still retain the bulk of their traditional support. But, where there is movement to the SDP, it will more likely come from Labour, and the danger therefore is of helping the Tories to retain power for much longer than they should naturally do.

Shirley Williams was the one real loss. I was sorry when she lost her seat in the Election of 1979, but I think that had she fought on within the Labour Party she would have found a seat. I believe the Party is poorer without her. As for the others, well, Roy Jenkins burned his boats, I thought, when he went off to Europe; Bill Rodgers, though he was Minister of Transport, was never much of a shining light—some of these lads become intellectuals overnight! And I think the other lad, David Owen, was pushed forward a bit too soon and too fast, and therefore became over-ambitious, with a false sense of his own importance. I don't think there's much future for him outside the Labour Party.

Now, it may seem strange to some people that I, as a long-time union leader, shouldn't have been delighted that the unions should have been given so much power in choosing the Leader of the Party. My first reason sprang from the purely constitutional aspect of it, because the argument was about choosing a Leader of the Parliamentary Party. It really doesn't make a blind bit of difference *what* the Party decides. The *fact* of the matter is that once MPs are elected to Parliament—by the whole voting population, not just that small percentage who are the enrolled members of any Party—then it is they who will choose a leader from among their own ranks to be Prime Minister. Because a Prime Minister can only function if elected to Parliament, and then if he or she commands a majority support in whichever Party holds the Parliamentary majority. That's the only way it can work, and I therefore believe that that whole Special Conference was kicking against a brick wall anyway.

The second reason is based on my view of the relationship between the Trade Union Movement and the Labour Party. It's a relationship which has frequently been misunderstood, and also frequently abused, and although it is a subject big enough for several books on its own, I will briefly put my own views.

I start from the position that, because of its origins, you can't have a Labour Party without the Trade Union Movement. Nor can you have a Trade Union Movement that is going to be of any value without a Party, which at the moment is the Labour Party. So it is naive for anyone to argue that the Movement should not be involved in politics.

Nor should anyone feel any guilt about that. When the Tories are in power, no one denies that they introduce legislation which accords with the thinking of their traditional area of support, namely big business. So why should we hesitate to persuade the Labour Party to bring in legislation which has been thrashed out at Congress, which, as well as representing the eleven million or so workers who want to be organised, also fights for the eleven million or so who don't? After all, the Welfare State, which benefits all, including millions who vote Tory, only came into being as a result of pressure which originally stemmed from the Trade Unions.

So, the first thing a Labour Government should do is to realise that any legislation it wants to get through should have the tacit support of the Trade Union Movement. But that is a very different thing from the bleating which always goes on, when Labour is in power, about the Unions running the country. When the Tories are in power, big business may try to persuade them about certain policies, but in the end it's still the MPs who have to make the decisions, and the same applies to Labour.

It's also true of both sides that if they *fail* to legislate in the interests of their traditional supporters, then they are likely to lose the next Election, though I think this is more so in the case of Labour. This is partly because I believe that the hard-rock, traditional Tory support is stronger than Labour's, and partly because there's undoubtedly a tendency among people, when they've improved their circumstances, to believe that voting Tory makes them 'posher'. They think that it will help consolidate their newly-achieved aspirations. But to me that's an irony, because in most cases it was the Labour Party which made those aspirations possible.

Not that I don't have a certain sympathy with someone in that position. Once a man feels that he has something to conserve, it can be hard to convince him that he ought to remain a Socialist.

So any Labour Government has to be wary about the sorts of laws it wants to make, if it is to retain the support it needs. And, in framing those laws, it needs to consult, among others, the TUC. But that *doesn't* mean the same thing as saying that the TUC can direct a Labour Government. What's more, I believe it's very important that the TUC should *not* be seen to be in the pocket of a Labour Government. That was why I was so annoyed when Denis Healey brought out a Budget, in 1977, whose provisions were conditional on what the Unions did in their wage negotiations.

As I said at the time: 'The way to present the Budget is to *present* the Budget, not put conditions on part of it which rely on the goodwill of somebody else.' In the end, the Government is there to govern.

That, too, was one of the reasons I was so opposed to the Social Contract. Yes, we went along with it for a couple of years, to help the Labour Government, but it put us in a false position. Our role in society is to look after our members, not run the country. What's more, I think the TUC overstepped its powers in trying to interfere with the authority of the individual unions. In point of fact, the TUC doesn't *have* any powers—it's a federation, and all its members are autonomous.

What particularly worried a lot of us at the time was that the Social Contract was organised by, and backed by, a few of the huge unions with big block votes, but who themselves do no negotiating. In fact, I said to Jack Jones of the Transport and General Workers Union at the time:'Keep out of my road, mate, because you don't negotiate a bloody thing. So get out of the way and let those who have to negotiate negotiate.'

The point was that they *don't* negotiate at national level. It's all done down the line, often at shop floor level. It's the same with the AUEW. True, they negotiate across the board for a flat rate increase which they think should apply. But, when you get a little shop with about twenty or thirty engineers in it, they can negotiate what the hell they like. It's outside the scope of any wages policy. There are thousands of small shops like that, and the managers are only too happy to negotiate generous bonus and incentive schemes to keep production up and attract the top craftsmen. Again, it's the same with the Municipal and General Workers Union, because they have different trade groups, and each group negotiates in its own right.

By contrast, the NUM is one of those unions which negotiate at national level. Agreements have to apply across the country, and on the same basis for all. So the Social Contract affected people like us much more than some of those huge unions with millions of votes. What's more, it only applied to those workers whose unions were affiliated to the TUC. But there were an equal number of workers *outside* that framework, and it didn't apply to them at all, so it was not only impractical from the start, but also unfair in its whole conception.

The trouble was that, as we have seen so often in the history of the Labour Party, the higher ranks were filled by people—they call themselves intellectuals—who have little to do with the grass roots of the Movement. I'm talking about people from the middle class, often from the professions, who have come to dominate Party thinking, the Harold Wilsons, the Barbara Castles, the Tony Benns, even the Michael Foots.

Now, I don't say that someone from those backgrounds can't make a good member of the Labour Party. I thought Clement Attlee made a first-class leader, and I even had a great deal of admiration for Gaitskell as a man who stuck to his convictions, even though those convictions were often not mine. But I do believe that they are essentially a different kind of Socialist from the man who has spent his working life wondering where the next butty, or the next pair of shoes, is coming from. They have never experienced that, and you cannot *imagine* experience. You have to experience experience.

Another trouble is that they usually start off as radicals, believing that they can change the world overnight, and then, when they get power, come around to a more middle-of-the-road point of view, realising that progress has to be gradual—well, it doesn't *have* to be gradual, but the alternative is revolution, and I don't happen to believe that Britain, with its basically liberal traditions, is a suitable seed bed for revolution.

But, to me, that middle-of-the-road, practical approach to progress is a ground that is more properly occupied by trade unionists. The whole experience of the Union Movement has taught us that basic lesson. So it's a matter of great regret to me that so few unionists have achieved positions of real power in the Party. I believe that they have a warmth, and an emotion, and a gut feeling of what the Party is all about, which is lacking in the 'intellectual' Socialists. Aneurin Bevan had that quality, and Jim Griffiths before him. Aneurin unfortunately died young, with still maybe twenty or twenty-five years of Parliamentary time in front of him. Had he not died, I believe that in the succeeding decade he could have moulded things completely differently.

And that would have been a good thing. I firmly believe that we are losing a lot of our traditional support because we no longer seem to be a Party of warmth and emotion, a Party not only of radicalism, but a Party of necessary change, and a Party which explained why that change was necessary. Somewhere, especially in the last decade, we have lost out, and there is increasing cynicism about the way in which Labour MPs, when they get into the House of Commons, seem to turn into different people from those who announced their platforms in order to get nomination.

Part of the blame may lie at the door of the Unions themselves. It always used to be the case that the Trade Union representatives on the NEC of the Party stuck pretty well together. As a united bloc, they were able to maintain a useful steadying influence on Party policies, preventing it from adopting some of the wilder schemes to which it later fell prey. But, from the moment that Jack Jones was nominated to the NEC, a division came in our ranks. He immediately sided with people like Ian Mikardo and Barbara Castle on political issues, and Trade Union solidarity was broken.

It's also true that a great deal of apathy has grown up among the rank and file. When I was in the pits, we would get two or three hundred members at a Branch meeting. Today, meetings would usually attract about a tenth of that number, and they often tend to be the Communists and their fellow-travellers. They are the activists, the ones who study all the possible arguments so that they can answer them, the ones who make sure they turn up to meetings. I don't blame them for that at all. They have their point of view, and they are perfectly entitled to put it, and if no one else turns up to the meetings, that's not their fault.

So ordinary, middle-of-the-road union members should be aware of the danger they run through apathy. Maybe they feel that the Movement has already achieved most of what they want, but they should be warned that, if they are not prepared to fight to preserve those gains, they run the risk of losing the lot.

Several other points should be made about unions. The first is that I have always believed strongly in one-union industries. I think that the position where an industry has to negotiate with a dozen different unions is quite absurd, leading to the demarcation disputes and the wage differentials which plague productivity. I would like to see us with a set-up like that of West Germany, where there are just sixteen unions. But that, of course, was a structure created from scratch after the War, and I can't see it happening in Britain. Personal ambitions and positions come far too much into the argument; too many leaders say, 'Ah well, if we amalgamate, my position will be lost.' There are the officials down the line, too, who have hopes that they will eventually be elected to the top jobs. So we just have to accept that we are suffering from history in that respect. Imposition of the structure by Government simply wouldn't be accepted, and it might be thirty years before we start to move towards what I would regard as sanity.

The second point is that unions, whether they like it or not, should be realists, and recognise that they exist within a capitalist framework. Now, the way the world works, you need money to provide jobs. Even in a Communist state, a worker doesn't keep everything he earns in his pocket. Some of it has to be held back for new machinery and the general betterment of the enterprise. Given that that is the case, and that the system demands that investment should pay dividends, the unions should long ago have got into the act so that those dividends would return, not to a comparatively few wealthy individuals, but to their members, the workers.

The NUM, for instance, through its pension scheme, which it administers jointly with the Coal Board, has vast investments, running right across the spectrum of industry and property. And we have put great emphasis on creating jobs in those areas which have been affected by a lot of pit closures—in the last two years of my Presidency, something like £70 million in the North-East and North-West alone. When the profits come, they return to the miners.

To me, that's real Socialism, sensible Socialism. And, if the Trade Unions had adopted that policy from the start, we would have owned three-quarters of Britain by now. There would have been no need for nationalisation. For years and years we were following some stupid point of so-called principle and lending money to people like the Co-op Bank at 3 and 4 percent. But *they* were then lending it to people like Charlie Clore, and the big property developers, and getting 9 and 10 percent on the money—*our* money!

If we had said, 'No, *we'll* lend the money, and *we'll* get the 10 percent', we could have owned the Clores and the lot of them. Instead, we just said, 'Ah well, that's not for us. We shouldn't be dealing with big business.' But of course trade unions *are* big business.

The final point I want to make is one which I have already expressed in so far as it relates to the NUM. But as a Socialist who also happens to believe in democracy, I would repeat it again and again and again. It is the people of Britain who decide who shall govern them. Not the unions. In the same way that I, as a union leader, was only there on a catch-as-catch-can basis. If they didn't like what I was doing, there were always democratic ways of getting rid of me.

So I say that, when the people of Britain have decided—irrespective of all the work and all the effort and all the arguments that one side or the other has put forward at a General Election—to vote Tory rather than Labour, no group of unions (and, after all, no more than 50 percent of them are affiliated to the Labour Party anyway) has the right to say, 'Well, the people have voted Tory, but we think they're wrong, and therefore we will immediately set out to destroy the Tory Government.' Because that leads to the total breakdown of democracy.

I want to lay to rest forever the ghost of the belief that it was the miners who brought down Edward Heath. It was not. He and his advisers brought themselves down. It was not of our doing, and it was certainly not of my wishing. Of *course* I would prefer to see a Labour

Government than a Tory one. But I would always want it done democratically, because if you haven't been able to persuade the majority of the people in the first place, the victory is an utterly empty victory.

In the early part of 1981, with the Tories' policies having brought the country to a ruinous degree of unemployment, a fellow union leader made a speech in Scotland in which he said that the whole Trade Union Movement should unite to bring down the Government. In my philosophy, that was a completely stupid thing to say. As I said at the time: 'What does he mean? I ask all those people who say the same thing, what is it they are waiting for? Are they waiting for the miners, knowing that theirs is the only union which is likely to be followed?'

If the miners, as a result of the row over pit closures, had got the bit between their teeth, they would have got an army of nearly three million unemployed following them. But for the wrong reasons. Not because of any argument relating to the miners, but with a view to changing the Government.

So, take the argument to its logical conclusion. Let's suppose that had happened, and that all the other unions had come out in support of us—not that they would have done; they would have forgotten all about *our* arguments—and that they had been backed by that army of unemployed. Then, suppose that they had succeeded in forcing a General Election. All this would have been very easy to achieve in 1981. It would have been *very* easy for the NUM to have appeared as a sort of national hero to all those unemployed.

But *then* suppose that the country, in all its wisdom, and through the votes of twenty-five million or so individuals, and having heard all the arguments, decided that it would re-elect a Tory Government. What would we have done? Would we have said, 'Let's have another go. Let's shift 'em again. Let's tell the people of Britain they're wrong?' Or it wouldn't even have needed to be a Tory Government. What if we didn't agree with what a Labour Government was doing? Would we do the same?

That way lies disaster. We would get to the position where other people would have to step in to take control, and that would mean, in my opinion, not a Left-wing Government, but an ultra-Right-wing Government, whose prime objective would be to destroy the Labour and Trade Union Movement—just as Hitler did. And it would take a hell of a long time to build that Movement up again.

So, when you have the position of leadership in a union like the National Union of Mineworkers, knowing the strength which that union possesses, knowing the large degree of public sympathy which it enjoys, you have to be sure to use that power very, very carefully indeed.

It has been said that the Miners are the soul of the Labour Party. Well, perhaps that was once true. But now more the conscience. That stems from 1926, when the rest of the Trade Union Movement abandoned the Miners, and left them standing alone, as a result of which they were defeated. They were defeated, but they were not destroyed, nor has that guilt which pervades the rest of the Labour and Trade Union Movements ever been destroyed.

So the Miners will always remain both the soul *and* the conscience of the Labour Movement. The Miners—what shall I say?—the Miners are at the heart of the matter.

Chapter Twelve

The Future of Energy

If a country is to succeed in the modern world, its prime need can be summed up in one word—Energy. Without Energy, the most grandiose of schemes falls flat on its face. It's pretty obvious that this must be true of industrialised societies. But it applies to agricultural societies as well, if they are to earn their living. Fuel for tractors and combine harvesters, power for milking machines or the tools of the timber trade—they are essential if a nation is to produce its goods economically.

The reasons why India is in the parlous state she is all boil down to the same thing—the speed of her economy is geared to the speed of the bullock. Until that is changed, she will never be able to solve all her problems.

Britain is blessed with abundant Energy. We have oil. We have natural gas. We have the scientific know-how to produce nuclear energy. And we have coal. We have coal to last for four hundred years. That isn't a guess; we *know* the reserves are there, even though in some cases, like the Vale of Belvoir, we may have to see off the likes of the Duke of Rutland to get at them.

The tragedy of Britain, especially since the Second World War, is that we have handled this national inheritance with the careful husbandry of the Prodigal Son, and the long-term strategy of the Grand Old Duke of York. In the Mining Industry particularly, we have been taken up to the top of the hill and down again like some sort of industrial yo-yo. And unfortunately, unlike the Duke of York's lads, for every ten thousand men who went to the top of the hill the first time, there were only nine thousand, or eight thousand, who remained to go back up it the second and third times.

The answer lies in something for which we have fought for decades—a co-ordinated National Energy Policy.

It is something in which I believe passionately, and something which I believe it is ludicrous in the extreme that we have not got. But, before I embark on the subject, and before anyone jumps to any conclusions about my fervour on the question, I have to state unequivocally that my beliefs are *not* some sort of selfish rationalisation from my origins as a miner. But they *are* founded on the experience I have gained as a miner and as an official of the Miners' Union.

For a start, I have to say that Energy should remain totally outside the political spectrum, and outside political debate. To many, both of the Left and of the Right, that will be anathema. They will argue that everything is political. Well, I don't believe that's true. I don't believe, for instance, that education should be subject to the swings and roundabouts of political fortune. There's no necessity for it. They don't vary the system in the United States just because a Republican is voted in rather than a Democrat, nor is it so in most countries. It seems to me patently absurd that in one year it is felt that we need one teacher for every fifteen pupils, and the next year, because of a change of government, one to thirty.

So I say that there *are* areas of our national life which should be excluded from the political arena, areas which should be organised by consensus, and then altered only by the decisions, in the national interest, of independent bodies. And Energy is most certainly one of them.

Now, I'm not for a moment saying that the blame for not having done this is the fault of any one political Party. In fact, if anything, the Tories have, when it came to the crunch, been more susceptible to the realities of the situation than Labour. We had Dick Marsh—known as the East End collier!—and Roy Mason, who came from mining stock, and Eric Varley, and Tony Benn. Yet only one of them, Eric Varley, chose to march into the Ministry and say, 'This is a load of nonsense. We have *got* to get Energy on a proper footing.'

On the question of imports, for example, Tony Benn knew perfectly well what our arguments were, and he could have acted to close the floodgates which Ted Heath had opened on imports. Instead, he argued that we had to be very careful on imports because of the dangers of retaliation. If he had been the strong man he pretends to be, he would have told the Cabinet, 'No way am I going to allow all these imports in. Either we deny them entry, or we subsidise British coal, or I resign.' But of course he didn't. The position was obviously more important than the case.

Yet the case could hardly *be* more important. It's like this. Our oil reserves are limited—maybe fifty years. Natural gas is the same. Nuclear power is obviously the great hope for the future—as a miner it may seem strange for me to say this, but the reason will be clear in a minute—but there are tremendous problems with the disposal of waste from nuclear fission. If we go on much longer without an answer to those problems, and the dangers of that material falling into the wrong hands, we're going to have many more thousands of marching feet on the roads.

Nuclear fusion, the hydrogen bomb harnessed, is clearly the ultimate target, since that uses the components of water as its fuel. With such unlimited power, you could then, for instance, use that power to make liquid hydrogen from water, as an alternative fuel to petrol for cars. Perfectly feasible—but we're a long way from being able to control the forces of nuclear fusion in an economic way.

There are also, of course, what one might call the 'fringe' sources of power—solar energy, wind energy, tidal energy, geothermal energy and so on. I can fully understand why the environmentalists are so keen on them, but for the foreseeable future they represent no real challenge, in a highly industrialised country like Britain, to the traditional fuels. Hydro-electric power does make a small contribution, with a few installations in Scotland and Wales, but it tends to be susceptible to seasonal variations. We just don't have the necessary huge volumes of water which are available in Africa or the Americas.

So we have to make the best use of what we *do* have, and that is, happily, a great deal, though by no means inexhaustible. Take natural gas. We have just converted the whole of Britain, cooker jets and all, to the use of natural gas. But that won't last for ever—perhaps no more than a few decades. Then we will be faced either with importing it—and at the moment the only two realistic potential sources are Russia and Norway—or we have to provide our own alternative.

The source for that alternative is coal. It is perfectly possible to use coal for making a synthetic gas which is equivalent to natural gas (as opposed to the old 'street gas'). The Coal Board have the expertise to do it. But it requires an effort of political will to provide the funds to make that possible, and to produce that gas economically. We should be doing that *now,* and mixing that synthetic gas with North Sea gas, so that the latter lasts longer, until we can build sufficient installations to replace it entirely.

That's not a gas pipe dream. In fact, it's essential if we are to avoid a gas pipe nightmare. Because nobody seems to have woken up to the fact that when natural gas runs out, the whole of Britain will be sitting on a bomb. We have one of the most comprehensive gas pipelines in the world, but those pipes have at all times to be kept filled. Otherwise, you get a lethal combination of gas and air. The only way of pushing that gas through those pipes is with more gas.

Then there's oil. At the moment we have the reserves in the North Sea, but we are still having to import a great deal of crude oil. Crude oil—there's the rub. People forget that, when you refine petrol from crude oil, you get a whole load of by-products which are essential for the chemical and other industries, and which cannot be obtained other than from the carbon fuels. So sooner, rather than later, when the Arabs have the expertise to make those by-products, they're not going to want to export crude oil. They'll want to export the lucrative by-products themselves.

So where will the oil come from? From coal. Already South Africa, faced with sanctions and the oil embargo, but with huge resources of coal, is almost self-sufficient in oil produced from coal. It's a highly-refined version of the method which the Germans used during the War. They are already three-quarters of the way towards self-sufficiency in oil, and within three years of the time of writing they will be totally so. Now, at the moment, they are exporting a lot of coal, but as soon as they perfect the art of conversion to oil to the point where it is economic in world terms—rather than the high cost forced on them by necessity—hey're not going to *want* to export any more coal, for obvious reasons.

Again, what South Africa can do, Britain has the expertise to do. But just as with gasification, this liquefaction process requires a great deal of costly investment. That is an investment I believe we must make. Nor is it just to get oil. When you make coke from coal, you get about twenty-seven by-products, similar to those from oil-refining, which is the reason why, for example, Courtaulds are one of the Coal Board's biggest customers. The trouble is, when there is a recession, there is less demand for steel, and therefore less demand from the steelmakers for coke, and therefore less of the by-products, and therefore people like Courtaulds have to go abroad for them—an industrial domino theory.

The point about turning coal into oil is that you get these by-products from *that* process, too. So I forecast that, by the start of the next century, coal will be regarded as such a valuable commodity that people will look askance at the idea of doing anything so crude as to burn it in power stations. In *fact,* you can get these by-products from natural gas as well! So there's the conundrum.

An industrialised society needs great amounts of power, but it also needs these by-products, on which it increasingly relies for producing everything from dyes to plastics. There's a very good case for saying that it is a criminal waste to burn either coal, or natural gas, *or* oil.

To this, people will naturally answer 'Yes, but to get energy we have to burn *something.*' And of course, unless or until we can get all our power from nuclear sources, that is undoubtedly true.

But it merely serves to underline what we have been saying for years, that Britain needs this National Energy Policy I was talking about. There's nothing very strange in the idea. After all, the 1974 Plan for Coal was passed unanimously in Parliament, even though it was later upset by the 1980 Coal Industry Bill. And this is exactly what I am arguing—that it *shouldn't* be subject to political whims.

Nor do I believe that it is anything other than extravagant and stupid to allow the normal market forces, and the tricks of the men in advertising, to play about with such an important national commodity as Energy. An example of this is the way in which Gas and Electricity compete for the housewife's favours. There are some cases in which gas is the most efficient fuel, in others electricity, in others oil, coal, and so on. They can't *all* be best *all* the time. What we need is a standing Energy Commission which will make these evaluations, and then insist in the national interest that their findings are adhered to. Such a Commission would also have to perform the difficult balancing act between the various natural fuels, bearing in mind what I was saying about their many other uses.

I know there are those who will complain, 'Oh no, not *more* State control,' but the truth of the matter is that we just cannot *afford* to indulge ourselves in the wanton profligacy of the past few decades. When it came to pit closures, I did not need any pressure from our lads to urge them out on to the streets. In fifty years' time, people will look at a pit like Mosley Common—whose closure I described in an earlier chapter—with millions upon millions of tons of viable coal buried under a bloody motorway junction, and they will simply say, 'Those people were mad.'

We need foresight, and we need to plan for the long term. That's why at the end of 1980 the NUM got together with the steel and railway unions to formulate a joint approach which we called the 'Triple Alliance'. With so many people unemployed—and *that's* a terrible waste of a natural resource, too—we felt that here was a God-sent opportunity to engage in large scale works in the long-term national interest, the electrification of the railways, the total modernisation of the road network, and so on. Indeed, when we met the ministers concerned, Jim Prior, Keith Joseph, David Howell and Norman Fowler, we felt that they were listening to our ideas with a great deal of interest and with more than sympathetic ears.

But then we came to Geoffrey Howe's Budget of 1981, and there wasn't even a hint that those ideas were being taken seriously. Not that the Tories were the only guilty ones. For years and years the Trade Union Movement and the Labour Party paid lip service to the need for a firmly-established British Coal Industry, and for a National Energy Policy, but lip service was all it was. They heard the words, but they didn't seem to understand what those words meant. Someone like Frank Chapple of the Electricians' Union didn't actually give a *damn* where the fuel for the power stations was coming from, as long as it kept coming.

So public attitudes have to be changed, if we are to make the investments we need, because those investments are huge and long-term. Nowadays, you can't do the smallest thing in a pit without it costing a million pounds. The great new pit at Selby, in Yorkshire, which recently started producing coal, cost £30 million before a lump ever came out of it—£30 million, and years of preparation.

And it's no use thinking about Energy in the crude economic terms for which I have so often attacked the mining engineers on the Coal Board. Shakespeare put into Richard III's mouth the cry 'A horse! A horse! My Kingdom for a horse' because at that moment on Bosworth Field all the riches in the world weren't worth as much as a mount on which to fight. To a starving man, a loaf of bread is worth all he possesses, and, to an industrialised nation, Energy is the sustenance without which it will surely perish, be it the richest in every other respect.

I believe these considerations apply to Europe, too, and when I was President of the European Coal and Steel Community, in 1976-77, I tried to put my ideas across in that wider context. I have already described my beliefs in internationalism, and I am pro-European too, though, I hasten to add, *not* pro-Common Market—I am convinced that our joining it has been little short of total disaster for Britain. But then, as a democrat, I accepted that the majority had voted for it in the referendum, and we as a Union decided that, as long as we *were* in it, the British Miners should play their part to the full.

I should also say that these strictures about Energy apply to the rank and file mining community too. There is still far too much of a feeling in the coalfields of 'Them and Us'. In my view, that is something which should have disappeared with Nationalisation. I have consistently urged that miners should feel that it is *their* industry. The Coal Board officials are not the bosses, in any sense of the word. They are the managers, and the NUM should always seek to work *with* them, not against them. In fact, over the past few years, many people might believe that the Union has run the Industry even more than the Coal Board has!

This is why, in wage negotiations, we have so often argued not simply that existing miners should be paid a proper wage for the job, but also for a wage which will attract men into the Industry—*our* Industry. And that is why I want the lads to get far more involved at pit level, all the time consulting with the management about how to make the pit work better, and how to get the maximum out of it.

I say 'consult' deliberately. I was pretty sceptical about the Bullock Report, and the idea of workers being involved in management, with trade unionists on the boards of companies and so on. How, for instance, could I honestly sit down as a member of the Coal Board? If there was an issue which I felt strongly about, on my members' behalf, but on which I was out-voted, how could I go back to my Executive and say, 'Ah well, we may be right, lads, but I was out-voted and therefore we have to accept it'? It would be an impossible position to be in. But worker-participation, with everyone feeling involved in the decisions being made about their pit, is quite a different matter.

I have used the word 'workers', incidentally, in the sense which people usually take it to mean, although it has never been very clearly defined. When I was a young man, it was easy to be led to believe that the working class starts and finishes at a certain level, and then you came to the middle class and the intelligentsia and so on. And it may still be very easy for people in the capitalist part of the economy, in the car industry for example, to hold to that view. But, now that the mines are part of a nationalised industry, I look around me and ask 'Where does it start, and where does it finish?'

To me, Derek Ezra is a worker. Coal Board managers are workers. I didn't stop being a worker when I first became a union official—in fact, I did more hours a day, and more days a week, as President, than I ever did as a miner at the coal face. So, to me, any man who has to work for his living is a worker, whatever he is earning. But that still doesn't mean that one should ignore the distinction between workers, or whatever you want to call them, and management. They are different roles, and it's just as important, if not more so, that managers *should* manage, and manage efficiently, as for the man at the coal face to extract the last possible lump of coal.

And how long will that man at the face need to remain there? It's a question I am often asked. If I said that I would like to see the day when there are no more men down the pits, it would be no more than a daydream. I hope it will come, but as a realist I know that that day is a long way in the future, even though a hundred years from now people may look upon men going down the mines as we now regard children sweeping Victorian chimneys.

Even now, every coal-producing nation is studying ways of extracting coal without the need for men. They've looked at the possibility of boring down to the seams and sucking the coal out in some way. They've looked at liquidising it below ground, or setting fire to it below ground and bringing off all the by-products that way. And they have developed robots which can do *some* of the underground work. More might have been done in these areas if it weren't for the fact that America and Russia, who could afford the vast investment necessary, have huge stretches of opencast coal to give them what they need.

So I believe we will need miners for many decades yet. Yes, we have machines to do a lot of the hardest work nowadays. Miners can honestly claim that they have never been Luddites—they have always welcomed the introduction of new and more efficient machinery. But it's still the toughest of jobs to get those machines into position, and then to move them as the coal faces move forward. And, in areas like Durham and Northumberland, there are *still* men working in seams which are so thin that you can't get machinery into them - seams so low that a man can't even crawl, but has to 'swim' along the floor, perhaps in inches of dust-laden water which permeates every pore of his body, in order to win the coal. And they do *that* by the archaic method of pick and shovel.

People might think, 'That's diabolical; such pits should be closed immediately.' Well, it *is* diabolical, but try telling those men you want the pit closed. For a start, they get used to working in those conditions, and their muscles become attuned to it, and if you put them into high seams it would kill them. Secondly, those seams are mostly the ones which produce the best, and most valuable, coking coal, and the men argue, 'Why put us on the dole queue when we're capable of producing good coal?'

I cannot argue with them, because of my firm belief that we need to extract every ounce of coal with which Nature has blessed us. But let no one be under any misunderstanding—coal-mining is a very dangerous game. Coal is a dangerous substance. You get slag-heaps which suddenly start to burn within them, especially in the areas of anthracite coals. To the public, this is astonishing. Miners know that it is because, when water starts to seep into those heaps, it has the opposite effect to the normal action of water. It actually ignites the build-up of methane in those heaps.

Again, machines are fine, but machines can go wrong, and maim and mutilate. We have gone a long way towards improving safety standards in the pits. But it's virtually impossible to go down a mine and not be exposed to dust. And sometimes, too, the lads get tired, or they're trying to speed things up a bit, so they take a short-cut and accidents happen.

So those who claim the miners are too militant, or that the miners are too demanding, or that the miners are overpaid, should remember this—the miner goes to work every day of his life under the threat of annihilation. It may be the long-term, but terrible, effects of the dust-diseases like pneumoconiosis. Or it may be the sudden fall of rock, or the explosion, which cuts Life off without further ado.

During my Presidency, almost exactly 600 men were killed in the pits. Coal is not cheap.

But if, during that same period, I succeeded in making the miners feel proud to be miners again, and in making the country realise the value of the Industry again, I will be able to look back and feel that I have achieved something worthwhile.

Above all else, I was *proud* to be the President of the National Union of Mineworkers.

Postscript

On Tuesday, December 8, 1981, at a lunch-break during wage negotiations with the Coal Board, the result was announced of the ballot to elect my successor. Arthur Scargill had won, in racing terms, by a distance. He got 138,803 votes, which represented just over 70 percent of the votes cast. His nearest rival, Trevor Bell of COSA, got a mere 34,075, which was just over 17 percent. Ray Chadburn, from Nottingham, achieved only half as many as Trevor, and Bernard Donaghy, from my own Lancashire, limped home fourth with a sad total of 6,442.

In the history of the NUM, there had never been a more decisive vote in a Presidential election.

The result came as no surprise to me at all. Arthur had effectively been running his election campaign for something like three years, and with precious little opposition. The 'moderates' on the Executive, who, I happened to believe, were much more truly representative of the great majority of the membership, failed to achieve any concerted effort to defeat him.

What's more, they were their own worst enemies. Some two years before the election, a meeting was held at my home in order to try to hammer out some kind of united approach to the problem. But the following day, that meeting was leaked to the Press, and straight away I had to tell the 'moderate' group: 'To hell with it. If we're going to be conducting this discussion in public, then I can't have anything more to do with it.'

It would have been naive, of course, for anyone to suppose that I *didn't* have my own views about who my successor should be, or that I would not help to give that person the best chance possible. I think that would be true of any union leader, as indeed it would be of any political leader. But these things have to be done discreetly. You can't have a situation where an elected leader appears to be spending more time politicking for his successor than in looking after his members' interests.

For some time it looked as though Trevor Bell would be Arthur's only opponent, but then, as the election approached, the 'moderates' woke up to the fact that the lads were unlikely to repeat the experiment of electing a representative of the COSA section, as Sid Ford had been. They would want me succeeded by another pitman. A couple of months before the election, Ray Chadburn, who had been dithering like the original reluctant bride, finally agreed to stand, and he was followed at the eleventh hour by Bernard Donaghy. But it was all too little and too late. Arthur, whether the men agreed with all his views or not, had at least established a clear image of himself—in which the media, for all his complaints about them, had given great assistance—and could be seen as a strong character who knew what he wanted.

The Press, of course, immediately assumed (and Arthur did nothing to contradict them) that the result ushered in a new era of extreme militancy in the pits. I believe no such thing, and for two reasons.

The first is the basic commonsense of the miners themselves. They've shown this again and again in pithead ballots. They will not be led into battles unless they believe the cause is just. Nor will they blindly follow the Executive's lead - sometimes they support it, sometimes they don't. They certainly won't allow Arthur to browbeat them into backing some of his wilder flights of political fancy, nor will he forget that there are methods for deposing Presidents, as well as electing them.

Not that I think it will come to that, because of my second reason, which is that men tend to mellow a little when they get power. Arthur may have made a lot of promises about how he will never change his philosophies and so on and so forth, but he will find out soon enough that you *can't* be fighting battles all your life. There do come moments in negotiations when you have to say to yourself,'This is all we're going to get, and there's no sense in pushing for any more.' Ever since he came on to the Executive, Arthur was among the 'antis', who would vote against anything, but again, he will soon come to realise that if *everyone* votes against *everything,* and that happens *all* the time, then nothing can be achieved at all.

My one disappointment—and it actually made me very angry—was that the election, and its immediate aftermath, led to a ridiculous game of 'chicken' in our wage demands and negotiations. The 'moderates', anxious not to be outflanked or outbid by Arthur, went along with his most extreme demands, lest they should be seen to be the first to give way to the Coal Board's arguments. And this even continued *after* the election, so that at our Special Conference on December 18, only *three* delegates, from Leicestershire, stood their ground against the calls for strike action. Even 'moderate' stalwarts like Sid Vincent gave way to the clamour, and I was appalled.

Press reports of the Executive Committee meeting which set up that Special Conference were confused and somewhat inaccurate in claiming that there had been a 'unanimous vote for strike action'. So let me set the record straight.

After lengthy negotiations, I had succeeded in getting the Coal Board to improve their original offer, by the addition of a further £2.5 million and bringing the service bonus forward by seven months. That represented an increase of between 9.5 and 10.5 percent. They said that was their final offer. They'd said that before, of course, but this time I believed them, and I made that clear.

When it came to the Executive, Tommy Bartle from Durham proposed that we accept the offer, but that motion only got seven votes, and was defeated. Then it was proposed from the other side that we call a Special Conference, and that was carried. But in the following discussion, concerning the wording of the resolution we would be putting to the Conference, it was generally felt that 'industrial action' was too vague a phrase—it could mean an overtime ban, or a work to rule, or a lot of other things, and the general consensus was that we should give a more positive lead to the Conference by recommending strike action.

Since we had already voted to call the Conference, and since no-one then seemed too disposed to argue on and on about the wording of the recommendation, we agreed that it would be 'for strike action' as suggested. But no vote was taken. I didn't see the point. If I *had* taken a vote, no doubt six or seven would have voted against it, and then we could have gone on all night arguing as to what the precise wording should be.

When the Conference actually took place, I was unfortunately unable to be there, and the Chair was taken by Mick McGahey, who decided to allow in several hundred men who had been picketing outside. I think that was partly my own fault. I had ruled that the Press could be present, and he took the view that, if the Press were present, there was no reason why the pickets shouldn't be there too. On the other hand, as I learned later, by no means all of those pickets were NUM members.

There seems no doubt that an element of intimidation took place, and, what's more, certain speakers made it clear that there was likely to be a degree of intimidation at the ballot, with people standing next to the ballot boxes and 'persuading' members to vote with the Executive regardless of their feelings.

As far as I was concerned, this was leading the Union into a very dangerous situation, especially since certain NEC members and others who saw things their way, had made it clear that they saw the vote as being on political as much as on industrial grounds - in other words, they wanted to use the miners as front-runners in persuading the TUC to move to bring the Government down. As I have already made clear in this book, that is *not*, in my view, what unions in a democracy are about.

The ballot was due to be held on Thursday and Friday, January 14 and 15. On the Tuesday of that week, the *Daily Express* approached me and asked if I would like to write an article for them setting out my views on the issue.

It was one of the hardest decisions I have ever had to make. I had always believed in the integrity of NEC decisions, and I had always seen

my job as representing those decisions to the best of my ability,
regardless of whether I agreed with them or not. On the other hand,
certain members of the Executive had always, during my term of office,
argued that they had the right, within their own Areas, to oppose
Executive decisions with which they didn't agree.

What's more, I felt hamstrung by the Executive. There I was, the
President, elected by the *whole* membership—not just a few—and
apparently unable to put my point of view to the members. So I decided
to go ahead and do it, believing that the members, almost by default,
were being denied an opportunity to think the matter out. I might, I
thought, perhaps be able to steady the vote a little bit.

The following morning, the *Express* published the article. It was
headlined 'Think—before you destroy what we have built up', and that
was a fair summary of what I had to say. I pointed out that over the past decade we had helped to restore coal mining as a strong and economically
viable industry. I also pointed out that, if we accepted the present offer,
miners' pay would have increased by some 40 percent in only 20 months.

But, to be fair, I didn't think I was telling miners anything they didn't
know already. I was merely reminding them of the facts. The miner and
his family are *far* better-off at the start of the Eighties than they were ten
years before, when I took office. That's as it should be. Quite rightly,
they enjoy cars, well-furnished homes, holidays abroad, and so on. But
those things have to be paid for, often by bank loans or hire-purchase.

The Left were trying to claim that a strike vote wouldn't necessarily
lead to a strike, but would be the lever to prise a couple more quid out of
the Coal Board. Well, miners have a pretty good fund of common sense,
and you don't need to be a mathematical genius to do the calculation.
Even though the minimum earnings of the lowest-paid surface workers
were still below the £100 a week we wanted, the fact was that their *actual*
earnings were somewhere between £110 and £120.

*That meant that if, through a strike, they got an extra £2 a week, it would take at least
a year, for each week on strike, for them to recoup what they would have lost.*

So I think that in this instance I was not so much persuading the
members as making a proper recognition of what their feelings were,
and I had always seen it as an important part of my job to travel up and
down the country, talking to the lads in the clubs and the pubs in all the
different Areas, so that I could really know what they thought about
things. That's how I knew we would win the strikes of '72 and '74, and
that's how I knew there was no feeling for a strike this time.

I knew the article would cause a rumpus, of course, and so it did.
Arthur called me all the names under the sun, including 'the betrayer',
but I wasn't bothered. I felt pretty confident in sitting back and letting
the ballot vote speak for me.

The vote itself was delayed, because the heavy snows had held things up in Wales, so when we came to the NEC meeting on Tuesday, January 19, the result still wasn't known, though the Left had already pretty well conceded defeat. Towards the end of that meeting, which was a fairly rowdy one, Arthur pushed a note across the table to Owen Briscoe, his Area Secretary, telling him, I believe, to move a vote of censure against me, which he duly did.

Immediately, Tommy Bartle moved an amendment to the motion, saying that the NEC noted the letters of criticism of me that had been received, and would take no action. I was asked if I wanted to say anything, but we'd already been at it for the best part of three hours, so I just said: 'No, let's put it to the vote.'

Tommy's amendment was carried by 13 votes to 12, and therefore the censure motion automatically fell and was never put to the vote, contrary to what was reported in a lot of the newspapers. What would have happened if it *had* been put, I have no way of telling. It may well be that some of those who put their hands up against Tommy Bartle's amendment would have had second thoughts if it had come to an actual censure motion against a President. I just don't know, and never will.

But I do know that when, on the morning of Thursday, January 21, the results of the ballot were declared, I had won my last great victory for common sense. Of the 205,142 miners who voted, representing an 82 percent poll, 45 percent supported the Executive, and 55 percent said, 'No—we don't want a strike.' It was a totally decisive result.

In their questions after the announcement, the Press lads were keen for it to be seen as a personal defeat for Arthur. Some also wondered if it was a 'victory for Maggie Thatcher and her policies'.

I refused to see it as either of those things. In my view, the miners simply took a rational view about an industrial situation, and as I said: 'I don't want to crow over anyone because of what's happened, and the Government would be very foolish if they did any crowing either.'

But I did also say that no leader comes to office blessed with complete wisdom. I had to learn my lessons as I went along. Arthur will also have to learn his lessons as he goes along.

If he takes those lessons to heart, I see no reason why he should not make an excellent President, and I sincerely hope that the members will give him the support which they always gave me.

Index

Aberdeen, NUM Conference (1971), 79
Airlie, Jimmy, 71
Aldridge, Alan, 75
American Miners, 62
Anderton, Jimmy, 53
Arab oil: embargo, 69; production cut, 127; price increase, 127, 131
Armstrong, Sir William (Lord), 124, 127, 131
Ashton-in-Makerfield, 1, 7, 9, 13, 19–23, 30–3, 35, 42, 47; Labour Party and Clubs, 8, 9, 35, 38–9; Urban District Council, 42, 43, 185
ASLEF, and picketing of oil supplies, 100–1
Attlee, Clement, 194; Attlee Government, 37, 115
AUEW (Amalgamated Union of Engineering Workers), 64, 73, 190, 191, 193

Bacon, Alice, 75
Barber, Tony, 115, 136, 137
Barnett, Joel, 146
Bartle, Tommy, 160, 209, 211
Basnett, David, 190
Battersea Power Station picketing incident with NUJ, 102
Belfast, 70
Bell, Trevor, 109, 115, 207
Benn, Tony, 194, 200; and NCB Chairmanship, 168; and coal imports, 200
Bevan, Aneurin, 187, 194
Bevin, Ernest, and 'Bevin Boys', 31
Bickershaw Brass Band, 20
Birmingham Trades Council, 105
Blackpool, 34; NUM Convalescent home, 67
Blackwell, Tommy, 21
Boilermakers' Union, 71
Bold Colliery, St Helens, 42, 43, 47, 48, 50
Bolton, 98, 153, 157, 158; Lancashire Miners' head-quarters, 43, 44, 49, 51, 72
Bonus shift system, 115–16
Booth, Albert, 146
Boston Colliery, 24–6, 35, 36
Bowman, Sir James, Chairman of NCB, 52
Boyd, Johnny, 73
Brezhnev, Leonid, 188
Brighton; TUC Conference (1974), 155; Metropole Hotel, 155
Briscoe, Owen, 211
British Association of Colliery Managers (BACM), 64, 146, 172
Britton, Frank, 167
Brown, George, 75
Brown, Tom, MP for Ince, 47
Bubbins, Arthur, 48–9
Bucharest, 187
Buckton, Ray, and picketing of oil supplies, 100–1
Bullock Report, 204
Burke, Wilfred, MP for Burnley, 47
Burnley Parliamentary Division, 47–8

Cadeby Power Station, 103
Calcutta, 185
Callaghan, Jim, 73–4, 120; becomes Prime Minister, 165; and the Social Contract, 165–6
Campbell Adamson, Bill, 110
Carr, Robert, 132; and the miners' strike, 104–9, 114
Carrington, Lord, 137, 138
Carter, Alan, 110
Carter, President Jimmy, 188
Castle, Barbara, 71, 73, 74, 194, 195
CBI (Confederation of British Industry), 110, 126, 128
Ceausescu, Rumanian leader, 187
CEGB (Central Electricity Generating Board), 174; and coal stocks, 90, 97
Chadburn, Ray, 207
Chapple, Frank, 63, 203
Checkweighmen, 17–18
Chile, NUM delegation to, 189
Clark, Jack, 19
Clarke, Len, 121, 122, 139, 149, 159, 166
Clegg, Professor Hugh, 109, 112
Clyde Shipyards, Upper and Lower, 70–1
CND, 47–8
Coal Industry Act (1973), 123
Coal Industry Act (1980), 148, 171–3, 178, 181, 202
Coal Industry Benevolent Trust, 155
'Coal Industry Examination, The', see 'Plan for Coal'
Coal Industry Housing Association (CIHA), 110
Coal Industry National Consultative Council, 146
Coegnant pit, Glamorgan, 177
Colliery Officials Staffs Association (COSA), 64, 66, 95, 97, 148, 207
Collins, Jack, 110, 138, 150
Communist Party, and Communists, 38, 49, 50,,54, 65, 72, 120, 138, 184–5, 187, 188
Concessionary coal, 29, 43–4
Contrat Social, Du (Rousseau), 159
Counter Inflation Act, 122
Courtaulds, 202
Cousins, Frank, 64
Crawford, Joe, 65, 120, 121
Crossley, Leon, 51, 53, 54, 58
Cumberland area, 66; loss of miners' jobs, 61
Cunningham, Billy, 21–2, 31

Daily Express, 138, 156, 181, 209–10
Daily Mirror, 154
Daivy Colliery, Wigan, 58, 59
Daly, Lawrence, General Secretary of NUM, 65, 72, 76, 78, 86, 89, 92, 113, 121, 128, 132, 138, 159, 160, 177; election as General Secretary; and the miners' strike, 97, 103–6, 115; and Wilberforce Inquiry, 109, 110
Davies, John, 71, 85, 105, 109, 113, 123
Day wage rates, 67
Delhi, Miners' International Federation Congress (1975), 185

Derbyshire area, 61, 66, 67; payment of strike pay, 99; incentive scheme, 152

Devney, Barrie, 138, 156–7; dubs Gormley the 'Battered Cherub', 156

Donaghy, Bernard, 207

Douglas-Home, Sir Alex, 52

Duffy, Terry, 190

Dunn, Jack, 150

Durham area, 48, 66, 160, 205, 209; loss of miners' jobs, 61, 63; unofficial strike (1981), 179

Eadie, Alex, 146

Effremenko, Soviet miners' leader, 189

Electoral Reform Society, Counts votes for NUM ballots, 51, 89, 167

ETU (Electrical Trades Union), 63, 65, 203

European Coal and Steel Community, 204

Evening News, 155

Extended Hours Agreement, 38

Ezra, (Sir) Derek, Chairman of National Coal Board, 81–3, 86, 87, 93, 97, 107, 110, 114, 116, 126, 146, 167, 171, 172, 176–8, 180, 205; reappointed, 168

Fatalities Scheme, 16, 17

Feather, Victor, 96, 97, 104, 105, 115, 128, 136

Fitch, Alan, MP for Wigan, 47

Five-day working week, 37

Foot, Michael, 143–4, 177, 194

Ford, Sid (Sir Sidney), NUM President, 55, 72, 76, 78, 120, 121, 207

Foster, Sammy, 51, 54

Foster, Wilf, 38

Fowler, Norman, 203

France, subsidy on coal, 174

Francis, Dai, 116–17, 138, 149

Fryer, John, 140

Gaitskell, Hugh, 194

Garnett, John, 109

Gandhi, Mrs, 185

Garswood Hill Colliery Company, 12

Gerard, Lord, 12, 21, 32

Globe Colliery, Fenton, 40

Golborne, 20, 22

Gormley, Frank, son of Joe, 22–4, 29, 33, 57, 99, 142; works in mines, 46; delegate to NUM Western Area Conference, 47

Gormley, Ian, grandson of Joe, 142

Gormley, Joe: birth, 1; parents and family life, 2–9; education, 9–10; work in the mine, 10–19; joins union, 11; wins singing contest, 19–20

courtship and marriage, 21–3; second man on coal cutter, 26; chargehand, 33; wartime negotiations, 33; leads strike, 36–7; national conference delegate, 38; branch President, 38; chairman of local Labour Party, 38–9; deputy's certificate, 39, 41; Urban District Councillor, 39, 42, 43, 47, 51; leader of Labour group, 43

in Staffordshire, 39–40; deputy, 41; returns to Lancashire, 42; standing delegate to Lancashire miners' meetings, 43; elected to NUM National Executive Committee, 45; on Area Executive, 47; parliamentary ambitions, 47–8

Lancashire area secretary, 48–9; moves to Bolton,

51; pit closures, 53–9, 62–3, 69; and Alf Robens, 63; and Sam Watson, 63; member of Labour Party NEC, 63–4; and Bill Paynter, 65; and National Power Loading Agreement, 65–7; plan for convalescent home in Majorca, 67–8; Chairman of Labour Party Organisation Sub-Committee, 35, 68, 74; on Shipbuilding Board, 70–1; defeated for NUM General Secretaryship, 72–3; and 'In Place of Strife', 73–5;

elected President of NUM, 76–7; first annual conference, 79–83; negotiations with NCB, 83–7, 91–3, 113–17; and the miners' strike, 97–118; Wilberforce Inquiry, 109–14; Labour Party International Sub-Committee, 119, 121; leaves Labour Party NEC, 119–22; NUM Conference (1973), 123–4; and Heath, 124–5, 127, 128, 130–2, 139, 144–5; and Whitelaw, 132–4, 137; on waiting and bathing time, 132–6; and Wilson, 133–6; and Len Murray, 136; Tory Government pay policy, 137; and TUC's offer to Government, 138; strike ballot, 139–40; and strike of Feb. 1974, 141–2, 144; and incentive schemes, 149–53

County JP, 153; racing and betting, 154; libel action, 154–5; reporters and Press stories, 155–7; ruling at NEC on sub-committee's wages settlement decision, 161; and the Social Contract, 162–3, 165–6, 193; 1975 NUM Conference, 163–5; ballot in favour of Social Contract policy, 166–7; declines Chairmanship of NCB, 168; on Derek Ezra, 168; and offer of 20 per cent (1979), 170; and early retirement for miners, 170–1; and Coal Industry Act (1980), 171

Confrontation with Tory Government, 177–82; question of pit closures, 175–9, 182; and coal imports, 179–82, 200; and interest charges, 179; and stocking costs, 181; and Jim Prior, 181–2

and Communism, 184–5, 187, 188; in India, 185, 186; in Rumania, 187; NUM international department, 188; Miners' International Federation, 188–9; International Miners' Conference (1981), 189–90

Labour Party Special Conference (1980), 190–2; and election of Labour Party leader, 191–2; and the SDP, 191; on Labour Party and trade unions, 192–3; on 'bringing down the Government', 196–8, 209

and a national energy policy, 199–206; coal reserves, 199; nuclear energy, 199–201; natural and synthetic gas, 201; oil and oil from coal, 201–2; 'Triple Alliance', 203; President of European Coal and Steel Community, 204; on workers in management, 204

election of his successor, 207–9; on likely consequences of Scargill's election, 208; article for *Daily Express*, 209–10; attempt to censure him fails, 211; and ballot against strike action, 211

Gormley, John, father of Joe, 2, 3, 6, 8–11, 24; in First World War, 5; chargeman, 5; death, 16–17, 170–1

Gormley, Lizzie, mother of Joe, 2, 4, 8–10, 12, 17

Gormley, Nellie (*née* Mather), 29, 31–3, 39, 42, 45–9, 51, 98–9, 142, 154–9, 168; courtship and marriage to Joe, 21–3; birth of children, 23, 32

Gormley, Winnie, daughter of Joe, 32

Griffiths, Jim, 194

Hall, Teddy, 48–9
Hammond, Jimmy, 49–52, 54–6
Harland and Wolff Yard, 70
Harrison, Terry, 100
Hart, Judith, 75
Hart, Major, 20
Hatfield Main Pit, 103
Haydock, 44; Haydock Park racecourse, 2, 3, 7, 32
Heath, Edward, 71, 75, 81, 87, 93, 94, 124–5, 127, 128, 130–2, 136–40, 200; and the miners' strike, 115, 117; and three-day week, 131–2; calls General Election, 140; defeated, 143–5, 196; Heath Government, 84, 122
Herbison, Peggy, 187
Holmes, Joe, 100
Horner, Arthur, NUM General Secretary, 65, 120
Howe, Sir Geoffrey, 169, 203
Howell, David, 171, 173, 177–80, 182, 203
Hunter, Professor Laurance, 109
Hurst Park, the Gormleys' house at, 98, 142, 157

Imports of coal, 174–5, 179–82, 200
'In Place of Strife', Labour Government's White Paper, 73–5, 81
Ince Parliamentary Division, 47
Incentive schemes, 149–52; Special Conference (1974), 149–52; Scargill and Yorkshire delegates walk out, 149; attacks on National Officials, 150–1; negotiation with NCB, 151–2; rejection by ballot, 152; NEC recommends acceptance (1977), 152; again rejected by ballot, 152; Area schemes adopted, 152–3; unsuccessful lawsuit against NUM, 152
India, 185, 186
Industrial Relations Bill (Act), 81, 93, 188, 124, 139–40
Interest charges, 179
International Labour Organization, 189
International Miners' Conference on Peace and Détente (1981), 189–90
Inverness, NUM annual conference (1973), 123–4
Isle of Man, NUM annual conference (1976), 167

Jenkins, Roy, 74, 191
Jersey, NUM annual conference (1979), 169
Joint National Negotiating Committee (JNNC), 83, 122, 125, 128, 144, 159
Jones, Danny, MP for Burnley, 47
Jones, Ernest, NUM President, 72
Jones, Jack, 193, 195
Joseph, Sir Keith, 203

Kempton Park racecourse, 157
Kent area, 61, 66, 67, 100, 138, 150, 152, 177; unofficial strike (1981), 179
Klebanov, Vladimir, 189

Labour Party, 8, 21, 30, 34, 38, 47, 61, 63, 65, 68, 98, 160, 184, 190–6, 203; Clubs, 34–5, 38–9; union block votes at Conference, 64; Organisation subcommittee, 35, 68, 74; Party Conferences (1966), 68; (1967), 79; (1968), 73; Home Policy sub-committee, 69; and the trade unions, 71–2, 192–3; Party Conferences (1971 and 1972), 119; International sub-committee, 119, 121; Special Conference (1980), 190–2; and the miners, 198
National Executive Committee, 35, 48, 63–5, 68–9, 73, 78, 106, 114, 119–22, 187; trade union representation, 195
Lady Victoria pit, Scotland, 175
Lancashire area, 43–5, 48–9, 66, 67, 207; and concessionary coal, 43–4; agents, 51–2; regrouping of pits, 52; loss of miners' jobs, 61; support for Gormley in election for NUM Presidency, 76–7
Lane, Frank, 187
Lee, Jennie, 187
Leicester area, 61, 208
Lever, Harold, 71
Levin, Bernard, 189
Lewis, John L., 62, 69
Life in the pits, 12–19, 26–8; lashing on and thrutching, 12–14; pillar-and-stall method, 16; fatalities, 16; checking system, 17–18; women workers, 18–28; coal-cutting and shot-firing, 26–8
Llandudno, NUM Annual Conferences (1960), 48
Lockett, Harold, 40
London Brick Company, 84
London Mercantile Corporation, offer from, 142
Lord's View, the Gormleys' flat at, 142
Lyme Pit, 35, 43; strike led by Gormley, 36–7

McGahey, Mick, 76–7, 79, 121, 128, 131, 132, 134, 138, 155, 184, 209; chairs meetings in Gormley's absence, 159–60; casting vote on wages settlement demand, 160; his conduct in the chair challenged, 160; Gormley's ruling, 161; propaganda against Social Contract policy, 166
McLean, Bill, 76, 138
Macmillan Government, 52
Maitland, Lady Olga, 154–5
Majorca, 67
Marsh, Dick, 69, 200
Martin, Albert, 76, 120, 121
Mason, Roy, 200
Mather, Levi, 21, 39
Mather, Nellie, see Gormley, Nellie
Matthews, Fred, 103
Matthews, Lord, 155
Meacher, Michael, 109
MGWU (Municipal and General Workers' Union), 84, 190, 193
Mikardo, Ian, 119, 195
Miners' Federation of Great Britain, 65
Miners' International Federation, 155, 188–9; support for miners' strike, 104; Delhi Congress (1975), 185
Mineworkers' Pension Scheme, 147, 196
Morecambe, NUM Annual Conference (1972), 148–9
Morris, Johnny, 43
Mosley Common pit, closure of, 52–7, 203
Murray, Len, 136, 137, 177
My Generation (Paynter), 120

National Association of Colliery Overmen and Shotfirers (NACODS), 64, 65, 95, 120, 146, 172

National Association of Labour and Socialist Clubs, 35

National Coal Board (NCB), 52, 58, 63, 67, 75, 79, 81–6, 88, 96, 104, 106–8, 110, 132, 133, 137, 140, 142, 161, 171–3, 180–2, 184, 196, 201, 202, 204, 205; and women workers, 28; and Mosley Common, 53–7; plans for the industry (1958), 60; negotiations with NUM, 83–7, 91–3, 107–8, 113–17; and Subsidised Transport Agreement, 88; and further NUM claims, 122, 125–30; and waiting and bathing time, 134, 135; and Pay Board Inquiry, 143; greatly improved offer to NUM, 144; 'Plan for Coal', 146–8, 171, 173, 179, 202; amicable relations with NUM, 146; and incentive schemes, 149–52; Gormley declines Chairmanship, 168; Ezra reappointed, 168; offer of 20 per cent (1979), 169–70; and question of pit closures, 175–8; and coal imports, 179–80; offer to NUM (1981), 208

National Economic Development Council, 136

National Power-Loading Agreement, 65–7, 83, 153

National Union of Mineworkers, *see* NUM

Nationalisation of the mines, 37–8

Natural gas, 199–201

Newcastle, International Miners' Conference (1981), 189–90

North Wales, loss of miners' jobs, 61

North-Western area, 48

Northern Ireland, 70

Northumberland area, 205

Norway, and natural gas, 201

Nottingham area, 61, 66, 67, 138, 139, 207; and concessionary coal, 44

Nuclear energy, 199–201

NUJ, and miners' strike, 102

NUM (National Union of Mineworkers': and women workers, 28; and concessionary coal, 44; differing Area systems, 51; and pit closures, 61–2; affiliation to Labour Party, 64; positions of the President and General Secretary, 72, 78; annual conference (1971), 79–83; negotiations with NCB, 83–7, 91–3, 107–8; and Subsidised Transport Agreement, 88; Special Conference, 88–90; Rules changed on majority for strike action, 89; strike ballot, 89; overtime ban, 90; new NCB offer rejected, 91

national strike, 94–118; Area voting, 95, 97; safety maintenance, 95, 97; movement of coal stopped by picketing, 96, 100–6; oil transport stopped, 100–1; rulings on peaceful picketing, 103, 105; death of a picket, 103; arrests of pickets, 103; Saltley picketing, 104–5; State of Emergency, 106, 109; discussions with Government, 106–7; Court of Inquiry, 109–15, 122, 125, 131, 138, 143, 149; NEC rejects Inquiry Report, 112, 114; ballot vote accepts final terms, 117

new pay claim (1973), 122; ballot vote turns down rejection of offer, 123; claim for large pay increase, 124, 125–30; and enhanced shift payments, 125; negotiations, 127–30; Special Conference, 129; Area ballot, 129; overtime ban, 129–30, 132; State of Emergency, 130; three-day week, 131–2, 136; waiting and bathing time, 132–6; strike ballot, 139–40; strike of Feb. 1974, 141–2, 144; Pay Board inquiry, 143; greatly improved offer accepted, 144

and 'Plan for Coal', 146–8; and productivity, 148–9; and incentive schemes, 149–53; Annual Conference (1974) calls for substantial increase, 159; largest percentage increase in history of NUM, 162; the Social Contract and ballot on its policy, 162–3, 166–7; further wage increases (1976–8), 167–9; NCB's offer of 20 per cent, 169–70; offer rejected by NEC but accepted by ballot, 170

and question of pit closures, 175–9; unofficial action, 177; NCB withdraws pit closure list, 178; international department, 188; overseas delegations, 189; and Russian unions, 189; and the Labour Party, 193; 'Triple Alliance', 203; election of Gormley's successor, 207–9; Special Conference and calls for strike, 208–9; pickets allowed into Conference, 209; ballot vote against strike, 211

National Executive Committee (NEC), 44, 45, 48, 54, 61, 62, 65, 69, 72, 73, 76, 79, 84–92, 99, 107, 108, 112–16, 122, 124, 126, 128–31, 138–42, 159–61, 165–7, 170, 172, 176–9, 184, 190, 207–11

NUR, 187

Observer, The, 98, 179, 182

O'Connor, James, 110

Oil: competition of, 52, 60–1, 137; by-products, 201, 202; from coal, 202

Orgreave pit, near Sheffield, 176

Owen, Dr David, 99, 191

Padley, Walter, 119

Paisley, Ian, 70

Parliamentary Group of miners' MP's, 131

Pay Board, 133–5; miners' claims referred to, 141, 142; Relativities Report, 143; Inquiry and report, 143

Paynter, Bill, NUM National Secretary, 50, 55, 62, 65, 69, 72, 73, 183; Communist Party member, 65; loses seat on TUC General Council, 65, 120

Periodic Chest X-Ray Scheme, 80

Pit closures, 52–9, 61–3, 69, 175–9, 182

'Plan for Coal' (1974), 146–8, 171, 173, 174, 202; Interim Report, 146; Final Report, 147–8

Plover, Laurence, 53

Pneumoconiosis, 80–1, 170

Price lists, 40, 65–7; disputes between areas, 40, 66; day wage rates, 67

Prices and incomes policy: Labour Government, 69; Tory Government, 124, 127–30, 132, 137

Prior, Jim, 181–2, 203

Productivity Scheme, 148–51

Rail unions, 97
  See also ASLEF and NUR

Rees, George, 151

Reid, Jimmy, 71

Retirement of miners: compulsory at sixty-five, 52; early, 170–1

Richard Evans company, 11, 43

Robens, Alf, NCB Chairman, 55, 62

Rodgers, Bill, 191

Rowe, Maurice, 79

Rugby League and Union, 20

Rumania, 187

Ruskin College, Trade Union Research Unit, 109

Russia, and natural gas, 201
Rutland, Duke of, 199

St Helens, 1, 2, 42; collieries, 44
Saltley Depot, picketing of, 104–5
Scarborough, NUM Annual Conference (1975), 163
Scargill, Arthur, 149, 162, 163, 166, 176, 184, 208, 210, 211; and Saltley picketing, 105; propaganda against Social Contract policy, 166; election as NUM President (1981), 207–8
Schofield, Sid, 76, 104, 106, 113, 115, 128
Scottish area, 66, 72, 79, 138, 166, 169, 184; loss of miners' jobs, 61; unofficial strikes, 76, 179
SDP, 191
Selby, new pit, 176, 203
Shephard, Cliff, 83, 146
Shepherd, Bill, 55, 116
Shipbuilding, British, 70–1; Board, 70
Six-Day War (Middle East), 69
Smethurst Colliery group, 9, 12
Social Contract, 159–60, 162–3, 165–8, 193; NUM ballot, 166–7
Socialist International Bureau, 119
South Africa, and oil from coal, 202
South Wales area, 65, 66, 116–17, 138, 139, 151, 152, 169; loss of miners' jobs, 61; unofficial strikes, 76, 177, 179
Soviet miners, and Soviet Miners' Union, 189
Special Case A? Social Justice for the Miners, 109
Staffordshire area, 39–42, 66
Steam trains, phasing out of, 61
Steel Board, 175
Stocking costs, 180, 181
Stones Pit, Garswood, 12, 20, 23, 78
Sunbury-on-Thames, the Gormley's house at, 157, 159
Sunday Express, 154–5
Sunday Times, 140
Swallow, Bill (Sir William), 70

Tait, Peter, 138
TGWU (Transport and General Workers' Union), 51, 64, 97, 193; and picketing of coal movement, 101
Thames Haven, picketing of oil supplies, 100–1
Thatcher, Margaret, 173, 176–9, 182, 211; becomes Prime Minister, 169
Times, The, 112, 136, 174, 178, 187, 189
Toon, Ken, 152
Torquay, NUM Annual Conference (1978), 169
Tribune Group, 119

'Triple Alliance', NUM, rail and steel unions, 203
TUC, 61, 63, 65, 73, 87, 104, 106, 126, 128, 155, 164, 165, 192–3, 209; General Council, 64–65, 72, 119–22; Mines and Quarries Section, 64, 65, 120; and the miners' strike, 96, 97, 105–6, 114; miners' nominations to General Council, 120–2; Special Conference (1974), 136; offer to the Government, 136–8; and the Social Contract, 160, 163
Tynemouth, NUM Annual Conference (1977), 168

University College, London, Rag, 161–2
Unsworth, Sammy, 51
USA, 200: and cheaper coal, 174, 175

Vale of Belvoir coal reserves, 199
Varley, Eric, 146, 200
Vincent, Sid, 122, 208

Waiting and bathing time, 132–6
Wales, Prince of, 186
Walker, Peter, 87, 93–4, 123
Watson, Sammy, 48–9, 63–4, 68, 78
Weaver, Mick, 54–6
West Germany, 195; miners' delegation, 155; subsidy on coal, 174
Whelan, Joe, 138, 139
White House restaurant, 155
Whitelaw, Willie, 132–4, 137, 143
Wigan, 19, 20, 33; Parliamentary Division, 47
Wilberforce, Lord, and the Court of Inquiry, 109–15, 122, 125, 131, 138, 143, 149; evidence, 109; Report, 112–13
Wilcock, Tommy, 38
Williams, Emlyn, 139
Williams, Ronald, MP for Wigan, 47
Williams, Shirley, 191
Wilson, Harold, 52, 68, 69, 71, 74, 124, 165, 194; and pit closures, 69; and waiting and bathing time, 132–6; returns as Prime Minister, 143; calls another General Election, 150; and the Social Contract, 159; resignation, 165
Women workers: in the pits, 18, 28–9; in canteens, 28
Wood Pit, St Helens, 11
Woodcock, George, 136

Yom Kippur War, 127
Yorkshire area, 61, 138, 149, 152, 163, 166–9, 184; and concessionary coal, 44; Saltley picketing, 105; ballot to fight pit closures, 176; unofficial strike (1981), 179